Don't Take It Too SERIOUS

[Memoirs]

Jerry L. Pittman

About the Author

Jerry Lane Pittman started writing his memoirs in 2006 when he fully retired as a practicing certified public accountant. He was born in Sweetwater, Texas, and graduated from Newman High School, where he played basketball and served as the student body president in 1962. He received his bachelor's degree in business and his Master's degree of science in accounting from Texas Tech University in 1966 and 1969, respectively. He married Susan Waits in 1966, and they are the parents of two sons, Julian and Joel Greer Pittman. He started his career with Arthur Anderson in Houston and later continued his CPA practice for 34 years in Grapevine, Texas. An Eagle Scout as a boy was elected and served six years in the Grapevines/Colleyville school district and nine years on the City of Grapevine City Council. He was chairman of the restoration of the historic Palace Theatre. He was named Citizen of the Year in Grapevine.

Dedication

This book of my life's Story is dedicated to our two sons: Julian Ross Pittman and Joel Greer Pittman and our four grandchildren: Noah Waits Pittman, Jack Caulder Pittman, Crawford Dill Pittman, and Adelle Elizabeth Pittman.

Acknowledgments

This book about my life has been proofed, edited, supported, loved, hated, despised, lived, and worked by my adorable, patient, and loving wife of 57 years, Susan Diane Waits Pittman.

Preface

A very trite expression today is "Have A Nice Day". You greet a friend, buy groceries, deal with a purchase online of any kind, a very common closing is one that includes "Have A Nice Day"!

This expression is so trite and worn out that almost no one means it. I have often wondered why most everyone uses it. It has always bothered me due to the insincerity of the statement. Several years ago, I started responding to this worn out

expression by saying "Don't Take it Too Serious". (Yes I know 'seriously' is more correct or perhaps more better, but after all, I am a Texan.) The response to my comments has been overwhelming, and popular, gaining a sincere response most every time.

It is an expression that I have adopted and one that describes me throughout this book. So you now know why I chose the title of my authorship. And when you get tired of reading my book or otherwise get trite in your thoughts. "Don't Take it Too Serious"!

Table of Contents

Chapter 1
It's Been A Good Ride

2/5/06

I wrote these memoirs, on the basis of chronological events in my life for the initial chapters, and then skipped to special events in my life for the following chapters. Some items have been covered in depth with a complete chapter while others have been brought up with a mere sentence or word to avoid a boring reader experience or over-inflation of my ego.

I married the love of my life, Susan Diane Waits, in 1966. She has edited every chapter, proofed every word, suggested titles, and influenced conceptual ideas throughout the book. This work would not have been completed without her support. One way or another, Susan has been in every chapter, in the details or in spirit. She is the apple of my eye, mother of our children, has the patience of Job, and is certainly the color of my life. It shows throughout these memoirs.

I write this for my heirs. I only wish that my grandpa, John Humphrey

Hastings could have imparted a little of his life for me to enjoy and relate to. Grandpa was a cotton farmer in Roscoe, Texas; a bank director at the Roscoe State Bank; and a trustee at the First Methodist Church. He married Lilli Ater, with whom he had eleven children. Wow! He could have left quite a story. I was the youngest grandchild of 24 on the Hastings side of the family, and the best looking, I might add. There were only 5 or 6 of us that graduated from college and I'm the only one to get a Master's degree.

JOHN H. HASTINGS and MR. A.M. DENMAN have been rabbit hunting on the Hastings home place West of Roscoe, Texas. Early 1900's. Johnny is driving. There are at least 3 greyhound dogs in the back seat.

My other grandpa was my father's father, Frank Prior Pittman, but he died long ago in 1950, and his wife, Grandma Pittman (Laura McCarty) died in the 30's, I guess. I know very little about their lives except that they lived on a farm north of Sweetwater, Texas, milked cows, cultivated vegetables, and grew cotton. They had three sons, Rafael, Floy Lionel, and my father, Roy Calvert Pittman. Floy Wallace Pittman, my first cousin, and son of Floy Lionel, later in life, tried to convince me that we were all related to Henry McCarty and his father was Patrick McCarty. Henry changed his name to William Bonney. He became better known as a famous gun fighter, 'Billy the Kid' of New Mexican vintage. My ancestry research into my grandmother Laura McCarty proved this to be untrue.

We lived in Sweetwater where my sister and I were born–Carolyn Ann Pittman in 1939 on Groundhog's Day and yours truly, May 12, 1944, during World War II. Daddy sold wheel balancers during the war and ran a gas station as he was ineligible for the draft for health reasons. Mother had her full-time job in the house: cooking, washing, ironing, and raising chickens. We lived on Avenue B when I was born.

Dorothy Brown lived nearby with her parents. Her then-husband of a very short time was killed at Normandy in World War II. Weldon was a paratrooper. They were married for six months and only lived together for two. Mother and Dorothy were best of friends, such that Dorothy changed my diaper probably as much as Mother did. I grew up loving Dorothy as though she were my mother. Later in life and a while after Mother died (about 1999), I reconnected with Dorothy in Fort Stockton near Fort Davis, our summer home site.

About an hour after I was born in the Sweetwater Hospital, my lifetime friend, Lawson Allen, was also born. We celebrated our birthdays every year thereafter throughout grade school and high school. Fortunately, our respective parents did not mix us up at the hospital because I ended up tall at six-feet-six in favor of my rather tall parents, while Lawson was always short in favor of his short parents. In fact, our classmates nicknamed Lawson 'Squirt,' a name that stayed with Lawson for the rest of his formative years. In 2006, Lawson became my banker as he was the president of the Fort Davis State Bank where we built our summer home. I do not call him 'Squirt' anymore (Much).

I had curly hair, just like my Daddy's hair, while Carolyn's hair was straight. Daddy said that my first barber must have committed suicide six months after cutting my hair for the first time, signaling that he did not want to cut it again! I kept my hair extremely short throughout grade and high school because I was too embarrassed for anyone to know that it was curly. It was in a crew cut or flat top with plenty of hair-arranger wax to keep it straight.

My best friend was Steve Smith. We were inseparable. He spent the night with me one night, and I with him, the next. We played baseball, dug foxholes, caught possum, wrote neighborhood newsletters, worshiped Mickey Mantle and Roger Maris, played miniature golf, spied on Carolyn and Nan, rode bikes, threw newspapers, and hunted dove and rabbits. When he moved to Odessa, we were both heartbroken, such that we wrote to each other every day and caught the T & P train to Odessa or Sweetwater for week end visits. We got over it eventually as we were heavily involved in sports, middle school and later, high school, but we still kept in touch nonetheless.

Chapter 2
Roots - Paternal and Maternal

2/5/07

THE PITTMANS

Floy Pittman and his wife, Audie, had two children–my cousins. Peggy Pittman was my age and her little brother, Jack, was about four years younger. Peggy and I grew up and went to school together. She married Elvis Wilson but divorced him after having two daughters. I never met her daughters. Jack went to Texas Tech, married Sue, and had two boys, Lucas and Justin Pittman. They live in Pottsboro, Texas at the time of writing this book. Lucas Pittman is quite a singer and guitarist; he may be famous and wealthy someday! I have had the pleasure of meeting both. The Pittman name will be carried on to the next generation along with Noah, Jack, and Crawford Pittman, my three grandsons.

Floy had a prior marriage. His wife died before I was born. They had two sons, Floy Wallace Pittman and Morris B. Pittman. Floy Wallace worked for Reynolds Aluminum in Portland, Texas, where he and his wife Joann, a school teacher, lived for many years. My daddy and mother loved Floy very much. They played golf and fished together. Floy and Joann owned a bay-front home in Portland, near Corpus Christi; we spent several nights on their pier catching ocean trout by the hundreds. They retired on a golf course at Wimberley, Texas. They had one daughter, Jan.

Uncle Rafael was my Daddy's country brother, who never moved to town. He and Aunt Pearl had two children, Wanda and Frank Lee Pittman. Wanda married Kenneth Justice and "Frankalee" (as we all called him) never married.

Growing up in Sweetwater was full of the outdoors! I loved to hunt. My country uncle, Rafael Pittman, and his wife, Pearl, lived seven miles north of Sweetwater in Fisher County. I would go out to their Dairy to help them milk their cows; then, afterward, I could go swimming in one of their tanks and hunt rabbits and doves all day. Aunt Pearl was a great cook and made her own bread so I stayed all day and sometimes all night. They owned Jersey milk cows and those cows had to be milked twice daily.

Morris B. Pittman was always called Bud. Bud was in the Navy in the early Fifties, stationed on the USS Los Angeles. He toured the Pacific on this vessel during the Korean War. One Christmas, he sent me a wooden bathtub-toy sized replica of the USS Los Angeles. What a thrill! You can only imagine who my hero was at that time. Bud married Jo and they adopted a daughter. They also lived in Portland, Texas, near the Whataburger, a new concept in hamburgers.

The first President of the United States that I remember was Harry S. Truman in the early 1950s. Somehow, I thought Daddy was saying "Harry Ass" every time he mentioned his name. I do not remember Franklin D Roosevelt or World War II, but I do recall a vacation we took to California to see some of Daddy's relatives. We went to Pikes Peak on the way and I threw Daddy's cap off the highest peak. He found it on the way down. We took this trip in our brand new '51 Cadillac with air conditioning, the kind that comes out of two tubes from behind the back seat.

We vacationed through Death Valley, California with a saddle bag of water hooked to the radiator of the new Cadillac. It produced the best cold water we could find in the 115 degree temperature. Once, we stopped to inspect the car only to find that the green paint on Daddy's new Cadillac was melting. Yes, running off of the hood like water! Wow, my Daddy was a real unhappy camper; in the next town, he bought a dozen eggs and tried to fry eggs on the hood!

We arrived in California and went to Fisherman's Wharf, where there were many unusual smells. I was eight and promptly held my nose due the obnoxious fishy smell everywhere. The little Italian anglers were selling various forms of scallops, shrimp, and fishes of all kinds. I was from Sweetwater, at least 300 miles from fishy smells of any kind. The more I smelled, the sicker I got. One particular angler kept telling me that these smelly things 'were better than candy.' He repeated it enough times that I threw up all over Fisherman's Wharf. Guess, I showed them!

Carolyn graduated from Newman High school in 1957. She and Nan took me to see Little Richard and Elvis Presley at the Sweetwater Municipal Auditorium in 1956. That was the only way Mother would allow Carolyn to go; she had to take her little brother. She did not want me to tag along as I was not the best brother. I used to spy on her and her various boyfriends–Jimmy, Robert Neeper, and others. Man, what you could see happening on the couch of Mother's living room! Carolyn would get so mad she chased me through the house. My defense was to throw a chair in front of her to slow her down.

Daddy and his brother, Floy Pittman, owned a floor covering store during the 1950s and that's where I worked during the summers. Pittman Floor Covering and Furniture had branch stores in Snyder and Colorado City, Texas. They had about five carpet crews that would install carpets at various parts of our trade area. I worked as a helper for the various crews. I also mopped and waxed the floors, delivered furniture, and later sold carpets and furniture. Daddy and Uncle Floy opened another store two blocks from the main Sweetwater store they called "Sputnik" after the Russian spaceship that went into orbit that year. I still have a picture of Daddy, Uncle Floy, and various crew members with their Pittman Floor pickups decked out in a Pittman Floor uniform.

THE HASTINGS

Grandpa Hastings, John H. Hastings was truly a pillar in Roscoe, Texas. He was a cotton farmer, director of the Roscoe State Bank, and long standing member of the Methodist Church. I'm guessing he and grandma thought children were cheaper by the dozen as he and Grandma had eleven children.

Grandma Hastings must have been quite a woman–great cook and a busy mother with eleven kids: Myrtle, Charlie, Olin, Homer, Leila, Jewel, Iona, Vesta, Merlin, Eugenia, and Mildred. When Grandma had my mother (Eugenia Bell), she was convinced that she was going to name the baby Mildred, but Myrtle, the oldest daughter somehow convinced grandma to name the baby Eugenia. About a year or so after that, Grandma had the eleventh child and named it Mildred–the only problem was that it was a boy! So, Mildred Hansen Hastings was his name. We called him Uncle Buddy and NEVER called him Mildred.

Charlie Hastings was the oldest. Charlie's children were Etta Bell and Harold Hastings, my cousins. Harold was a motorcycle police officer in Sweetwater, and later owned a carpet store in Hurst, Texas. In retirement, he was owner of the concession at Lake Bridgeport. The family called him Audrey but everyone else called him Harold.

Myrtle Hastings married Emmitt Mathis and they had one child, Melvis Mathis. They lived in Dallas near SMU, where my Aunt Myrtle taught ceramic painting at SMU. Melvis owned a carpet store distribution warehouse in Dallas. He had two children, Ken and Gloria Mathis. Aunt Myrtle's house or Melvis's house were great stopping places for me as I was periodically pursuing parties or women in the Dallas area (including Susan Waits).

The fall of 1981, a number of things happened. My Aunt, Myrtle Mathis died. She was my Mother's oldest sister. Aunt Myrtle lived in Dallas and taught ceramics at SMU. She and her husband, Emmitt Mathis, provided a place to stay when I visited Susan in Dallas.

Homer Hastings died early in his life, and I never met him, nor did I know any of his children.

Olin Hastings married Florence. They were both schoolteachers in Roscoe. They had two children, Rodney and Beth Hastings. They attended and graduated from Hardin Simmons College in Abilene, Texas. Beth married and taught school in Sweetwater.

Jewel Hastings married Aubrey Taylor and they lived in Fabens Texas where they had three children, Betty Lee Taylor, David Taylor and Jimmy Taylor. David lived in St Paul, Minnesota, last I heard and worked for Northwest Airlines. Betty Lee attended Wynona Taylor Dommert's funeral in 2007 and I was able to visit with her then. Her brother Jimmy Taylor is living in a nudist Colony in North Carolina someplace.

Lelia Hastings married Inman Taylor (the brother of Aubrey Taylor above); they lived in El Paso and had four children, Glen, Jack, Nita, and Wynona. Glen worked for El Paso Natural Gas Company until he died in the 60s. Jack lived in Albuquerque, New Mexico and later moved to Salt Lake City, Utah while Wynona married Howard Dommert and lived in Inverness, Florida, as Howard was a career military man. Later in life, they moved to Kerrville, Texas. Howard and Wynona had two children, Janice and Stan. We were always in touch with Nona and her family. Nona died in 2007 in Kerrville, Texas. I attended her funeral and learned more about the Hastings family.

Iona Hastings married Golden Bennett and lived in Roscoe. Aunt Inie and I were really close, but she loved all of her nieces and nephews equally. She and Uncle Golden never had children so we all belonged to her. Uncle Golden–sometimes we called him Uncle Pete–was a cotton farmer west of Roscoe. I used to help harvest cotton with Uncle Pete and got paid $.25 per hundred cotton I pulled or picked. I worked hard in hot conditions and never really saved money at that rate. Aunt Inie attended Texas Tech but never graduated.

Vesta Hastings married Lee Stephens and lived in Van Horn, Texas, where Uncle Lee worked for the Texas and Pacific railroad. They had two sons, Donald Lee and Kenneth Ray. Donald Lee Stephens and his wife live in Coppell, Texas, where he worked as a school bus driver, and Kenneth Ray Stephens lived in Alpine, Texas, and helped Aunt Vesta with her floral shop in Van Horn. Kenneth never married. He was gay and died shortly after Aunt Vesta died in Van Horn, Texas.

Merlin Hastings married Althaea; they were both teachers in Kress, Texas north of Plainview, Texas. They never had any children. Fat chance! Uncle Merlin had a girl by another women that Grandpa bought off! The illegitimate woman found Lynda Hastings Stafford's DNA through Ancestry proving that she was another cousin. Uncle Merlin and Aunt Althaea both graduated from Texas Tech, which was one of my ambitions to attend.

Mildred Hastings was called Uncle Buddy for obvious reasons! He married Theda and they had two children. Maurice Hastings was about three years my senior and Lynda Jane Hastings was the same age as I. Uncle Buddy and Aunt Theda lived on the Hastings home place and farmed cotton west of Roscoe. This was the place that Grandpa Hastings owned. Uncle Buddy later worked for several years in Sweetwater for a distribution company owned by Jimmy Carson's father. Maurice Hastings lived in Garland, Texas, while Lynda Jane married Butch Stafford and live in Dublin, Texas.

Grandma and Grandpa Hastings gave each of us grandchildren $1.00 for Christmas. We always gathered at the Roscoe home in town for Christmas lunch. I was so impressed that I had so many cousins–twenty six of them. Kenneth, Maurice, David were similar ages, while Donald Lee, David, Jimmy and Rodney ran together, and Carolyn, Donald Lee, and Beth were best buddies of a similar age.

I was the youngest, the baby, and of course, the best looking!

Once, I climbed on top of Grandpa's windmill. He was to catch me when I came down. Instead, I fell, scraping my wrist and arm against the stucco garage next to the windmill. Worse, it scared me out of my wits! I was five years old. I was afraid of heights from that point onward in my life.

Grandpa Hastings was a trader. He always had a knife that he wanted to trade with me so I always took about three knives to negotiate with him. Each time, I returned home with a new knife, many times with more knives than I brought. Grandpa stood out on the front porch with all of his sons and sons-in-law smoking cigarettes. He did not smoke but would light one up and hold it with two fingers, trying to act like he was smoking. He was, I am sure, trying to bond with his sons and sons-in-law.

Grandma Hastings made the best pies and cakes! She always worked hard in the kitchen and was a great cook.

Grandpa Hastings died in 1954. I was ten years old, and his was probably the first funeral I had ever attended. It was really hard on me as Grandpa and I were good friends. The Methodist church in Roscoe was packed with friends and of course, family. All of the children and their husbands and wives along with all of the children gathered to celebrate Grandpa's life. Grandma Hastings died in 1960 in her bed at home in Roscoe. I met most of my twenty-six cousins at Grandpa's funeral. Only three or four of us grandchildren graduated from College–Rodney, Beth, Lynda and Me.

My Daddy also liked Grandpa but called him 'Mr.' Hastings. He had less respect for other members of Mother's family. Aunt Inie always called Mother on the phone using a collect call feature, which reverses the charge for the long distance call to the person being called. Now Aunt Inie lived seven miles away in Roscoe, but Mother would reply to the operator that "if she can't afford the call, I will pay for it." It was all of ten cents for the entire call. Daddy referred to the Hastings in general as tight! I believe he would say that they were tighter than a chigger's ass!

The Hastings family still had family reunions periodically. Buddy Hastings, Iona Bennett (Aunt Inie), Vesta Stephens, and Mother (Eugenia Bell Hastings Pittman Freeze) were the remaining members of the twelve Hastings family from Roscoe, sons and daughters of John and Lillie Hastings. The twenty-six grandchildren and many more great grandchildren were eager to attend the Hastings reunion. Susan and I had been married about ten years and she had witnessed at least two or three of these, so we decided to host the reunion at our home in Colleyville during the summer of 75 or 76, with Mother's help.

The invitations went out and we were anticipating as many as sixty people to enjoy our back yard, swimming pool, games, and all. Jay was excited about meeting more of his cousins. Greer was only two years old, but he was ready for anything! At that age, Greer was always ready for anything; thus, Susan and I needed to be prepared!

The day arrived, but the only problem was that it rained several days before the party and our septic tank was full. The commodes would not flush. The sinks would not carry the water out; we could not wash dishes. And we had 60 guests! It was really embarrassing and disgusting. Many took trips to the local service stations; others used the backyard discretely.

Mother kept up with Inie, Vesta and Buddy better than the others and I remember some unusual stories about them.

In 1994, Aunt Inie, who now lived in a rest home in Roscoe, died, which was twelve days before Mother's death. Since Aunt Inie had no heirs, she gave her entire estate to her then living siblings. The only ones left were Uncle Buddy, Aunt Vesta, and Mother (Eugenia Bell). Since Mother died twelve days after Aunt Inie died, Mother's estate became heir to one third of Aunt Inie's estate, to the dismay of Buddy and his wife Theta as they commented.

I was a practicing certified public accountant in Grapevine at the time, and Aunt Inie had previously asked me to be the co-executor of her estate along with her brother, Buddy. I then found out what my Daddy meant about how tight the Hastings were when Uncle Buddy and Aunt Theda asked to be reimbursed mileage for their travel (as co-executors) from their home in Early, Texas, to Roscoe to visit Aunt Inie in the rest home WHILE she was living! I refused to pay them mileage out of the Aunt Inie's estate for the period while Aunt Inie lived but paid them mileage out of the estate for the travel to help me conduct the marshaling of her estate. I received no compensation whatsoever–and certainly no mileage from Grapevine to Roscoe.

Several years later, Aunt Althea was in a rest home in Kress, Texas. Buddy and Theta were all over that in that they decided to have her moved from her rest home to one in Early or Brownwood, Texas, telling me that money could be saved by doing so. Aunt Althea died six months after they moved her. I was not an heir of her estate, but Buddy called me several times on her estate and the probate process required marshaling her assets. Buddy told me that Aunt Althea had changed the beneficiary of her Texas Teacher life insurance policy to Lynda Hastings Stafford (Buddy and Theta's daughter). This spiked my interest in the estate further, so I contacted the County Clerk in Brown County and received a copy of Althea Hastings' probate estate. That's when I found out that $30,000 was left out of the estate before settlement with the remaining heir, Vesta Hastings Stephens in Van Horn, Texas. I had no interest in the estate other than trying to attain justice, so I when I visited Aunt Vesta and told her about the missing $30,000, she replied, "If he can live with it, then I can live without it."

Buddy and Theda died in early 2000 or so. I did not attend their funerals as I had no respect for them either. It probably alienated Maurice and Lynda, my cousins.

She made me the co-executor of her will and when I called my high school best friend, Lance Hall who was a practicing attorney in Sweetwater to probate my mother's and Aunt Inie's respective wills–he did both for the price of one! That is really what I called "a twofer!"

Once while I was in Sweetwater working on settling the two estates, I met with Buddy and Theda at the bank and learned why they were bitter at me. My Aunt Inie's will left her estate to her surviving siblings and they were Buddy Hastings, Aunt Vesta Stephens in Van Horn, Texas, and my Mother, Eugenia Pittman. Theta and Buddy, in a very subtle way mentioned that if only my mother had died before Aunt Inie, then her remaining estate would have been divided two ways instead of three ways–obviously more for them!

By this time, I was very curious to see how much Buddy reported as probate to Brown County (Brownwood) and how much my Aunt Vesta got after the Estate was settled. I also did not trust Buddy. So, I called the County Clerk of Brown County and asked if she could send me a copy of my Aunt Althelea's probate record. I sent her $10.00 for the copy and when I received it, I was not surprised to find that Buddy had reported $30,000 less than the total cash and certificates of deposit that were on hand and previously discussed with me at the time of death!

Aunt Vesta was the last to die, a few years later. I flew out to Midland, rented a car, and attended her funeral. I picked up Carolyn in Odessa, who went to Van Horn with me.

Susan and I purchased two memorial stones at the Merket Center at Texas Tech in memory of Iona (Inie) Hastings Bennett and Merlin Hastings—both either attended or graduated from Texas Tech. Aunt Inie attended while Uncle Merlin got his degree there and became a career teacher in Plainview and later in Kress, Texas.

Aunt Vesta Hastings Stephens had two children, Donald and Kenneth Stephens. Donald lived in Coppell, Texas, and in his later years, drove a school bus, while Kenneth lived with his mother, Vesta, in Van Horn, Texas. Susan and I played golf with Kenneth at Marfa periodically when we would travel out there. Kenneth was a florist and caterer. He was never married and never came out of the closet to my knowledge.

Kenneth died suddenly a year or so after his mother died. Donald called me to tell me. I planned to drive out for the funeral, but Donald said that an autopsy was being performed. When I called back a day or so later, he told me none was performed, and that the funeral was the day before.

Chapter 3
Carolyn Ann Pittman Selinger

8\8\10

CAROLYN ANN PITTMAN SELINGER

One Easter, I was given a purple chicken. We already had about two hundred chickens in the backyard, but Daddy figured I needed a pet chicken. The baby chick was dyed purple, so I named him Purp. Of course, his purple color went away as he got older. His feathers turned white. That fact did not matter, since Purp and I had bonded. Purp followed me everywhere I went, and I fed Purp a special diet separate and apart from the other chickens. You see, Purp was special. My sister is five years older and well, she and, shall I say, never bonded. So, I taught Purp to not like Carolyn. Purp chased Carolyn with vengeance all over the backyard, pecking at her ankles and legs. The only place she could seek safety was on top of Mother's car and she screamed for Mother to referee the melee.

I love my sister and always have, but I was always her dumb little brother. Her pals, Nan Williams and Carolyn Templeton would team up to give me trouble, so Purp was my best friend.

One Saturday morning, Mother had fried chicken for dinner, much to Carolyn's delight, as it was Purp. I did not speak to either of them the rest of the day.

Carolyn did not marry Jimmy or Robert, but instead went off to SMU to pursue a college degree in 1957. SMU was an expensive place to go, but Daddy and Mother buckled down for the fun. I guess that since she was a blonde, she had to pledge 'Delta, Delta, Delta,' which was imagined in my mind later when I attended Texas Tech, that the Tri-Deltas only pledged blondes! She was never initiated into the sorority because her grades began to decline or perhaps, they never got high enough to even stay in college.

She must have had a good time at SMU; perhaps she was pursuing her MRS degree as it was suggested later. By the beginning of the spring semester, Mother and Daddy had received her grades and they were not good! She continued this trend for the second semester. One morning at breakfast, I noticed that my Daddy was crying. I had never seen him cry…only to learn that Carolyn had flunked out of SMU.

I was two years from Graduation–a junior at Newman High School, when Carolyn and Chuck would come home to Sweetwater on visits as they lived in Fort Worth. Chuck owned a slick 1959 apricot-colored Ford convertible. Wow, it was really a 'hot' car. Wow! I had visions and dreams of driving around Sweetwater, especially around the courthouse square so all my friends could be green with envy in that hot convertible. Chuck would not allow it. In fact, the convertible top never came down on their visits to Sweetwater.

Carolyn and Chuck had four children. Tanner, Suzanne, Eric, and Richard were their names. All of them graduated from Permian High School in Odessa. Tanner married Darlene and they had two great children. They are divorced now. Suzanne married Brian and they had two children. Eric married twice and had one child by the second marriage. He is divorced now. Richard lives with a woman, and they have two children. They have never married.

Over several years, Mother helped the Selingers out financially in many ways as that was a real trend. She guaranteed a loan at Don Brown's Savings and a loan in Wichita Falls and over a period of years, Chuck defaulted on the loan and Mother had to use her CD's to liquidate the loan.

This default embittered Mother. Mother worked hard for her nest eggs and wanted Chuck to repay the loan. It never happened. She never had much appreciation for Chuck. She even recommended that Carolyn divorce Chuck. Mother went to her lawyer and changed her will. She set up a trust for Carolyn's share of her estate after her death. The trust would dole out necessities to Carolyn so long as she continued to be married to Chuck. She named me to be the trustee of Carolyn's trust.

Mother sent me a copy of the draft will. The will upset me very much when I asked her if she had discussed the trust and its purpose with Carolyn. She replied that she had not. I resigned as trustee and told Mother that I refused to do be a party of any kind to inform Carolyn of the trust AFTER her death. She did not want to tell Carolyn and I refused to do her 'dirty work!'

I recommended that Chuck should sign a promissory note to her bearing a reasonable rate of interest and that the note would be paid out of Carolyn's share after Mother's death. The draft will was changed, the trust was eliminated, and paragraphs added identifying that $24,000 was to be paid out of Carolyn's share of the estate together with 6% interest. She never prepared a promissory note and really did not want to upset Carolyn and her relationship with the grandchildren. Carolyn never knew about the trust either. She merely put a note in her will instructions to collect the money from Carolyn's share which was done.

Chuck had many jobs and borrowed money from my mother and never paid it back but he also stiffed me when I bought a cell phone following Carolyn's request and never reimbursed me despite my pleas. Carolyn was a registered nurse in Odessa. She developed dementia and died in 2012, unexpectedly. She was 73.

Chapter 4
Small Town Texas – 50's Style

7/17/07

Newman High School was named after Mose Newman, a local rancher that donated the land for the school. The Newmans lived across the street from our home at 308 Ragland, a big fancy house with white columns on the front porch. Mose Newman had died long ago, but the Newman family still lived at the house on Ragland. It was not far from the high school, so I presume that the Newmans owned all of the land to and beyond the high school. Newman was a name we often associated with the popular magazine 'Alfred E. Newman' so we nicknamed the high school 'Alfred E. Newman High School.' The school board changed the name of the high school, several years after I graduated in 1962, to Sweetwater High School. They also tore down the old two-story brick building that was the place for the infamous 'Library Run' when I was a senior there.

I played basketball in high school. In West Texas, basketball players were second-class athletes compared to football players. We ate hamburgers on our road trips while they ate steaks. They traveled in Greyhound buses while we would travel in school buses (Yellow hounds). I often remember having a flat tire on the inside of the rear wheels on the way back from long basketball trips like Lamesa, Snyder, or Lakeview. An inside flat tire meant that the outside tire had to be removed before the inside tire could be repaired. It was also bitterly cold when the yellow hound decided to have a flat tire, and we all had to get off the bus while the spare was installed.

Lance Hall and I became best friends. We were inseparable! He was elected president of the state's 'Future Teachers of America,' and the only way I could attend the state convention in Austin with him was for me to play the Star-Spangled Banner during the opening ceremony of the convention. I had been taking organ lessons for the past three years, so I thought I was qualified. My lessons were on a Hammond Organ, but the convention organ was a Baldwin. It did not go very well that morning since Lance and I had been up the entire night before. Someone said that the bass notes sounded like Elliott Ness breaking down a door.

We played basketball together, drove around town, thought about pretty girls, and drank beer. Sweetwater was not 'wet' according to the Texas liquor laws; in order to buy any alcohol, we had to drive to Impact, Texas, to a legitimate liquor store, or drive to the local bootlegger, Curly. It was a crude drive through and around his house. Curly lived in the west part of town, where most of the other Hispanics lived. When you drove over to Curly's, you would feel a little uneasy because you just knew that every house had a spy watching your every move. Curly had a lot of friends looking after him. He was illegal and so were we, buying beer from him. I really think the police turned their head and allowed Curly to conduct business as usual. A quart of beer cost $.50, fifty cents, or four bits. Lance and I took our beer to either the Midway or Rocket drive-in outdoor theatres. The sound was on a speaker box wired to poles in the parking lot that hung on the window and allowed us to watch the movie on large screens. The beer would last us the entire movie and the evening. A quart of beer was plenty for us as we could feel the buzz.

Mrs. Zelma Hulse was the librarian at Newman High School. She was a unique teacher at the high school in that no one liked her. She had too many rules, played favorites, and intimidated most of the students. Lance and I decided that we should celebrate National Library Week in style at Sweetwater High, so we designed a 'run on the library.' We asked everyone in the high school to check out a book or several books and then turn them all back in to the library on a particular day during Library Week. At the time, Lance was still the president of the FTA and I was president of the Student Body. Well, the 'library run' went off with a few hitches. Zelma Hulse was elated that so many students were actively checking out books in celebration of the National Library week. Her assistant librarians all chose to be ill the day the books were to be turned in, so Zelma had it all to herself!

According to the plan, all books were to be turned in at a specific time. Books were all over the floor of the library. People threw books through all three doors of the library. Since we had no air conditioning, the windows were open, so books were received through the windows! It was wonderful, and although Zelma did not have a nervous breakdown, the message was clearly delivered. 'The Library Run' was the name of the Event and it is talked about this day! John White was the principal of the high school, and he gave me and Lance three days of suspension from the high school and three points off of every grade. It was worth it!

I was a student guest of the Sweetwater Rotary Club as a member of the student senate, and president of the student body during my senior year. My friends included Nancy Price, Tommy Leonard, Kenny Eads, Lawson Allen, Buddy Aldridge, Lance Hall, Richard Green, Diane Young, Linda Taylor, and Bill Shaw, naming only a few. I got involved with thespians and had leading roles in the one-act plays, 'Little Women, Meet Me in St. Louis,' and 'Harvey.' I played Elwood P. Dowd in 'Harvey' and tried it again in Grapevine for the Runway Players in 1986.

Daddy was on the road, traveling most of the time, selling carpet and linoleum. He discovered a mole on his left arm near his wristwatch and consulted with a chiropractor in Odessa, Texas. The chiropractor burned it off, only for the growth to return some three months later, which the chiropractor again burned off. A knot or two cropped up in his left arm and his doctor, TD Young, sent him to M.D. Anderson Hospital in Houston. He was diagnosed with melanoma cancer. They removed most of the lymph nodes in his arm and armpit, but to no avail, as he did not live beyond a year from the diagnosis. Daddy had a fair completion. He had moles on his body. Sun exposure with these characteristics will more than likely produce melanoma, as it did for him. Roy C. Pittman died on January 30, 1962–only four months prior to my graduation from high school. We buried Daddy at the Garden of Memories in Sweetwater. He was forty-nine. I was seventeen.

Playing Elwood Dowd in Harvey helped me recover from the shock of my father's death. The summer after graduation, I worked at the cement plant at Maryneal, Texas, and helped Mother manage the carpet store. I continued organ lessons at McMurry College.

Mother was a real trooper after Daddy's death. She had never worked at the store (Pittman Floor Covering, Inc.) her entire life, but the Monday after we buried Daddy, she stepped right in to conduct the affairs of the retail carpet store. Daddy had previously bought controlling interest of the store from his brother, Floy Pittman, in anticipation of his death.

Graduation from Newman High school was in May with the usual events of partying, getting graduation gifts, and drinking beer. I got $50.00 for graduation from Floy Wallace Pittman and another $50.00 from Bud Pittman–they must have thought it was a miracle that I was graduating! Lance and I celebrated by going to Curly's for a beer. Neither of us had girlfriends to speak of, since we had intentions of leaving Sweetwater and going off to college as soon as possible. I dated Lynn Hixon, Linda Taylor, and Diane Young periodically through high school but never got serious with anyone.

Mother and I took a couple of vacations that summer. Mother needed a break after my father's lengthy illness with cancer and his ultimate death. We flew to Seattle and attended the World's Fair. We dined in the famed Space Needle, the icon of the Fair. We drove a rented car to Victoria and took a ferry down Puget Sound through Vancouver and finally back to Seattle. We also went to New York and Harford, Connecticut, where Carolyn and Chuck lived with their son and my nephew, Tanner Selinger. We saw 'Golden Boy' on Broadway in New York, starring Johnny Mathis.

Lance was a National Merit Finalist and received a full scholarship at the University of Denver. I graduated from Sweetwater High School in the top ten percent of my class and got accepted at Texas Technological College. Daddy had left me an insurance policy for $5,000 which was to help me get started in college, and Lyndon Johnson had pushed legislation through congress to supply monthly benefits for children of deceased social security members. This benefit lasted for two years after Daddy's death. I promptly went to the Chevrolet dealership and bought a brand new 1962 Hardtop Chevrolet Impala with the money–surely this would impress the girls at college! It had bucket seats, and I had a cushion made to fit between the buckets with a big double-T on it so the girls could sit closer to me when I was driving!

Chapter 5
College

I enrolled at Texas Tech in the fall of 1962. I had never been to a college football game, never attended a pep rally with 4,000 kids, and never attended an English class with 400 other students. I moved into Carpenter Hall on the Tech campus and had a roommate from Burkburnett, Texas who was a Caucasian acting like a Hispanic.

We played Texas University for my first football game. Our coach, J.T. King, decided to punt the ball back to the Longhorns on the kickoff, which we did! We went on and lost that game 49-7. I guess Coach King had seen the elephant and decided to play defense. We went on that season and won one game at the end of the season against Colorado in the snow! We were 1-9! My first college football season!

I got a job, selling clothes at Dom's Limited, a popular men's clothing store one block off campus. Bill and Jean Neal were the owners and a lot of fun. Bill drank Canadian Club whiskey every afternoon and showed up at the store with a red face, assuring us, the salesmen, that the rush was coming from downtown and Dillard's at any time. My wardrobe improved substantially while working there–alligator shoes, belts, Gant shirts, and blazers–yes blazers, blue and black blazers! White shirts with a ton of starch were extremely popular. I met a lot of people while working there and learned a lot about retail clothing sales. My first acquaintance with Jay Stanley was through Dom's Ltd, as his mother, Millie, would come into the store to buy clothing for Jay. They lived in Lubbock, but Jay was a burnt orange student at the University of Texas. Jay and I were of similar build and size, so his mom would use me to try on—you guessed it blazers. Jay and I became best of friends several years later and this friendship is very dear and special to me today.

My first English paper (in my class of 400) received an F, a failing grade. So did my second one. I was taking 16 hours in my first semester. My first history hour quiz was an F, also a failing grade. I wasn't doing well in Botany or Algebra either. My roommate Robert Eaton was no help since he kept asking several of his Latino friends in Lubbock to come over so he could have conversational Spanish with them. I ended up studying most of the time at the Tech Library. Finally, after coming to my dorm room one night to find one of his Latino friends sleeping in my bed, I drew the line and asked him to leave, letting my roommate know that I did not approve of his Spanish betterment procedures. At the end of the semester, I requested a new roommate.

By Thanksgiving, I was a bit discouraged, if not depressed. I was failing two subjects and not doing well in the others. The only friends I had on the dorm wing were not doing well either, such that all they did was go out and drink beer. I was studying hard but finding myself in a tailspin, often thinking that I was not capable enough for college. Sweetwater was two hours away, but my mother, who had not attended college, and whose daughter had flunked out of SMU, was little help with my predicament. I missed my father for the first time in a real big way. If I could only talk out my problems with him.

During the Thanksgiving break, Mother set up an appointment for me to visit our family doctor, Dr. Frank Barker, in Abilene, Texas. Dr. Barker was a trusted friend as well as the family physician. He was one of Daddy's pallbearers at his funeral, the year before. Dr. Barker agreed with me at once that I was not college material. He suggested that I leave Tech and join the Army or Air Force.

Well, Vietnam was the order of the day, and everyone who joined the army or air force was shipped over there. Several of my high school buddies had gone and returned to Sweetwater in body bags! I was not ready for this. After Thanksgiving break, I went to the Dean and dropped five hours of study. Since I was not failing Botany or History, they had to go and nothing would be appended to my transcript other than a W-P (withdrew passing). I turned English and Economics around and I made a 2.9 on a 4.0 system for the semester.

The sage advice of Dr. Barker was, in effect, reverse psychology and it worked! It got my attention and was the next best advice compared to my father that I could have had. I finished college without failing one grade and made the Dean's list several semesters!

I hated to drop Botany, because I had a friend in class with me that was doing worse than me. His name was John Deutschendorf from Fort Worth. John's problem was that he did not attend class often; instead, he would be in his dorm room playing his guitar and singing songs. He was quite good and played with the Alpine Trio–a group of fraternity guys who played at various smokers (rush parties) and other parties. John was also cutting his other classes such that he flunked out of Tech by the end of the semester. It was a year later that I heard John was still playing and singing, but he had changed his name to John Denver!

One day in November, 1962, I was on a lunch break, eating a Monte Christo sandwich at the Broadway Drug, when I heard the radio announce that President John Kennedy had been assassinated in Dallas, Texas. What a horror, the President being shot in my home state! I kept my eyes on the television for the rest of the weekend during the aftermath, mourning the loss of a great leader. Flags were half mask for the rest of the month, and everyone was in shock.

For the second semester, I had enrolled in 17 hours, this time with improved attitude, scheduling my time diligently, getting a new roommate, and with renewed confidence. I got a job playing the organ at the Plainsman Hotel on Friday nights and later they asked me to play Saturdays as well. After dinner, music is what their guests wanted so I played and played. I got another job later playing for Ritz Funeral Home for every day (or almost) everyday. Ritz would have a 2 pm funeral, so I played the organ, usually repeating the same songs–In the Garden, I love to tell the Story, and The Old Rugged Cross. I got paid $5.00 per funeral and that was enough to take a date for dinner and a movie. One day, I arrived at the funeral home early, long before the 2 pm service, so I decided to practice a new organ piece that I had acquired. It was John Phillip Sousa's Stars and Stripes Forever. The body in the casket certainly did not care what I played, I was merely practicing; however, the family walked into the parlor as I was playing. Mr. Ritz was not pleased, and I was really embarrassed—oh I guess I was. I almost lost my job! With three or more funerals each week, I was breaking even! Bread cost twenty-five cents, as did milk, and a six-pack of beer was seventy-five cents, while I got my shirts washed, ironed, and starched for $1.35 per dozen!

The second semester brought rush parties, and I considered pledging a fraternity. I was really getting to like college life. I was being rushed by three fraternities, Phi Psys, Phi Delta Theta, and Phi Gamma Delta. I really liked a lot of the guys going through rush with me and many of us confided that if certain things happen, we would or would not pledge this or that. One that I remember clearly was if Roland Anderson pledged one way, several of us would go the opposite way. Roland was squirrelly.

Bid day arrived and I pledged Phi Gamma Delta (the FIJIS) along with twenty-five other men that I was getting ready to know and know well—guys that I would know and love for the rest of my life. Bill Ed Abraham, Jimmy Adams, Jerry Breed, Ralph Timothy Evans, Donald Bruce Davis, Ronald Mack Jackson, Ranny Greebon, Charles Perry Wright, Craig Sutton, Michael Gireau Moore, Jack Robbins, Jerry Steven Rawls, Jic Club, Clark Pfluger, Lee Wooten Williams, Robert Smith, Craig Sutton, Trent Humphrey, were my new pledge brothers.

This semester was to be our test as to whether we would luck out and become a member of Phi Gamma Delta. We would have to secure the signatures of each and every active member in the interest of getting to know each. Some signatures were truly memorable, and others were tough, with various tasks needed before a signature could be attained. We had much to learn, memorize, and many meetings—both social and business-themed. Our pledge trainers were Richard Pfeiffer, and Robert Paulson, both of whom I developed the highest respect for, if not fear and hate.

The fraternity encouraged scholarship by supplying a study hall for all of us and tutors if necessary. If we did not make our grades for the semester, we would not be started into the fraternity. Pledges were considered the lowest form of fraternity life possible. We had our own pledge retreat, or pledge cut as we called it. We would go to Pfluger's ranch in New London, Texas. We drank a lot of beer, drove jeeps around the ranch, and got to know each other much better. We crowned Craig Sutton and began calling him "blinky" because he blinked all the time with contacts, Perry Wright became "W.A" which stood for 'Wise Ass'. Don Davis became "Jigger"; Mike Moore became "Gireau" because he had such a cool middle name. My nickname became "Bo" as in Jerry-bo, I guess. That was a lot better than Jughead, the label that my Daddy gave me around the floor-covering store. Bill Ed Abraham was from Canadian, Texas and Lebanese, I suppose, but we were convinced he was a Mexican-Jew.

"Candy-ass or taffy ass" meant you were hooked on some girl and could not see straight. A dirty leg was a girl who had a questionable reputation. I did not date much my freshman year since pledging the fraternity, holding down two jobs (Dom's / funerals), and maintaining good grades with 17 hours was enough. We ate the dorm food until we moved out at the end of our freshman year; the food was not that good, but the milk was great—all you could drink from the Tech dairies.

I made my grades and finished my pledge duties. Don Davis and I played tennis that last day of school–why I put this in the book, I am not sure, except that is exactly what we did. We were both excited about returning to Tech for our sophomore year to be started in the fraternity and take some new pledges that we could harass! I worked all summer long at the cement plant at Maryneal and helped Mother with the duties of the store. I loved to hunt so I spent a lot of time in the country north of Sweetwater, hunting whatever I could in whatever season was open. Dove season starts in Texas on September 1 and with few exceptions, I have rarely missed opening day.

Football at Texas Tech improved during my second year. All of the Fijis sat in generally the same area for the games as it was quite a social occasion. Everyone dressed up for the games including a coat and tie, and freshly polished shoes. The football games were quite eventful as well as history defining. We played SMU in a hailstorm. It was hailing so hard that players could not hear the signals being called on the field. The game was delayed at least 30 minutes until the hail and rain subsided. My date was Mary Beth Diers, who wore alligator shoes to the game, and I had to carry her out of the stadium while she protected her precious shoes. I did not date her again. Another game that season was with Kansas and a storm blew in from the North together with high winds. It was the beginning of the third or fourth quarter when a tornado was sighted north of Lubbock. Tech was leading the game and the Kansas team decided to go home! I have heard that was one of the very few games that were never finished in the Southwest Conference.

I moved out of the dorm and into the Lubbock Apartments on Fifth Street with my new roommate, Jerry Rawls. Jerry was from Houston Bellaire High School and was majoring in mechanical engineering. He and I had pledged Fiji together and we seemed to have a lot in common. We both had a desire to study and get good grades, we liked to party not to excess, and we were both poor. We would alternate as to who would drive out to the famous strip to buy beer and we looked for ways to save our pennies. We ate one meal per day at Ma Tyler's boarding house, six days per week which cost $35.00 per month. Ma Tyler was a crusty old and big woman that took no shit from anyone. She made the best yeast rolls and on Fridays, she always served roast beef.

Our neighbors next door at the Lubbock apartments were Jack Vanderburg and Marvin "Hog" Stephens. Jack and Marvin were rarely sober and partied a lot. They were bad influences for me and Rawls. Jack is now president and owner of a bank in Spearman, Texas. Marvin married up and became an orthodontist who now lives in Tyler. The apartment manager at the Lubbock Apartments began stealing beer out of our refrigerator while we were away at school during the day. After we had enough of this, I took three beer cans and punched one hole in the top of all three. I placed a note under the three beers saying that one of the beers was full of arsenic–and that it would be his guess as to which one. He never stole beer from us again. We drank all three beers.

That Fall of 1963, I continued to work at Dom's Ltd and my wardrobe continued to improve. I continued to play the organ for funerals at Ritz Funeral Home and I went to work for Mrs. Baird's bakery, driving a bread truck on Sundays. This job not only provided some badly needed cash but kept me and Rawls with ample bread and milk. You see, I got to know the milk drivers on their Sunday routes, and we swapped bread for milk.

My major was always business. Since I had dropped Botany, I decided to take Foods and Nutrition and Horticulture as my science requirement. Both courses were far more practical than Botany and Zoology. I have found that as an adult who owns a home with gardens and flowerbeds, the horticulture course was the most helpful.

I knew I did not care for economics; it was too theoretical for me. Micro and macroeconomics were so idealistic and not scientific enough for my brain. I had to have four courses in economics so I made an A, B, C, and then a D in the final one. I was thankful that my degree plan did not need five courses in Economics! I declared my major to be financial management, which was oriented towards banking, but required four accounting courses. I took elementary accounting and liked it, so I moved into intermediate accounting with little effort.

Chapter 6
College 3rd and 4th Years

I joined Saddle Tramps, a spirit organization for Texas Tech. We wore red shirts and carried a cowbell on a piece of wood to all the games. We had a special place to sit at football and basketball games and that came in handy as the Tech basketball team during the Spring of 1964 was quite successful with Dub Malaise, Harold Denny, Glen Hallum, Norman Reuther, Billy Tapp–some of the ball players that came within one game of winning the Southwest Conference. We were declared ineligible for the season, the results of Norman Reuther's grades or his class load.

It was difficult to attend church because I was too busy delivering bread for Mrs. Baird's bakery. When possible, I would attend the evening service of the First Methodist Church on Broadway. I missed going because I was brought up in Sunday school and church as a kid. Mother and Daddy took us to church every Sunday and we always went home afterwards to eat roast beef and potatoes. I was a member of MYF (Methodist Youth Fellowship) and their president during my senior year of high school. I also attended several summer church camps.

Lyndon Johnson was sworn in as President of the United States after John F. Kennedy was assassinated in Dallas. The war with Vietnam was still very serious with jungle warfare–a war no one thought we could or would win. A lot of my college buddies were drafted and went off to Vietnam. My junior year at Tech was full of fraternity, Saddle Tramps, women, football, and work among other things.

Money was not plentiful. Mother was a great help with tuition and books, but I had to work to provide almost everything else. I worked at the Cement plant during the summer and saved my money. I was doing well in accounting courses so Dr. Doyle Z. Williams hired me as his assistant. Thus, I was engaged in grading papers and doing research for him when I had the time. Dr. Williams was an associate professor of accounting at

Tech and provided encouragement for me in the accounting arena.

Mrs. Baird Bread Company hired me to deliver bread on Sundays to about 25 grocery stores. The job consumed Sunday mornings until the Fiji intramurals started in the afternoon. Then, at about 4 pm I had to make my rounds again and restock the bread inventory at various stores.

I began driving a "sound truck" for Mrs. Baird's bakery on the weekends. Mrs. Baird had a van with speakers on the top with a fairly sophisticated amplifier inside that furnished the sound truck to various functions in the Lubbock area. A public address system is exactly what various rodeos needed to provide sound on Saturday and Sunday afternoons and evenings. Brownfield, Littlefield, Lamesa, Sudan, Idalou, and others all had rodeos periodically, and I provided the van and the sound!

Texas Tech lost to Georgia Tech in the Gator Bowl, and we had wagered with the Fijis there regarding the game, so we provided them a purple Fiji blanket with lettering that signified the loss. Oh well, at least we were not punting the ball back to Georgia Tech like we did with Texas U on the kickoff that year! Donnie Anderson was our All-American football player, and with the passing arm of Tom Wilson, our team had a fairly good season.

I don't remember all the women that I dated except a few, and it is just as well. None of them meant anything except a date. My dedication to completing my degree with good grades and keeping myself financially stable was paramount. I do remember going to the Kappa Kappa Gamma and Pi Beta Phi black tie formals with Mary Beth Diers and Pat Rolf respectively. My date for the annual Fiji Island dance was the most memorable, since that was the last time I ever drank straight whiskey. I had a date (her name was Carolyn (something), a Zeta, and I am really glad I am unable to remember her name. She drove my super sport to her dorm that night without me. All I remember is that I got it back the next afternoon somehow. Drinking alcohol was never a big event for me after that for the rest of my life.

I ran for office and was elected to the Student Senate at Texas Tech in the

Spring of '65 where I got to know a lot of new people outside of Saddle Tramps and the fraternity. The student senate governed student affairs and worked closely with the Tech administration. It was a good experience and exposure for me as I was developing a real desire to branch out to new horizons beyond the fraternity. Some of the people I remember meeting and getting to know include G.W. Bailey, Tommy Craddick, Roland Anderson, Mike Horridge, C.C. Willis, Johnny Ayres. G.W. Bailey later became an actor in Hollywood starring in M.A.S.H. and The Closer, while Tom Craddick became a rather worthless Republican and Speaker of the Texas House of Representatives. John Ayres died in Vietnam tragically, by suicide. He was the President of my fraternity and a Captain in the Army. I never knew what traumas he had in Nam.

Sweetwater became somewhat famous for their annual Rattlesnake Roundup which was conducted the first weekend of March each year. I participated annually in the event. Rattlesnake custom was to hibernate through the winter months in caves and rock embankments. During the spring of each year, they would begin to squirm out of their dens, seeking the warmer sunshine. Gasoline sprayed into their dens created a loss of oxygen for them, thereby forcing them to come out more rapidly. Special hooks were used to catch the snakes and put them in 55-gallon empty oil drums. The snakes were carried back to the Sweetwater Coliseum to be entered in the annual contest. There would be a banquet on Saturday night of the big weekend and Miss Snake Charmer would be crowned to hold office for one year until another would be so anointed. At the Coliseum, snake demonstrations of all kinds were on display, including cooking and eating rattlesnake meat. It did not taste too bad, sort of like fried chicken. One could learn how to milk the venom out of a snake. The venom would be used medically to create a snakebite cure.

The biology (Zoology) department of Texas Tech expressed a desire to have some rattlesnakes to study, dissect, or whatever. Somehow, I got the word and considered it my mission. So, I crated eighty-eight snakes to take back to Lubbock for their benefit.

Jerry Rawls and I had moved into an efficiency apartment that had one kitchen, one bath, and one large bedroom. The snakes were in a wooden box in the back of my car. They were dormant since it was bitterly cold outside. All were asleep and not a creature was stirring, but I felt sorry for them, so I moved the entire box inside to the far wall in the kitchen where the only light switch was. I then got ready and went to pick up my date. Rawls was taffy over Sally and had already left for his date, presumably a FIJI party.

Rawls came home first from his date, and I arrived a few minutes later to find Rawls sitting in his car, shivering and cursing a blue streak about rattlesnakes all over our apartment! He knew nothing of the box or even that I had brought these snakes to Lubbock. But he did know that I had something to do with the snakes. He was not happy!

I merely opened the kitchen door and walked across the room and turned on the light switch above the box of snakes. And yes, the snakes had waked up—rattling rather loudly. All the snakes were still in the box with the locked gate still shut. They were no longer dormant, however, and neither was Jerry Rawls. So, I had to put the snakes back in the trunk of my car. I was a little surprised that Rawls did not make me sleep with them that night!

We went skiing in Ruidoso, New Mexico on the weekends during the winter. We left our dates out at midnight on Saturday, and drove five hours to Ruidoso, skied all day and then drove back to Lubbock on Sunday evening. Many of us would cut classes on Monday!

Chapter 7
Susan

7/20/07

I met Susan Waits that spring. We had crossed paths several times before, but this time we were in the Tech senate together. Prior times included fraternity smokers or Saddle Tramp functions. We had one coke date before the semester ended and agreed to reconvene in the fall. She was to work at Camp Longhorn as a counselor, and I was planning to attend summer school at Tech.

I met Susan at the Tech post office one late summer day just before the second semester of summer school. She had just finished the first term at Camp Longhorn and arrived in Lubbock for the second summer session. She was going to be the rush captain of the P.I. Beta Phi sorority and accordingly she had prepared for the occasion. She looked great with a fresh tan, beautiful hair with a sleeveless dress on. I asked her out on a date that night and Susan said yes. I was thrilled.

Susan and I went to church together mostly on Sunday nights at the First United Methodist Church since I had to deliver bread for Mrs. Baird every Sunday morning. We were both Methodists. Her home was in Dallas, but she had lived in Sulphur Springs until her junior year. Sulphur Springs was about the same size of Sweetwater with many similarities. We soon discovered many common interests. We played tennis, we went to the movies, and we went out for coffee. I took her on several sound truck excursions as I needed assistance in setting up the sound equipment at Brownfield or, Littlefield or other towns around Lubbock. Those trips were particularly romantic! Being a Saddle Tramp I was fortunate to sit in special sections of the football stadiums or basketball courts with our dates that of course, included Susan. We soon became more than boy/girlfriend. We became best friends.

Christmas time was generally two- or three-week vacation, the fall semester concluding with finals when we returned in January. I went to Dallas after Christmas to see Susan. I stayed with my Aunt Myrtle and Uncle Emmitt who lived near SMU, not too far from Susan's home at 4114 San Carlos. Aunt Myrtle was my mother's oldest sister, the one who convinced Grandma Hastings to name Mother something other than Mildred. She taught ceramics at SMU and Uncle Emmitt was a handyman for several widow women near their home on McFarland.

I met Susan's parents and sister, William T., Elizabeth Waits, and Linda Waits. Her father worked for the FAA at Love Field, and her mother was a teacher at Bradfield Elementary. Linda was a freshman at Tech and had just pledged Pi Beta Phi. Imagine that with her sister as rush captain! Linda was dating Mart True, a Sophomore at Rice who played baseball for the Owls. Mart was gaga over Linda, and Linda was totally indifferent! I thought Mart was a bit squirrelly. We had a double date or so and played cards at the Waits home. That was when I witnessed how cutthroat Susan and Linda were at cards including Linda saying "cheater, fibber,-----, liar" which she would kill me for putting this in my memoir, but it was the truth. Susan's mother was a great host and cook, she always welcomed me in their home. Her father was also genuinely hospitable and was always talking about their dog, Cookie.

W.T. Waits

The New Year was 1966. Little did I realize how the events that occurred during this year would change and influence the rest of my life forever!

Susan and I attended all basketball games at the Municipal Coliseum where Tech was doing quite well with Dub Malaise, Norman Reuther, Glenn Hallum, Billy Tapp, and Harold Denny basketball players. They had a great drive and motivation. It was evident that we might be Southwest Conference contenders, except that Norman Reuther's grades were inadequate and Tech was declared ineligible. All in all, it was a good effort.

The Tech Senate was involved in trying to get the University's name changed to something more creative like Texas State University. The student body was in favor of a new name but the board of Regents opposed the decision and the compromise was Texas Tech University.

Susan and I spent as much time together as we could. It would be dates on the weekends and at least coffee every night or so. She lived in Weeks Hall and the curfew on Fridays was 12pm, Saturdays 1pm, and Sunday 11pm. We wanted to hang out together to the last minute for many of those curfews. We loved to dance and went to some honkey Tonks at the end of the strip where Hank Thompson was playing providing great country swing music. I was star struck in love with that woman. We were best friends and I asked her if she would wear my FIJI pin, which is the same as asking her to marry me. Susan and I spent as much time together as we could. She accepted. Wow! I felt as the happiest and luckiest guy in the world and I think she was equally thrilled and accepted.

Susan and I spent as much time together as we could. It would be on the weekends and at least coffee every night or so. She lived in Weeks Hall and the curfew on Fridays was 12 pm, Saturdays 1pm, and Sunday 11pm. We wanted to hand out together to the last minute for many of those curfews. We loved to dance and went to some honkey tonk at the end of the strip where Hank Thompson was playing, providing great county swing music.

Two attorneys in Sweetwater, Jim Pearson and Zollie Steakley, a member of the Texas Supreme Court, were instrumental in getting me the C.J. Wrightsman Foundation Scholarship to attend the University of Texas Law School. They obviously knew of my financial plight (my mother knew them well) and they further wanted me to return to Sweetwater to practice law with them. The scholarship covered everything—books, tuition, room and board. Further, it started during my senior year at Tech! So, most of my financial pressure was off. My life was getting more complicated, as outlined below. I quit my organ work at Ritz Funeral home.

Jerry Rawls and I found a house to rent located at 1502 Avenue M with two bedrooms and one bath. We invited Dennis Rawls and Keith Winslow to join us as roommates. Dennis was a sophomore and Keith was a junior, and both were FIJIS. Keith was my roommate in the back bedroom, and Dennis was in the front bedroom with Jerry. Keith was from Menard and supplied us with fresh venison throughout the year. I supplied the bread from Mrs. Bairds. We slept in double beds without any thought of anything else except a place to sleep.

We had a 12-inch black and white television, which was the source of much entertainment, including our dates. Gasoline was 25 cents per gallon, and beer had to be purchased south of town at a place we called "the strip". Rawls and I flipped a coin as to who would be traveling to the strip to purchase the week's supply of beer, which cost all of 3 to 5 dollars per case. Bread was 25 cents per loaf, and milk cost 50 cents per gallon. Many times, I swapped bread for milk with a milk truck driver I met on my Sunday delivery.

On Wednesday nights, at the VFW Hall in Slaton, Hoyle Nix and his band played good country music, and we loved to Dance! Country music and dancing was especially great, with everyone two-stepping in a big dance circle to music like Faded Love, Waltz Across Texas, Maiden's Prayer, or Six Pack to Go to name a few. Hoyle Nix had a fiddle (violin) player that was especially good only if he was sober enough to play it. His name was Bob Wills.

All seniors at Tech were preparing to either go to graduate school, go into the Service or interview with companies or go on campus trying to interview and hire for permanent employment. I took the LSAT test (Law School Admission Test) and did not interview very much since I was planning on going to law school in Austin. I did interviews with a couple of companies and was offered employment by Shell Oil Company in Houston.

Spring rodeos and the sound truck offered entertainment on Saturday nights when the Pi Phis or FiJIs were not having functions. We attended the FIJI Island Dance, the big dance of the spring where pledges prepared the decorations and seniors were able to relax and enjoy Lightning Hopkins or some other band/entertainer for the annual dance. Pictures were always a part of parties like this and we still have pictures of my fraternity brothers with their respective dates, many of whom became their wives soon after graduation, including Bill Ed Abraham and Margie, Don Davis and Linda Six, Mike Moore and Sandra, Trent Humphrey and Pam, Ronnie Vance and Myrna, Ranny Greebon and Jackie, and Jerry Pittman and Susan Waits.

As graduation from Tech approached, Susan I got busy setting a date for the marriage. I gave her an engagement ring, we visited Sweetwater to meet my mother and a few of her friends, and I decided not to go to law school. Susan planned to work for Camp Longhorn for the first term and I had agreed to go to work for Shell Oil in Houston. I wanted to pursue accounting more than to be a lawyer. Attorneys Pearson and Steakley said that they understood. The scholarship was great, but I had changed my mind and I might add, I was very in much in love with Susan and wanted to get married and pursue a career in accounting.

I moved in with some Rice students (that Steve Smith knew) near the Rice Hotel and went to work for Shell Oil. Long-distance phone calls were rather expensive, so we solved this problem with Shell's toll free number that we used to plan the wedding. We planned for our honeymoon to be in Acapulco, Mexico. We had six bridesmaids and six groomsmen, and each of them needed to be contacted regarding the wedding plans. My groomsmen included Keith Winslow, Dennis, and Jerry Rawls, and I am unable to name them all—there were no pictures of the groomsmen, only bridesmaids. Steve Smith was to be my best man and Linda Waits was to be Susan's maid of honor. The wedding was to be at Cox Chapel at Highland Park United Methodist Church on August 13, 1966.

It rained on our wedding day. Steve and I drank Heineken beer at North Park and I had breakfast with John Wayne all on my wedding day. He was dining in the same restaurant that morning and I like to say that we had breakfast together. Susan and I drove to Austin to spend the first night and then caught a plane to Acapulco the next day. We stayed at the Las Brisas hotel right on the bay, we had our very own pink jeep and private swimming pool, but the room was equipped with twin beds. Needless to say, these twin beds had to be pushed together because we both had a double bed in mind!

We went deep-sea fishing in Acapulco on a boat named the Ma Cristina. Before the boat was to depart we ran into Glenn Jennings (a Fiji at Tech) in town. Glenn was rehabilitating from a severe car wreck back in the U.S. He had a least three pins in his legs and was on crutches, living with two women from New York. He went fishing with us. We were in the smallest boat in the entire bay and caught four sailfish more than any other boat going out that day. The fish Susan caught was eight feet four inches long from the tip of his sword to his tail. We caught three other sailfish that day and flew four red flags on return to the dock. Our captain was very proud. I spent most of the day calling 'Buicks' over the side of the boat. Sea sickness had taken its toll on me. Glenn caught a sailfish, as did the other honeymooning couple on board with us.

It was going to cost too much to stuff, package and ship this big fish home, such that we donated the fish to the local people. We left Acapulco and spent two days and one night in Mexico City on the way home. We were planning on touring Mexico City, but Susan was not well so we limited our visit. We did discover the musical orchestra by the name of Villa Fontana and purchased their 33 1/3 album which we cherished for many years following. When we arrived back in Houston, we had just enough money left to buy some toilet paper for our apartment on Wake Forest in Houston.

I returned to Houston and began learning how to use a calculator by adding up telephone numbers without looking at the keys. My title was staff assistant and I soon was assigned numerous duties. I observed oil inventory on top of oil tanks owned by Texaco at midnight on the last day of the year (December 31, 1966), I counted cash in a bank, and reconciled accounts receivable at Getty Oil Company. Getty was the first audit that I worked on during January of 1967.

Susan and I had gone to Dallas for Christmas. We celebrated the New Year in Dallas by going out to eat at the Flight Deck near Love Field airport. We ordered Chateaubriand steak for two. We stayed up long enough to celebrate the New Year but I developed an upset stomach. This may have been an omen for later in life since that was one of the last times we stayed up past midnight, and it was not the last time that one of us developed some sort of stomach illness on New Year's Eve. Perhaps celebrating New Year's was not heavy on our agenda.

Susan's secondary education training did not come in handy for her first year of teaching, in that she was assigned by the Houston Independent School system to teach at Houston Gardens Elementary. The school was across town in the Houston shipyard area. It was not the best part of town, and neither were her students: she had 25 to 30 students equally divided among Caucasian, African Americans, and Hispanics. Her students were colorful, to say the least. She won them over by playing sports with them during recess. The kids did not understand this teacher who liked to play basketball, hit baseballs and generally compete with the best. During the spring of 1967, she invited me out to participate in a softball game with the kids. I was on one team and Susan was on the other. I played centerfield and when she hit a home run over my head, the kids went crazy in enjoyment. Needless to say, my team lost, but the students had fallen in love with their teacher.

We had purchased a Volkswagen Beetle. We named the car B.C. "for baby car." One day, when she was driving home and, she and B.C. were sandwiched by two cars on Kirby in Houston. The front and rear of B.C. was damaged. She did not have her driver's license when the police arrived, she invited the police officer to our apartment, where she called her mother to get the license number. She had accidentally left her DL at home in Dallas. She made coffee for the police officer and he agreed to take the license number to write his report. The police officer would have thrown the book at me, but she got away with it with her charm and coffee.

We went to see the Astros play baseball in the new Houston Astrodome. We went to see Aretha Franklin in the Houston East side where we were the only White Crackers in attendance. We played tennis and began a walking routine of sorts. I gave Susan a set of left-handed golf clubs for Christmas. When the Houston Rodeo came to town, and we had to go. We parked our car in the Astrodome parking lot but when the rodeo was over, we could not find the car! The police, rather patronizingly, assured us that we merely could not remember where we parked.

Well, so much for the 1965 Blue Chevy as it was stolen. We took a cab home only to learn that the car was discovered on Mt Houston road about four days later, completely stripped: no dashboard, no tires, no golf clubs, and no ice cream maker that was in the trunk as well. The golf clubs had not been paid for yet, so it was an expensive lesson and rodeo.

We moved to a new apartment out in the Memorial area, The Winrock Apartments. By now, Susan had started teaching secondary which was in line with her major and teaching certificate. We visited Dub and Jane in Dallas periodically, on one occasion, we purchased a new Oldsmobile Cutlass two door coupe. It was blue and white and quite a car. It was not ready for delivery when we were in Dallas, but Dub and Jane drove it down to Houston the following weekend. They arrived to see us that weekend at about 4 am and waited in the parking garage until we awakened at about 8 am to surprise us. Jane slept the whole way as Dub drove all night! That's the way Dub operated, very excited to deliver our new car.

Susan and I joined the ST Luke's Methodist church in Houston and promptly became involved as sponsors of the Methodist Youth Fellowship (the MYF). We talked the youth into going snow skiing at Estes Park, Colorado. About 30 young people went on the trip with us as sponsors, along with one other couple as sponsors as well. The bus driver left a lasting impression on everyone as he lacked the maturity and skills needed for a bus driver. We did make it to Estes Park and the kids really enjoyed skiing. I spoiled the party for a few of them one night as I had to pour their vodka down the drain. We continued the MYF sponsorship for the rest of the year.

Mother's floor covering store was not doing very well as the cotton crops in West Texas were progressively bad. Mother called me a lot regarding the finances of the store, her employees, or her various debts. Susan and I made several trips up to Sweetwater to assist her throughout the next three years. The phone calls stopped when she met and married Eddie Freeze, thank goodness!

Susan and I tent-camped to Florida one summer in a Volkswagen. We stopped to stay with her Uncle Buddy Waits and his roommate, Jerry, in New Orleans. They were restoring an old house not far from the French

Quarter. Cajun food and Cajun coffee were all good! Our trip was for one week and it seemed that no sooner we pitched a tent to camp, we were up and running many miles the next day.

Chapter 8
Arthur Andersen

10/22/08

Working for Shell Oil was tedious and highly routine. It had been a great place to work while we were planning our wedding and enjoying our honeymoon, but something had to change. I got a call from an old friend of mine from Roscoe (Jerry Riggs), who worked at Arthur Andersen; he wanted me to apply there for employment. The interview went well. It was one of the big eight CPA firms in the world, with offices in almost every country in the world, with offices in nearly every country in the world. Business hats and white shirts had been hallmark clothing for employees; however, when I was hired in the business, the hat routine had been dropped a few months earlier- thank goodness. Within a week, Arthur had me flying to Chicago to attend the auditor boy-wonder HOSTS (Home Office Staff Training School) in downtown Chicago, two blocks from the home office of the Playboy Club. I met many guys working from all parts of the US; during the day, we would be drilled on auditing, and by night, we would enjoy the benefits of our new membership at the Playboy Club. I met a friend from Utah who liked the scenery at the Playboy Club but could not drink beer or Coke because of his Mormon religion. He had completed his two-year sabbatical with the Church of the Latter-Day Saints; his dedication to his religion was fascinating to me. He did like the women at the Playboy club!

The first time I sat for the CPA exam was in Galveston. The exam had four parts: auditing, tax, theory, and practice. Galveston was fun-filled with seafood and much study for the exams. I was working on the John Mecom job and left for the exam the next day without any significant study for the exams. I did not pass even one of the four parts!

As mentioned, I had been assigned to the John Mecom audit. Mr. Mecom was a multimillionaire who owned the New Orleans Saints professional team, oil properties worldwide, two ranches, and various airplanes, autos, and other toys. Jim Gunter and Jim Rash were my bosses on the job, and Kirby Simmons, Ken Smith, and I were the staff assistants.

Because Mr.Mecom was having trouble refinancing some of his debt, Chase Manhattan Bank required that Arthur Andersen be assigned to the audit to adjust the books to realistic reporting. We were required to work long hours seven days per week. Susan and I would eat breakfast at Brennan's on Sundays, and then I would return to work. The pay was good, but the long hours got old quickly.

Mr. Mecom had an elevator in the back of his building to carry him and his automobile to the top of the building where his office was. We really never knew when or whether he was in, especially since we were working in the basement. One evening, the phone rang in our room where we were working. I happened to answer the phone, and on the other end of the phone was Governor John McKeithan, then the governor of the state of Louisiana. The New Orleans Saints had just signed Jimmy Taylor, a free agent running back, to play for the Saints. Governor McKeithan wanted to talk to John Mecom right then. I told the governor that I did not know the whereabouts of Mr. Mecom, and after the governor that I did not know the whereabouts of Mr.Mecom, and after the governor insisted that he talk with Mr. Mecom again and again, I informed the governor that I was a member of the night janitorial crew and that all I knew was "mop, mop, mop." Upon hearing this response, the governor hung up. My colleagues in the office got a kick out of my response such that they told the other members of Arthur Anderson's office, and I was labeled as the "mop mop" auditor.

My assignment in Florida was undoubtedly unique. Mr. J.K Stuart was a very wealthy businessperson, citrus farmer, dairyman, and investor. His office was in Bartow, Florida. He and his brother were the fifth largest citrus (oranges and grapefruit) farmers in all of Florida. And he had a massive diary in Waco, Texas.

My assignment, however, was rather unusual. Mr. Stuart had given $100,000 to each of five different stockbrokers/money managers nationwide. After each money manager had invested their respective $100,000 and sold stocks, bonds, and other paper for over a year, it (WHAT IS "IT"?) got somewhat confusing to Mr. J.K., who, in turn, called his old friend, Pete Wehner, at Arthur Andersen to send someone to Florida to determine who won, lost or tied the ballgame! Mr. J.K. had given the money with the understanding that the one that made the least amount of money of his money would be replaced (or "fired," as Mr. J.K. stated). This was my job! I was successful in my assignment, but Fayez Sarofim from Houston lost his opportunity, and his remaining money was returned to Mr. J.K.

I was also assigned the responsibility to improve the accounting for the diary in Waco. I installed an accounting of milk pounds as a measurement of cow productivity and designed a worksheet (before computers) to track mother cows' breeding cycles and milk cycles to lower the downtime for breeding and increase the milk production cycle.

I was in Bartow for five weeks. After two weeks, I was entitled to fly home, but Mr. J.K. had different plans. He called Pete Wehner and told Pete to have Susan fly to Bartow (really Tampa) on the next flight! Mr. Wehner was the partner in charge of the entire Houston office of Arthur Andersen, and particular undivided attention was given to one staff person, namely me, when the Houston office had a staff of at least four hundred others. Mr. Wehner had never met Susan, much less even knew who she might be, but he found out very quickly. Susan was on the next flight to Tampa first class, while Arthur Andersen personnel was accustomed to flying only coach!

Mr. and Mrs. J.K. entertained me and Susan for the entire weekend. We were informed that Florida had outdoor theatres (drive-ins). They took us out to experience southern cooking and informed us of this unique Florida drink called the 'frozen daiquiri.' Mrs. J.K. was quite the investor since she only invested in names with Dixie, Confederate, Southern, and the like.

The manager of the job and my boss was Jim Rash. Typical of many managers and partners at Arthur Andersen, he was in the process of getting a divorce from his wife. Arthur had a bad habit in those days: they fully expected employees to sacrifice for the firm. Being married to Arthur Andersen took a higher priority than being married to your wife. Extensive overtime, late nights, and travel on short notice were hallmarks of the firm.

Jim came to Bartow, reviewed my work for about ten minutes, and announced that we were leaving for the Bahamas! And that we did! We drove to Fort Lauderdale and caught a shuttle airplane to the Grand Bahamas. We toured the gaming tables, drank island drinks, spent the night, and took the shuttle back the next day. Jim caught the red eye back to Houston that night.

During my five weeks, I purchased a bushel of grapefruit and began squeezing grapefruit juice for breakfast in my motel room. I was entertained regularly by Mr. and Mrs. Stuart and Mr. Stuart's brother. Mr. Stuart took a liking to me and offered me full-time employment as his financial assistant. I had informed him that I had planned on returning to college to seek my Master's degree in finance or accounting. He countered that by offering to send me to the Wharton School of Finance in Pennsylvania. I told Susan about the generous offer, but we concluded that we both loved Texas too much to leave her. So, I turned the offer down.

It was just as well because a few days later, an event occurred that convinced me that I had made the right decision. I guess this was late summer of 1968 when civil rights leader Martin Luther King was murdered in Memphis. The next day, Mr. Stuart draped a Rebel flag over his desk in celebration of Reverend King's death and began lecturing me that he knew of at least five more "n____s" that should be shot as well. I was in shock! Later that day, Mr. J.K's secretary told me that Mr. J.K and his brother had been the most significant individual benefactors of Erskine College until the college enrolled their first Black student.

I returned to Houston, completed my work papers, and awaited another assignment.

President Lyndon Johnson ushered in his programs called "The Great Society," and the civil rights act was passed in 1964. Integration of Blacks with whites with the abandonment of separate dining and drinking fountains, the end of the back-of-the-bus seating, and the enrollment of Black students in previously all-white schools were topics of new media and general discussions. My hometown of Sweetwater closed the separate high school, Booker T. Washington High School, and integrated those students with Sweetwater High School students. It was and still is a volatile topic all across the United States, such that it took generations to completely heal.

I retook the CPA exam and passed auditing but made a below passing on the other three parts. Again, I did not have much time to study. I was assigned the Suniland Furniture Audit, spent some time on Getty Oil Company, Tenneco, and Texaco audits, and was assigned to the tax department for two months during the spring of 1969.

Enough Susan and I decided to move to Lubbock, and I would pursue a master's degree while she taught school.

Chapter 9
Master's Degree 1968-1969

1/14/08

I asked Arthur Andersen for a leave of absence to work on my Master's degree back at Texas Tech. Susan secured a teaching position at McKenzie Junior High, and I was hired as a Teaching Assistant at Texas Tech University. I enrolled in the Master of Science program at the Business College, where my concentration was accounting, with a thesis to be written for the final six hours. I was to teach elementary accounting levels one and two each semester. Thirty hours were required for a master's degree.

We had our first dog, a dachshund named Virginia. Virginia slept at the foot of our bed, generally under the covers, keeping Susan's otherwise cold feet warmer. She started wearing socks to bed later, and that habit has never changed; her feet have not warmed up either. Our landlord did not allow dogs, but he melted and changed his mind once he met Virginia. Gin was the most convincing!

Jay Stanley had returned to Lubbock to complete his Masters as well. I previously knew Jay through his mother, Millie, when I worked at Doms Limited, a man's clothing store. At that time, Jay was a University of Texas in Austin student. Pat Stanley, Jay's wife, was also teaching at Mackenzie Junior High, and Susan and Pat became friends immediately. In fact, their association probably brought Jay and me together while in Lubbock.

MY fraternity learned that I was on the faculty of Texas Tech and immediately asked if I would be their faculty advisor. It was an opportunity for Susan and me to attend parties. We also chaperoned the Pi Phi's annual trip to Santa Fe on a skiing weekend. Jay, Pat, Susan, and I decided to go skiing in Ruidoso, New Mexico, for a long weekend. We stayed in the Dan Dee cabins and skied up and down the Ruidoso Ski slopes, later renamed Ski Apache. The skis in those days laced up to your boot and were exceptionally long. No snap-in footings would snap loose in a bind.

The ski range in Ruidoso was owned and operated by the Mescalero Apache Indians; their motive was to make money at all levels. Jay and I had developed a taste for scotch whiskey, and since the Apache accommodates adult beverages at the bottom, middle, and top of each slope, we felt that we should participate at each level. Skiing became much more accessible, and the moguls were smaller, so I did a summer salt over some monster moguls and had a big-time fall. My skis stayed attached to my boot, and my knee made all the needed adjustments. Another scotch and another run down the mountain were in order. I knew when it swelled so much. We went to a cocktail party after skiing, and later that night, as the scotch wore off, my knee throbbed with every heartbeat. Susan said I was disturbing everyone in Dan Dee's Cabins. I wore a cast on my leg and knee on the ride home. The knee got better, and no surgery was called for.

Linda Waits King was now married to Kenny King, and they were still at Tech finishing up their degrees. Kenny had worked during the summer before they were married on the ship Brown and Root. One of the most memorable funny moments regarding Kenny was when he shipped some fish to Jane and Dub, but somehow ribbon fish (bait fish) was in the package they received. Being the proverbial diplomat, Jane Waits bragged to her new son-in-law to be regarding what a delicacy the fish were. I am still not sure how Jane found out.

Another event involving my mother-in-law, Jane Elizabeth Sanders Waits, came in the fall of 1968 when Susan and I had returned to Tech for my Master's degree. Linda and Kenny had also returned to Tech as well to complete their senior year. The only problem was that Kenny had flunked out of Tech the previous semester (he liked to party). And since I was on the faculty at Tech, it was the consensus (Linda, Susan, Jane) that I should assist Kenny in getting off of scholastic probation and back in school. So, Kenny and I went to see Dean Floyd Boze, who was the

Dean of Admissions. Kenny was in his last semester; the fact that he had to work throughout college, etc., were the reasons we used to gain readmission. However, somehow, nothing registered with Dean Bose until we told him that our mother-in-law was Jane Elizabeth Sanders, who went to ET (East Texas State College). That's that "Liz was a beautiful woman." They had both attended ET together in years past. Dean Bose immediately granted Kenny readmission and dismissed us from his office. I think he was still saying, "Liz was a beautiful woman," as we left.

I taught elementary accounting for freshmen during the four semesters that we were in Lubbock. I studied for the CPA exam again and passed two parts --- auditing and theory. When you only pass one part, you get no credit. Once you pass two parts, you get to keep those in anticipation of passing the remaining two parts. But if you do not pass the other two before five years expire, then you lose the two you passed, and you have to start all over.

Teaching accounting was fun. My students respected me as I returned to college to teach after spending three years with Arthur Andersen. Accordingly, taking graduate-level courses was also fun and relatively easy for the same reason. Accounting, unlike economics, was rather scientific; read the chapter, learn the nomenclature, and work on the problems at the end of each chapter. Most students comprehended and were able to pass with flying colors. However, some students would not work on the accounting problems at the end of each chapter and did not do well in the course. Practice sets went with each course and represented a set of books of a fictional company. The company had cash disbursements and cash receipts journals, journal entries, general ledger, trial balances, etc. It represented a great way to learn and practice accounting. It represented quite a bit of work, and I gave my students the option of working the practice set for an extra grade for the course; for the most part, those who did get the better grades. I warned my students not to copy (cheat) the practice set, and if they did practice or plagiarize the exercise, they would flunk the entire course. In other words, work it for a better grade, or don't work it and not be punished.

Those students who copied the practiced set would be detected very quickly---erasures, coffee and Coke stains, and wrinkled papers. They did not pass accounting. I had a few FIJIs take my course, and while most took the course seriously and studied accordingly, one particular student, also a Tech football player, took my course with the attitude that I would be more lenient with guys from my own fraternity. His name was Louis Brewer. Lou did not heed my instructions and copied the practice set. He flunked the course.

Susan was teaching and drawing paychecks from Lubbock Independent School District, and I worked for Tech drawing paychecks as well. I borrowed money from the Texas Society of Public Accounting (TSCPA) under their student loan program so we could purchase a huge console television. The year was 1969, and NASA would put a man on the moon. We did not want to miss it! We watched Neal Armstrong plant the US flag on the moon with "One small step for man and one giant leap for mankind." It was exciting. I think Sally Halley and Linda King were there with us as we had them over from time to time to play Tripoli.

I had very little trouble completing my Master's requirements. Most of the courses were reasonably thought-provoking and fun to participate in. The professors enjoyed having me in their classes as I had returned from Arthur Andersen, bringing actual experience to their classrooms. I made straight A's for my entire Master's degree except for the last course I took, being taught by Dr. Roberts. He had learned of my perfect record and refused to allow it to continue, giving me my first B in graduate school. ASSHOLE!!

I shared an office at Tech with Johnny Walker, another graduate student who is also teaching accounting. Johnny was from Greenville, Texas. He and I started a Lubbock tax practice in the spring to make a little money. In the Lubbock Avalanche-Journal, we advertised that we could keep books, prepare tax returns, and pick up and deliver them all for $5.00 per hour. Our partnership was called P & W Tax Services. We were relatively prosperous and made a little money; it was the beginning of my first business enterprise. Neither of us had passed the CPA exam then, but we were undoubtedly aspiring graduate students who aimed to please.

Dr. Kenneth Fox was the professor in charge of my thesis. All of my work had to be coordinated through him. I was previously acquainted with Dr. Fox in one of his graduate courses. He taught Income Taxation, and while he had a bit of a speech impediment, he would also get confused about some things. One time, when he was trying to make a vital point involving the IRS (Internal Revenue Service), he built up the conversation by saying, "And if you do this or that or if you don't do this or that, then the FIR will get you, er, I mean the IRS." We graduated students loved to mimic and mock Dr. Fox.

Dr. Fox, using a red pencil, completely butchered my first chapter! Every page had red marks. Principally, his comments involved grammar, punctuation, and structure–not content. Well, Susan, who had proofed the copy, was livid! He was wrong, and that was all there was to it! So, she used a blue pencil and marked over his red pencil and, in the margin, cited chapter and verse of some grammar handbook of sorts.

And it was my job to take my red and blue first chapter back to Dr. Fox and explain that he was wrong. And I did. However, the correction obviously did not work well with the professor when he responded with a muffled "Humph." The thoughts racing through my head then were that I was destined to be kicked out of Tech–which was all over! After a few more muffled words, characteristic of Dr. Fox, he told me that he would look over the paper and let me know. I sweated it–big time!

About three days later, Dr. Fox called me to his office. He slid my first chapter across his desk toward me, asking whether my wife planned to prove my thesis balance. I replied that she would. He then murmured, "Proceed." The remaining five chapters were all turned into Dr. Fox, and never did I see one red mark for the balance of the thesis.

During my Oral Exams with about six professors before completing my Master's thesis, I fielded several questions regarding earnings per share calculations of oil and gas production payments from the various professors. Dr. Fox never asked one question!

I sat for the remaining two parts of the CPA: auditing and practice. I passed them both and completed the requirements for the CPA certificate. Susan and I celebrated this victory at Brookshire's (a restaurant where Kenny and Linda worked) with Joe and Jay Stanley. Jay's father, Joe Stanley, was one of the most genuine and sincere men I have ever met. His interest included the water business he owned and operated in Lubbock, and he loved flying his airplane.

Chapter 10
Life of Hunting

2/08/09

Daddy and I got away many late afternoons to go dove hunting or rabbit hunting on one farm or another where the doves would be flying. Many days, we both reached our limits long before sunset. Mother cooked them for supper. Dove season always starts in Texas on September 1, and with a few exceptions, I have rarely missed opening day.

Bill Shaw, who was in school with me, accidentally killed Rodney Cliff one day when they were playing with pistols. The accident was awful, and several years later, as I tried to get to know him better, he and I went dove hunting together.

We went dove hunting one day in Fisher County with no license. We were sophomores in college, and both were home for the weekend. A license was not required for Nolan County residents, our residence, but we were hunting barely in Fisher County. When we were about to leave the hunting pasture, we ran into a covey of quail that truly was out of season, and we lowered the shotguns on them, too! Got 6 of them! And as we were pulling out of the pasture to go home, the game warden was there at the gate. I was busy with the quail out the window, but it was too late as the game warden dutifully picked them all up and put them on the hood of the car. Bill met the County Judge and was fined $78.00, but I was sent to the Justice of the Peace court and was fined $145.00. This was more than Bill because I had claimed the quail so we both wouldn't have to. I hated to make the check to EF Branson, a man who was really old and could not hear. I told the judge that I hoped this money would put meat on his table for 6 f-----g months. He asked again what I said cause he could not hear me and I repeated it. He fined me another $50. We left, and I did not pay the contempt of court charge without his pursuing it; he must've been too old to do so. Mother assured me later, as we were barbequing the six quail, that I could have purchased ten or so years of licenses with that hefty fine.

We hunted dove and deer at the PK ranch. Greer shot a 10-point buck on our ranch. For the Boy Scout gathering each year in the fall, I always cooked the chili, having plenty of venison chili meat; I cooked it with crispy fried bacon, heavy in cheese, Wick Fowler's chili fixings, lots of tomato juice (even tomato soup), jalapenos, and beer to add flavor. Everyone loved my chili, or at least they were too intimidated to tell me it was bad.

Greer and I went hunting in Sonora at the Texas A&M research center with Sid Cavanaugh. Sid owned the maintenance company that cleaned my office buildings. All in all, we went hunting at this prescribed hunt about three times over the same number of years. They placed us in our blinds and provided a rather controlled hunt on their rather large research facility, housed us, and provided great meals for a three-day hunt each time. We had a grand time each time we went, but Greer Pittman got the trophy deer of all time there on our last visit. We had traded for a 7mm rifle for Greer Pittman earlier that year. The 7mm rifle had an unbelievable range, and Greer got the most out of it by shooting a monster buck deer with it! At the end of the hunt that evening, Greer told me he shot at a large buck deer but was not absolutely sure the deer was down. We searched for the deer, and after dinner, we searched again in an area quite a way from where Greer blind was. We found the deer lying in the road, and it truly was the largest white-tailed deer I had ever seen with huge horns. I was so proud of Greer and his expert marksman site, and so were Sid Cavanaugh and Butch, the ranch foreman, who also could not believe the size of this deer. The shot had to have been over 600 yards!

That year (1980), I went deer hunting with Brian Snowden in Fredericksburg, Texas. I continued my love for hunting and the out-of-doors. Brian was a client at the time. We continued to hunt together every fall, and I would bring back venison each year for our family to consume.

Paul Moore and I both liked to hunt. We went fishing at Rockport, Texas, with a guide named David Nesloney. David was an outfitter and offered a combination duck hunt and fishing trip to Rockport for as many as 25 people in the fall. We took him up and asked all our hunting/fishing friends to join us. It became an annual affair for the next five or so years. We flew by Southwest Airlines to Corpus and then on to Rockport. David took us in airboats out to the duck blinds early the next morning, and he picked us up mid-morning to feed us fried fish for lunch and then fishing again in his boats for ocean trout in the afternoon. We hunted, fished, drank beer, ate well for two days, and then we would fly home with iced coolers full of fish and duck. We had great fun!

The trip increased in size, and within two years, we had 30-35 men enrolled on our hunt. David Nesloney always reserved the opening day of duck season for us. It was very profitable for him. Paul and I always hunted together since we were the organizers. One particular year, that part of Texas had received a lot of rain prior to opening day, with a lot of water following the various rivers and streams into the Gulf. David took Paul and me to our blind. It was before daybreak. We placed our duck decoys out in a "J" routine as we were instructed. Paul and I laughed about that because we always got a limit and then some, whether our decoys were in a straight line or some sort of a "J" arrangement.

The blind was in knee-deep water (we wore hip waders) and camouflaged with reeds, twigs, and leaves. We climbed into our blind, loaded our 12-gauge shotguns, and waited for daybreak. About the time daylight was breaking, I looked down on the wood floor of our blind, and there beside my ammunition box was this HUGE SNAKE all curled up and undisturbed. I said to Paul that we had a snake in our blinds! We both moved a little more to Paul's side, and Paul decided he was going to shoot the snake with double ought buckshot. I told Paul that we needed to move my ammunition case away from the snake before he shot, or we might be blown to kingdom come! Very carefully, I nudged the box away from this big snake. The snake never moved. It was asleep or very sick but clearly not dead. At least until Paul shot him. The shotgun blew that corner of the blind to bits with the snake. Our blind was listing afterward, but the snake lay dead in the water. We then got our limit and then some in ducks. When

David picked us up in the airboat, he identified the snake as a water moccasin that had floated from freshwater streams into the salt-watered bay where our blind was. The snake was probably sick in this foreign environment. Water Moccasins are only freshwater snakes.

We have had many laughs about this since. Paul has assured me that if the snake had bitten me, especially in the ass, I would more than likely die. He had no plans to suck the poison out of my ass!

The annual duck/fish trip became quite a routine for Paul Moore and me. Participants included Mac Jamison, Bill Crabtree, Bob Stephenson, Scott Keeshin, Ed Fulbright, Roger Cloud, and many others for as many as 30 at a time. It was a truly coordinated effort to arrange air, transportation, airboats, and fishing boats, not to mention feeding the entire lot as well. David Nesloney always aimed to please and arranged for all the means. One special request included Scott Keeshin's father-in-law; thank goodness I have forgotten his name. Scott had invited him (I will call him Bob) to go on the hunt but called David to arrange for a prostitute to meet Bob on the morning of the opening day duck hunt. David arranged for two prostitutes to fly from Houston to Rockport to accomplish this special request.

Paul and I learned about it that morning when we were ushered to our blinds. We had one missing participant—Bob. David informed us of the details. Scott had arranged everything. When we went back after the hunt, we learned that the two prostitutes had stiffed Bob; during the night, they tried to negotiate a better price but instead stole his wallet and all his clothes, including his shoes. He was really pissed! He showed up at the lunchroom when we returned with no clothes! By this time, everyone knew of the incident. Scott was a lawyer and wanted to sue the prostitutes! The incident got funnier as the day progressed. Scott and his father-in-law went home that afternoon while we continued our afternoon fishing for ocean trout. I never knew why two prostitutes were hired to serve; the other one was Scott's, I guess. That was our last Rockport trip.

Scott Keeshin had another rather immature occurrence with me. His law office rented space from me across the hall from Pittman, Harris & Co.

Money had been stolen from his office, and he accused the janitorial crew! We called for a lie detector test to be conducted of all people who had master keys—Kirk Hardin (janitor), me, Barbara McSpadden (my receptionist), David Harris, Scott, and his secretary. The lie detector man started his process and interviewed everyone down to Scott when Scott called the process off and admitted that he stole his own money—yes, he paid the company hired to do the tests and issued written apologies to everyone else. He said he forgot!

After hunting for several years at Doss, Texas, I moved to on new deer leases at Senora, one captained by Fred Joyce and the other by Gary Fickes. The Galbraith (Fickes) was a large lease with about 8 hunters. Greer and I had many good times cooking out and hunting deer on the Galbraith ranch. We harvested several deer and turkeys there.

Chapter 11
Julian Ross Pittman

3/12/09

We moved to Dallas to live at 3912 Purdue in January 1970. I went to work for Centex Corporation as a CPA in their Corporate Development department. Susan and I walked a lot while she was in the last three months of her pregnancy. Dub and Jane lived at 4114 San Carlos, which was about a mile from us on San Carlos in University Park.

Centex Corporation is where I worked on the 46th floor of the Dallas Bank of the Southwest building. I was in their corporate development department. Centex-owned J.W. Batesman Company has just completed building Texas Stadium in Irving, Texas, the Dallas Cowboys home. The owner of Centex was the Murchison family, who also owned the Dallas Cowboys. I was involved in the purchase investigation and ultimate purchase of Fox and Jacobs, a home-building company, as well as large tracts of real estate purchases in Dallas, Texas, San Jose, California, and Fate, Texas.

Centex went through an initial public offering to be listed on the New York Stock Exchange about a year after I started to work for them. By this time, I had been promoted to assistant controller and was responsible for the accounting of 13 companies. Three assistant controllers (all CPAs) each had about 12 to 15 companies for which they were responsible. And each of us had at least four to six bookkeepers we supervised in the massive consolidation of Centex's financial statements. This consolidation occurred monthly with special quarterly reporting required by the SEC (Securities Exchange Commission) with a publically held company.

Having completed my master's degree and having had special courses involving corporate equity issues, I got involved with upper management regarding the calculation of earnings per share. This was when I realized that I was put in quite a pressure position with the big push to increase earnings per share, a critical factor in stock analyst's attitude in valuing the company's performance, but I was confident in my training and stood firm with my calculations with upper management grading my performance daily.

Dr. Brunken was Susan's doctor in Dallas, and our baby was to be born at Baylor Hospital. We had paid weekly for her visits to cover the amounts that the insurance had not covered. We both met with Dr. Brunken at least twice during these last days of the nine-month period. We had rehearsed for the trip and knew that the day was near. It was late April of 1970 when, one morning, she had the call of contractions. So, we called Jane and Dub and proceeded to Baylor.

Susan's labor at the hospital was long and drawn out, lasting all day. She imagined she was on an airplane with intermittent bumps and rolls. She thought the nurses were flight attendants (they were called Stewardesses in those days), with, I guess, the doctor to be the pilot. I heard all kinds of language in the labor room area, with other women cursing their husbands and being mad at everything. Susan was uncomfortable, but she never expressed anger, only wanting to know when the plane was to land!

The baby was born at 7:21 pm and weighed 9 pounds 13- and one-half ounces. We named him Julian Ross, not any family name, only names we both liked. It was a caesarian birth because Susan had labored for at least 12 hours with such a big baby. The doctors had consulted both of us, and we were ready, and so was Jay (the nickname we liked as well). I nicknamed him "Big Boy" and have called him such since.

Jane and Dub (soon to be renamed Gram and Dede handles that would stay with them forever) had waited most of the day with me in the father's waiting room area, and they, too, were exhausted as much for Susan as themselves.

I was so proud. My son had been born! He was so healthy. I called my mother in Sweetwater and cried as I told her. I could not help myself. Jay wrote his grandmother (soon to be called Grenna) in West Texas a letter while he was in the hospital, bragging about how he was the biggest kid in the wing and had managed to beat up all of the other kids as he waited impatiently for his mother to feel well enough to get out of the hospital. He was feeling fine, and he did express his dismay with his father that the only time he cried was when his father wanted to count his fingers and toes right after he was born. My, Jay has such talents!

Dub and I went to Sears and purchased a washer and dryer for our home to accommodate all the diaper washing. We installed them while Susan was still in the hospital. We bought them on credit and made monthly payments after that.

Susan reminds me that a tree had fallen on our house at 3912 Purdue the night before we went to the hospital. Somehow, I had forgotten this event as I was preoccupied with getting her to the hospital in time. But that tree became a real focal point for our new son as time went on. When the landlord sent someone with a chainsaw to cut the tree down, we discovered that the loud noise outside Jay's new bedroom was well-liked by Jay. The noise put him to sleep immediately! In fact, the more noise we had in the house put the boy to sleep. We kept the vacuum cleaner in his room to turn on to put him to sleep.

We used cloth diapers mostly. Pamper diapers were recently (in the past 10 years) invented using safety pins, while the tape was invented several years after Julian R. We were proud of our washer and dryer but not so proud of our stove in that it had only one temperature-creating many burned delicacies. During the summer of 1971, Jay was over one year of age, and as soon as Susan would leave me to stay with my son, he would immediately surprise me with the mother lode by pooping in his pants. He loved it when we would go into the backyard, and I would hose him down with the water hose! Susan, Gram, and Granada certainly disapproved. Mrs. Sanders (aka Granada) was Gram's mother from Sulphur Springs) did not approve of many things employed in rearing Jay, especially the occasions of drinking beer from our beer cans.

Susan and I joined the University Park Methodist Church and attended every Sunday. We joined a Sunday school class there and made many friends, including Vic Shaw, Eddie, and Ellie Morrison. Eddie was a new medical doctor doing his internship at Parkland. They both were graduates of SMU and knew Dallas well. Ellie was a Pi Phi, while Eddie was a FIJI at SMU. We became particularly good friends with them for the rest of our lives. It helped that they became clients of mine as CPAs after they moved to Waco. I served on the Administrative Board and had some involvement with the finance committee.

My mother had lived a lonely life in Sweetwater since my father had died in 1962. She relied on me quite often for problems she encountered while operating the retail carpet store. But then along came Eddie! Mother had fallen in love with Edward Earl Freeze, and a wedding was being planned for the Christmas of 1970. Eddie had been a star football player for Sweetwater during the late 30s or early 40s as a halfback and went to Texas A&M on a football scholarship. He spent four years with the Navy during World War II. He returned to Sweetwater after working in California for about 30 years. He had been previously married and had two children, Eddie Jr. and his daughter. They were very much in love with each other, so Susan and I talked our minister, Jim Scott, into marrying them in our home during the Christmas holidays.

Eddie Freeze

Eddie immediately purchased one-half of the retail carpet store and stepped in to help Mother sell carpets all over the Sweetwater area. Eddie was a great stepfather for me, and the only grandfather Jay or Greer ever knew from my side of the family.

During those days, Lyndon Baines Johnson, a Texan, was President of the United States. He succeeded to the office when John F. Kennedy was assassinated by Lee Harvey Oswald in Dallas. Johnson gave a stirring speech on television saying that he did not want to run for reelection. He went on further, saying that the Vietnam War was a part of his decision. The war had dragged on for several years with many American casualties and much monetary cost for the United States. War protests had broken out everywhere. Young men and women were dodging the draft, and anti-war riots were common. Robert Kennedy, the attorney general, was running for President, and he, too, was assassinated. He was John Kennedy's younger brother. Richard M. Nixon was elected president, the first Republican president our country had since Dwight Eisenhower preceded John Kennedy.

Chapter 12
Centex And CPA 1970-1972

12/23/08

Before Centex went public, I was instrumental in their choosing Arthur Andersen & Co. to replace Grant Thornton as their auditing company. It was the Dallas office of Arthur Andersen that got the new audit of Centex Corporation. It was a good move for Centex since their intent was to take the non-private shares public as an IPO Initial Public Offering. I did not know many of Arthur Andersen's Dallas offices since I had worked only for the Houston office (a much larger office).

I was granted some stock options for the public offering, and I borrowed money from Jay Stanley or Craig Sutton to purchase more Centex shares in the public offering. It paid off. Susan and I made a bundle of money, the stock was sold, the loan paid off, and we purchased our first home with the profits!

We had lived on Purdue for almost two years before we felt the need for something larger. Purdue had one bath and two bedrooms. I had gotten into mowing, edging, and fertilizing the yard. Dressing up the flower bed, etc., but Purdue had only one bath and two bedrooms.

We started looking for a larger home and went off the deep end!

Our new home had six bedrooms, four and one-half baths, two car garage, a three-story, and a swimming pool! The home was in foreclosure, and we basically stumbled across it, made an offer to assume the seller's back monthly payments, and gave him $500.00 to move out. The house address was 2612 Sherburne in Dallas in the Lake Highland area near the intersection of Skillman and Audelia. It had a game room, a restroom downstairs with the garage, and a dumb waiter from the garage to the kitchen to convey groceries from the car to the kitchen. There were three bedrooms upstairs and three bedrooms on the main floor. The living room was perfect for Jay's new electric riding train. Besides, we did not have any formal living room furniture anyway. We had a lot of empty rooms! We had purchased some furniture at the Dallas Furnishing Market thanks to my mother's contacts. The swimming pool was fairly new, with a fenced-in area that we landscaped. Susan and I repainted the entire home and purchased new carpet from Mother and Eddy, and we chased plants, landscaping media, and furniture when money was available.

I tried my hand at wallpapering in the dining room adjacent to the kitchen. I set up a table to cut the wallpaper and to affix or paint the glue with. Wallpapering did not go down with me too well. Things started not to match as well as the written instructions said they would glue everywhere, including on me, and Susan learned a new language she had never heard before from me. It was the last time I ever wallpapered anything.

Jay was beginning to form his words, and he was into almost everything, creating plenty of home entertainment. He loved to ride his train. Reading to him was beginning to be a challenge because he would memorize the stories, and if we even thought about skipping a page or so, he would let us know that it did not go that way! Jay got an electric train for Christmas. Santa brought it. It had a 12-volt battery, it had two or three cars, and you could ride it. The train was a huge success. Jay got several other toys, but he loved the train the best. Our house was so big we had a special room just made for riding the train. By now, he was talking, walking, and getting into almost everything. We went to Fair Park to see the trains and to the airport to witness the airplanes taking off and landing.

Jay and Pat had returned from New York, with Jay acquiring a job with First National Bank of Dallas, where Craig Sutton (my Fiji pledge brother) worked as well. Pat was seeking employment as a teacher in the Dallas area and asked Susan to join her in interviewing Farmers Branch ISD. Susan and Pat were both hired to teach, but Pat turned the offer down and accepted a teaching job at Plano. And Susan started to teach again.

We had discussed the merits of her returning to teaching and weighed the importance of what development concerns our son needed. Daycare was ruled out, so we decided to hire a Nanny who could either live with us or come early and stay late to look after Jay full-time in his own environment. Along came Betty Robinson! She was hired as a full-time employee to be Jay's Nanny. Betty's full-time job was to teach, play, love, and develop our young son. That she did! She taught him, cooked for him, got on the floor to play with him, and walked on the sidewalks and curbs with him. She laughed with him, cried with him, and worried for him when he was not feeling well. They bonded.

She also made the best chocolate chip cookies for me.

Betty was divorced and had four children at home, with her mother helping her. Tyrone, Silvia, Carmen, and Shaunee were their names, and they were the best kids. We got to know Betty better and knew she and her character had much to do with raising the best. We entertained them all periodically by dining and asking them to come over and swim with us in our pool.

My travel with and for Centex was both fun and rewarding. I spent quite a lot of time in California acquiring a company called Creative Travel and Leisure, a travel-related company and landed near San Jose, California. I spent two or more weeks out there during one trip and lived in Sausalito, California, at the Alta Mira right on the bay. I used the daily morning ferry to get to the downtown area, where I was conducting a purchase investigation for Centex.

I also spent many days in the Chicago downtown area reviewing our books and common joint ventures with the Pritzsker family interest. Centex (I am sure it was the Murchison's) had joint ventured industrial parks in suburbs of Chicago with the Pritzsker family. The Pritzker owned and still owns the Hyatt Corporation's nonpublic common shares. They also owned a controlling interest in Hammond Organ Company. The family was fascinating; they were friends or associates of the mayor of Chicago, John M. Daly. On the front door of their office was the name "Pritzker and Pritzker, Attorneys at Law," but very little public practice of law was ever conducted there among these Russian lawyers, only investments. I met and worked with Si Zunaman, their comptroller, and at least four of the Pritzker's while I was there.

Susan had started her second year at Vivian Field Junior High School in Carrollton. Teaching was truly fulfilling for her as she enjoyed it very much, not unlike her mother. We discussed the merits of teaching or raising children and concluded that a happy balance could be reached, especially with the help of Betty.

Susan gave me a Rolex watch for Christmas. She borrowed the money for the purchase from Jay Stanley and paid $64.00 a month for six months to pay it out. I loved it.

It was in the fall of 1971, and I was getting bored at Centex. I had been in the Controller's office as an assistant controller. I had about 13 different companies for which I was responsible, including consolidating them into a combined balance sheet and income statement for the ultimate consolidation of Centex on a quarterly basis. The SEC required quarterly reporting. I had about 9 people, mostly women, who worked for me in the bookkeeping responsibility. One or more of them would be sick at the wrong time when I needed them the most. So, I would do their work for them, which got boring.

Chapter 13
Grapevine

12/23/08

I had a desire to start a CPA practice. My father had always been self-employed, selling wheel balancers during World War II and later starting a furniture carpet store in Sweetwater. It was my dream to own and operate my own business. Susan and I deposited Jay with Gram and Dede one day, and we went to the Dallas Public Library and researched the entire Dallas area via the Yellow Pages for areas that might need a CPA.

We found Grapevine. It was the location where the Dallas Fort Worth Airport authority had decided to build an international airport to serve Dallas and Fort Worth. Grapevine was a small town with about 5000 people. It had no CPA, only a bookkeeper who kept books and prepared tax returns.

I met Gene Smith, who worked in the tax department at Centex. He was also a CPA and expressed a desire to start a CPA practice. He knew Bill Reed in Grapevine and wanted me to meet him. Gene and I worked on budgeting at the start of the practice, realizing the money was needed to survive the first year or so before a profitable practice could be developed.

A developer named James Biddle contacted me regarding being his controller for a planned community development in Carrollton. His compensation offer was substantial, and I viewed it as a way to build up a nest egg for the practice. So, I quit Centex in November and went to work for James Biddle. I worked for Mr. Biddle for about two months before I realized he was borrowing money for his home-building development and redirecting the money to his personal ranch and other unrelated expenses to the project. After confronting Biddle regarding the redirection and the need to report properly to the bank regarding the application and use of the borrowed money, I soon realized that I would be short-lived as his controller. I felt that Mr. Biddle was dishonest in his dealings with the banks and that his enterprise would soon fail.

On Valentine's Day in 1972, I started the CPA practice in Grapevine. Gene Smith was to assist me with some money during the beginning months of the practice, and he agreed to help with tax return preparation on a need basis with the ultimate goal of a partnership for us both.

I rented a small office from Bill Yancey, owner of the Yancey Insurance Agency, and hung out my CPA certificate, waiting for a client to walk in the door. Bill was the best property owner one could have, and he helped me by taking me to Chamber of Commerce functions and inducting me into the Grapevine Rotary Club. My only competition was Tommy Alexander, who had a bookkeeping business employing several employees across town. I was the first CPA to practice in Grapevine, a town of 5,000, in 1972, and the first CPA to retire in 2005.

I went to both banks—American Bank of Commerce and First National Bank of Grapevine. The two banks were arch rivals, with Joe Box and Harold Kaker running First National Bank. First National was owned by Joe Box and was considered the icon of Grapevine. The original and "only" bank, owned by pioneers of the town and a bank that was big and strong! The other bank, American Bank of Commerce, was owned by a group of medical doctors, including Ed and Minnie Lee Lancaster, Carlton Pittard, Mike Simmons, and Sam Gladney. It was operated by Pat Patteson, Bob Stewart, and Neva Frymire.

First National sued the banking commission in Austin to prevent the formation of the new bank ABC. The logic was that Grapevine did not need a second bank. Today (2020), there are at least 12 banks in Grapevine, with a population of over 50,000.

The two banks did not swap or exchange mutual checks on a daily basis. All checks written on either bank had to be cleared through the Dallas clearing house before they would be presented to the other bank. They did not associate with each other and generally bad-mouthed each other when the occasion arose. I elected to open a bank account in each bank, trying not to offend either. I borrowed $1500 from Pat Patteson with ABC to purchase used office furniture and equipment. As collateral, I pledged our Volkswagen, life insurance cash surrender values, and the listing of office furniture and equipment.

I purchased one executive desk and chair, one secretarial desk and chair, four sitting chairs, one IBM Selectric long carriage typewriter, one filing cabinet, waste baskets, two-hole punchers, and files, all for

$1500. I rented a Xerox copy machine from Xerox Corporation—the first Xerox ever in Grapevine! Advertising was prohibited in my profession by the Texas State Board of Public Accountancy (the licensing bureau) or by the American Institute and Texas Society of Public Accountants. An announcement card two columns wide and two inches long was allowed by the State Board. The card could be published three times in an area newspaper. I contacted Zena Oxford with the Grapevine Sun and purchased the advertisement.

The announcement read:

Jerry L. Pittman

Certified Public Accountant

Announces the opening of his

Office located at

1340 South Main

Grapevine, Texas

817-481-7505

Don Gerschick, a local optometrist, took me to Rotary, where I made many acquaintances, including Millard Dilg, Luther Hillman, Pearce Horton, Dennis Hraninsky, O.C. Mike Taylor, Pat Patteson, and Bill Reed. I joined Rotary. We met in the Civic Center downtown every Wednesday at lunch.

Willhoites Texaco station was the gathering place for all men in Grapevine. Ted Wilhoite, the proprietor, provided a few chairs and hot coffee every day. That's where I became acquainted with the older men.

Jerry and Lura Tarwater were clients of mine, and later, I met their son, Scott, with his enterprising spirit.

Chapter 14
Colleyville

2/28/09

At about this time, Linda and Kenny went to New York for some kind of job assignment for Kenny. They left us Lulu, their beagle. Lulu liked to dig and bark, much to the boredom of our dog, Virginia. I had planted 36 wax leaf legustrums plants around the swimming pool only to come home from work one day to find that Lulu had dug all of them up and was commencing to eat the roots of each. Before Lulu met her maker, and before she was to be crated up and sent "collect" to New York, where Linda and Kenny resided, Susan rescued her and took her to Jane and Dub's house. What happened to Lulu after that? I was not sure, and I certainly did not care!

Virginia, our dachshund, died on one of our many trips out to see Eddie and Mother. She jumped out of the car when we arrived and ran across the street, only to be run over by a passing car. We buried Virginia on Eddie's land outside the city limits. Susan and I cried all night long. Virginia (Gin) was our first dog. She slept with us at the foot of our bed, mostly keeping Susan's feet warm. (Perhaps that is why she now wears socks to bed during the winter, continuing the tradition that Gin started.) It is hard to lose the dog you love, as I learned later with our other dogs. Jay was too young to be concerned about our dog. Besides, Grenna and Eddie were always ready to entertain him. That they did! Susan and I went to Lubbock the next day to see the Texas Tech game.

Betty Robinson continued to look after Jay daily until the fall of 1973 when he enrolled in a prekindergarten school in Farmers Branch. I took him to school every day since it was on my way to Grapevine, and Susan would pick him up in the afternoons. We either did not have seat belts or car seats or did not use them, but it did not seem to bother us. We sang songs every day going to school: "She'll be coming around the mountain;

jingle bells, shotgun shells; I love you a bushel and a peck; here we go loop de loop, here we go loop de lie."

Driving daily to Grapevine in a Toyota Corolla was quite a venture. Highway 114 was merely a two-lane road with lots of traffic. In particular were aggregate truck haulers, taking the concrete base to the new airport—DFW. The contractor that was building the runways at DFW called for a truckload of rock to be delivered every two minutes! So, the rock truck haulers were not interested in speed limits, safety, or Toyota Corollas en route. The construction of the airport started in 1971, with the completion to be in 1974. The DFW airport was one of the main reasons I chose Grapevine for my practice.

I first met Connor Lam at the café across from Mac A Go Go grocery on the southeastern edge of Grapevine. Connor was an attorney starting his practice in town. He was eating breakfast at the café every morning, and I stopped to drink coffee with him almost daily. He told me stories about Grapevine and the various personalities, including Bill and Sue Reed, Pearce and Beverly Horton, Millard and Helen Dilg, Joe and Cecilia Box, Harold and Eunice Kaker, Don and Gayle Gerschick, Bill and Betty Yancey, and of course, buy your boat from Wilbur and Alma Goltz.

I shared one of the better stories with Connor when I described one of my first clients who wanted me to prepare their tax returns. Lena Mae Perry and daughter Hazel Joyce Henderson walked in the door along with Hazel Joyce's two daughters, Melissa and Trisha, ages 11 and 8. We began talking about their "A-PART-MENTS" that they owned at the end of Main Street in Grapevine. I examined their hand-posted ledgers and started taking down the particulars when, all of a sudden, little Trisha stood up and commenced to urinate on the carpet in my office. And the water flowed straight down under her dress as though she had no panties on. Her mother, Hazel Joyce Henderson, responded by saying, "Oh my, I knew you would do that here. What am I to do?" After utter amazement, I felt that was my cue, so I suggested she take little Trisha to the lady's restroom to teach her what bathrooms were all about and bring some towels to clean my carpet. Upon hearing this story, Connor said, "Jerry, welcome to Grapevine!"

Gene Smith continued to work at Centex while I started the CPA practice. He did not help me much in practice, with the exception of some tax advice and certainly no money. The CPA practice was developing slowly. Joining the Chamber and the Rotary Club helped a bunch. I felt like I needed to walk the streets and kiss babies to generate business.

Bill Reed owned a real estate company, William K. Reed and Associates, in Grapevine and was the guru of real estate for the entire area. The whole area was wild with development prospects, what with the DFW airport well under construction. He would purchase a piece of land—10 or more acres in the Grapevine area, and then sell it to investors for a profit. He was very wealthy and a bit eccentric in that he was extremely sloppy, kept very few records, had one bank account (First National), and needed an accountant very badly.

When I started to work for Bill Reed, I learned that there were at least 25 joint ventures (partnerships) of land with as many as 15 different partners in each. Some of the partnerships had been oversold, that is, a partnership of 10 people, but as I was cleaning up the records, I learned that more than one had more partners than 100% of ownership. I insisted that he open a bank account for each of the twenty-five partnerships. He asked me to contact a banker he knew at Greenville Avenue State Bank in Dallas, so I did, and he gave me a check for $1900.00 to open nineteen separate bank accounts. The check was payable to me, which I deposited. So, I went to Dallas and wrote my personal check to open the separate bank accounts, only later to find out that Bill's check bounced! He later made it good, but that was a hint about my future with Bill Reed.

Bill and Sue Reed would have lavish parties out at his beautiful home on Lake Grapevine. His wife Sue was the former Sue Garner, and even later Sue Crabtree, and finally (perhaps) Frank. The parties were mostly black-tie affairs with named entertainment, wonderful food, and drinks for all. Susan and I learned a lot about the social scene in Grapevine by going to these rather lavish parties.

Bill also was involved in selling lots allegedly owned by his grandmother. He would go to one investor and ask him to purchase a lot for $3000 and later reported that it was sold for $3800 the following week. The following week, he would bring that investor $3800 and tell him that he had another lot costing $4500 that was closed for $6000 in two weeks. At the same time, he sold to another investor a lot that cost $3800 for a closing that was going to happen next week for $4800. This Ponzi scheme carried on to as many as 15 investors for some time, with the last lot investment of $25,000 and up to $35,000. These investors were successful businessmen, including Mike Taylor, superintendent of GCISD; Sid Pruitt, principal of Grapevine High School; Pearce Horton, insurance agent; Don Gerschick, optometrist; and, of course, me. The last ones holding the bag lost the most, and fortunately, I did not lose any money because I got wise to the "Rob Peter and paying Paul" routine long before his kingdom folded.

During Bill Reed's peak of financial fortune and during the summer of 1973, I borrowed his brand new Winnebago motor home for a long week in colorful Colorado. Jay and, Pat, Linda, and Kenny joined us for travel and camping in Colorado in this new motor home. Little Jay was two-plus years old and was just as happy to stay with Gram and Dede in Dallas. Dede had an Airstream travel trailer and loved to travel to the coast of Texas and make friends with fellow travelers. Jay liked that, too.

Jay, Pat, Linda, and Susan caught the steam locomotive at Ouray, Colorado, while Kenny and I drove the Winnebago up to Silverton, where the train was to arrive later that day. I decided to take a shower in the Winnebago while Kenny drove, and that was the most bruising affair! The only other thing that was most memorable was the time that our septic tank was gaggingly full and Jay Stanley's baseball bat to the tank. The mother lode shot out like a cannon, much to all of our relief.

Much scotch and beer were consumed on the trip—fun was had by all. As planning for our family continued, Susan and I decided to have another baby. We were still living in Dallas, but the obvious need to move to Grapevine was becoming important. Susan was not too sure of some of the social scenes that Grapevine offered, but I assured her that all of the people in Grapevine were not like Bill Reed and Pearce Horton. I even promised her that I would purchase a sailboat that we could sail on Lake Grapevine.

We decided to go to Mexico after Christmas for a driving tour to Guanajuato and San Miguel de Allende. We planned our trip to drive and prepared BC for the trip. As you recall, we had more than one BC, a Volkswagen beetle that met our needs to a point until the family came along. This was to be a big Christmas for Jay as he was involved with G.I. Joe and all that G.I. Joe had to offer. He loved to build things, including Legos and related designs, and construct model airplanes. Santa gave him a G.I. Joe helicopter for Christmas, and on Christmas Eve, the night before we were to leave for Mexico, Susan and I constructed the helicopter. He called it the" hell of a copter" or something like that. We stayed up most of the night trying to make sense of helicopter construction and finished shortly before Jay woke up on Christmas day. Grenna and Eddie were really happy to keep Jay while we drove to Mexico.

It was our second trip to Mexico, the first being our honeymoon to Acapulco. We used a travel agent to make our hotel reservations in Guanajuato and San Miguel. We toured the shops, visited the art galleries, and took many walks. I spoke limited Spanish, enough to get along in Mexico. Many Americans live in San Miguel, and English is spoken everywhere. We drank their cerveza and Mexican drinks like Margaritas and Tequila sours. We had no problems until the last day when I wanted to attend the local Rotary Club in Guanawato. They were having their annual Christmas party and decided to convert their entire program that evening to English in our honor.

The Rotary Club in Guanawato was most hospitable to us. The Rotarians there, however, loved to drink. We had cocktails before dinner, during dinner, and, of course, after dinner. The meal was some sort of soupy meat substance that looked like it might not go down too well with me. We retired to our room in the hotel in Guanawato after more drinks and a basic celebration with many Rotarians still drinking at the restaurant.

Fortunately, Susan did not drink or eat too much of the food. She was four months pregnant with our second child at the time and exercised good judgment, but I did not, as I got sick in Mexico again! Some call it Montezuma's revenge as the whole Mexican war fought once again in my stomach. We had to call for more toilet paper around 3 am because I was still going at both ends!

We tried to drink only bottled cokes and beer and to order purified water (aqua purificado), but in Mexico, the water is generally impure with ice, lettuce, tomatoes, and salads, all rather risky with bacteria. You really cannot be too careful in Mexico. Some better hotels can be trusted with pure water, and as we learned later in this account, all of the water in Parras de la Fuente is pure.

Quietly and slowly, Susan drove us out of Guanawato the next morning to head north to Sweetwater. It was a little rough at first, with a couple of stops on the way home. It was about 800 miles to the border as we were scheduled to cross the frontera (US border) at Cuidad Acuna or Del Rio, Texas. We spent the night with Grenna and Eddie, played with Jay, and then the next day, we went home to Dallas.

The practice in Grapevine was still going well. I became the City Auditor, and The Airport Cities Chamber of Commerce asked me to apply for their exempt status with the IRS, and I was elected treasurer of the Grapevine Rotary Club. I needed to move to Grapevine to become more involved there. So, Susan and I started on the weekends looking for a new home in Grapevine. The Reed addition was too far from town even though it was close to the lake, and there were not many housing additions near town. It was January of 1974. The airport was still under construction to be completed this year, and there was much discussion regarding the development of the area.

We started to look in Colleyville and Southlake. The City of Southlake received its charter to be a city in 1956, and it had very little infrastructure, streets, and schools. The Grapevine Colleyville

Independent School District appealed to us for Jay to enter school in another two years and probably preschool there as well. We found a new, used home at 5612 Oak Top Drive in Colleyville and put a contract on it subject to the sale of our home in Dallas. We had the home on Sherburne listed the week before, and it was getting a lot of interested parties. It sold quickly; we made a profit and completed the purchase in Colleyville. We moved in late March, with Susan expecting our child in early May.

Since we had a swimming pool in Dallas, we had to have another. Our new neighbors to the south were the Devereaus. They had two boys named Wally and Jeff. Wally, Jeff, and Jay were inseparable. They explored the field behind the house, hunted, played games, and tried to fish out to the hole dug in the backyard for the new swimming pool. Somehow, it was filled with water that came from rain and other sources as well. This area of Colleyville was one big rock, and septic tanks would not perk! Perhaps they were fishing for floating turds. Who knows? Thank goodness they never caught anything. I purchased a riding lawnmower because our home included one-half acre with most of its grass. Jay loved helping me with the yard duties as he would say that, "Daddy is mowing the Lard." He had trouble with his 'Ys." Bill Yancey was called Mr. Nancy, and the color was not yellow; it was, "Lellow."

Our next-door neighbors to the East were great people. John and Louise Ramey. And became great friends. John helped me with our water well, gave me advice for my garden, and always had the right tools that I needed at the time. Their son, Michael Ramey, was a freshman at Grapevine High School. They all loved Jay and really enjoyed having him visit next door as he did quite frequently. He also visited the Stellmachs across the street and met Ben Utley, who lived next to the Rameys to the East. Ben was Jay's age, while Jay was between the ages of Wally and Jeff, who lived to the West of us.

The swimming pool was completed; we built a shelter hut and installed a water well. I bought a rotor tiller and planted a garden. Susan purchased strawberries and started a strawberry and asparagus patches. They all grew well in the sandy soil. She was 8/9 pregnant, with the baby due soon.

Chapter 15
Joel Greer Pittman

3/11/09

It was my birthday on May 12 when we were scheduled to go to Baylor Hospital in Dallas. Our baby was to be delivered by appointment since it was to be a caesarian birth. We did not know the baby's sex or any of the particulars, except for the fact that Susan was very healthy, and she had met all of the dietary and other rules known by anyone on that day. Sonograms were nonexistent, or maybe we just ruled out the opportunity. I certainly was not interested in being in the delivery room with Susan any more than she wanted me there. Dr. Robert Brunken was Susan's doctor who also delivered Jay in 1970.

Eddie and Ellie Morrison were good friends, and we met them during our Sunday school class at University Park Methodist. Eddie was working on completing his residency in pathology at Parkland. He and I were both former Eagle Scouts. Both of us had gone to Philmont when we were younger, and he also was a Fiji from SMU. Ellie was a Pi Phi at SMU, so she and Susan had much in common. Eddie was from Carthage, Texas, and Ellie was from Waco. We had previously arranged for them to keep Jay on the day of delivery. So, we delivered Jay to the Morrison's and were off to the hospital.

Joel Greer Pittman was born at 9:43 on the morning of the 13th of May 1974. He had blond and somewhat curly hair, the best I could tell. The only reason Greer was not born the day of my 30th birthday is that Dr. Brunken wanted to play golf on that Sunday and made a scheduled time to deliver Greer on the next Monday. Certainly, a valid and good reason since golf is so important to me today!

Greer Pittman was as healthy as could be. He was ready to go home long before Susan was. I picked up Jay and told him of his little brother, who was born that day. I took him back to the hospital, up to the baby ward, and there, through the glass, was Greer Pittman. Jay was four years old, and as he beat his hands on the glass, he shouted, "Joel Greer Pittman, Joel Greer Pittman, I am your big brother!" He was so excited, and so was I. Another son! Wow! Jane and Dub were there as the Morrisons.

We took Greer home along with his mother so that we could live in our new home at 5612 Oak Top Drive in Colleyville. John and Louise Ramey were among the first to greet us and give us a warm feeling from our neighbors. Jane, more fondly known as Dainty Jane, was truly a trooper assisting Susan while she was convalescing. The boys were soon to start to call their loving grandmother Gram. And Dumpy Dub would be called by the boys "Dede."

While Jay was happy to have a little brother, he had his own agenda-- mainly Wally, Jeff, the backyard, the swimming pool, and helping Dad "mow the lard." Jay also enjoyed going on camping trips with Gram and Dede. Dede had acquired an Airstream trailer, and they desired to travel and camp all across the state and country. And they were eager to take Jay with them.

The summer of 1974 was filled with swimming, boating, mowing lawns, attending to Greer, and working in the garden. I had purchased a rototiller, and we were growing potatoes, tomatoes, okra, onions, squash, and strawberries. The fall was full of football, and we secured babysitters for Jay and Greer on special occasions when we wanted to step out. Babysitters included Cindi Turk and Gaye Arrington.

The Fall included a couple of trips to Sweetwater to see Grenna and Eddie and their cows. Eddy was raising Murray Grey cattle and was eager to tell us all of his stories and introduce us to his cows, and he had names for each! Mother and Eddie were very much in love, or at least Susan and I were abundantly aware of the differences in my mother as the pre-Eddie and post-Eddie involvements were different, including the reduced telephone calls, etc. The fact was that the floor-covering store was turning a profit, and everyone was happy. We would spend some time at the store where they worked—Pittman Floor Covering, Inc. in Sweetwater. Jay climbed up and over the carpet rolls while Grenna held and entertained

Mr. Greer Pittman.

Mother loved for us to come out for a visit as she cooked her usual big meals: brisket, potato salad, creamed squash, red beans, pecan pie, and peach cobblers: yum! She kept us all entertained, either playing gin rummy or cutting out doors and windows for Jay in a shoe box. He was mesmerized with the fun she had to offer and loved her Delaware Punches. During the fall months, we drove to Sweetwater, left the boys, and went to Lubbock to see a football game when Tech was playing, probably Texas or A&M. Other times, we would merely listen to the game on the radio in Grenna's living room.

Living in Colleyville was okay, but some annoying problems developing in 1975-76 were beginning to get on my nerves. The roads were rough at best–city streets with lots of potholes and a government that was reluctant to spend money fixing them. In another vein, the city had a bond election to provide a city-wide sewer system to collect the effluent and process the stuff, only for the electing public to turn down the vote! At the time, I blamed the City Council because they were not enthusiastic about the sale of the bonds to the public. Perhaps they enjoyed having the slimy green water running in the streets. Colleyville was established on a big rock that absorbs nothing. It was not designed for septic tanks with lateral lines disbursing the effluent.

As he grew older, Greer started exploring his environment as he grew older. I built a three-foot fence around the swimming pool. We were not ready for his voluntary swimming objectives. He had quite a wandering mind and body. Susan and I learned early on that we needed to keep an eye on him, or else he would wander off. He loved his big wheels and rode them all over the driveway. When he first got the big wheels, he wanted to take them into his bedroom to spend the night with them.

Greer's first grade was rather eventful. He came home on the first day and announced that he had a full and tiring day and wanted a beer! It was obvious that Greer Pittman had heard his mother many times when she returned home from school.

Our next-door neighbors were PKs, also known as Preacher Kids. I believe their name was Darnell, and the two PKs were trouble. Other young boys were on the block, all of whom Greer attached as friends. Some were older, while others were his same age. Cannon Elementary was right across the street from our house on Pebblebrook, so the boys had a vast playground to keep them entertained. It was also a good place to fly kites, walk and train dogs, and generally hang out. We never worried about the whereabouts of Jay or Greer, nor did we keep track of them hourly or otherwise. It just seemed that it would happen when we needed them or they needed us.

One day, Jay came into the house and said that we would not believe what Greer had said. He wouldn't tell me, but when I questioned Greer, he told me that he had broadcast loudly in school that certain people were "Assholes!" I asked him if he knew what that meant. He wasn't sure, and he told me he heard the word from the mouths of our neighbors–the PKs. Well, I informed Greer that assholes were not an acceptable word, nor customary in conversations of any nature. I felt like he needed an explanation, so I told him that an asshole was the place where big potty came out. I told Greer to grab his ankles. Both boys knew when I told them to grab their ankles that it was time for corporal punishment– namely, my belt. Greer got two licks and was informed not to use that word again.

Not too long after that, I learned that Greer had dropped his drawers and mooned someone at school or on a bus. Well!

Yes, the source was the PKs and his friends down the block. And he was informed that this behavior was unacceptable, and accordingly, he had to grab his ankles again.

When Greer later called some other kids "Mother Fuckers", his mother and I almost went in orbit! We were devastated, not knowing what to do, who was teaching our son such a language, and how we should control his friend's influence. Once again, he was told that this language was not acceptable, if not downright awful, and to grab his ankles and hold on!

I did not want to bother to tell Greer what the term meant. He was only six years old.

On still another occasion, either that year (his first) or the next, I got a call or a note from the principal at Cannon Elementary that she wanted to visit with me regarding Greer's most recent behavior. According to her, Greer apparently punched out a girl in the first grade. It was a rather awkward meeting for this principal, I am sure, given that I was on the school board, I assured her that I would discuss/discipline our son so that she could expect better behavior in the future. This time Greer did not have to grab his ankles, especially when I heard his side of the story. Greer's report was that this girl hit him first. And his mother and I had heard of this little girl's behavior earlier. So, we told Greer to steer clear of any confrontation with her in the future.

The main lesson I learned here was that there are always two sides to every story and that I should never react foolishly hearing only one side. This lesson carried on for the rest of my life, involving my tenure of six years on the school board and nine years on the city council.

We went to Salt Lake again in March of 1983 to ski Solitude and Brighton, rent a Rent-a-Wreck, eat at Bill and Nada's, and sleep at the Skyline Motel with the hot tub and swimming pool, we didn't have a lot of money, but we knew how to have fun.

Greer finished Tech with a business major in MS and marketing. He was unsure what he wanted to do at that time as he was considering more studies and perhaps a Master's degree. He had spent the previous two summers at Philmont Scout ranch, helping young hikers and scout troops explore the 18,000-acre ranch near Cimarron, New Mexico. He was a Ranger for Philmont those two years and learned to love the out-of-doors even more during his tenure there.

He also had a yearning to learn Spanish better and enrolled in a four-to-six-month study of Spanish in a Cuernavaca family school. Cuernavaca is a small town about one or so hours south and east of Mexico City. He loved it, and so did his mother and me. We went to Cuernavaca while he was there and enjoyed the charm and warm hospitality of Hector and his host family. Greer's total emersion into Mexico with this family and with the people of Cuernavaca, including the children at the Zocolo, gave Greer perspectives and dimensions never encountered before. We toured much of the countryside with Greer, including Xtapa, and even thought he had a girlfriend at one time in one of the nearby villages.

In August 1989, Susan and I celebrated our silver anniversary. On our anniversaries, we were almost all very quiet and usually did nothing. Rocky Gribble and his band played in our backyard party for our annual Dog Day's dance at our home again, and Greer started two-a-day's football practice. He was to be a senior and the tight end for the Grapevine Mustangs. He was a great tight end; he blocked well and caught many passes, thrilling his mom and dad! He was also elected as Homecoming King–a very prestigious title and award.

GREER PITTMAN'S TRI AT MAUI AND ANGIE

During Bush's presidency, airplanes piloted by Arabs crashed into the World Trade Center's, destroying both buildings and also crashed into the Pentagon. Over 6.000 US citizens died. The event was called 9/11 because of the date (Sept 11), and everyone remembers where and what we were doing at the time. This provocation is what caused us to declare war on Iraq. It changed the world, causing the establishment of Homeland Security and many new travel requirements.

Greer was planning a triathlon at Carmel, California, and travel plans were solidified. Airfares for me, Susan, Greer, and Dainty Jane had to be cancelled, as well as $1200 of golf tee times at Pebble beach and other golf courses where Greer and I were planning to play. Because of this continued terrorist threat on our entire country, the airlines, and hotel people were most conciliatory in refunding our money.

The next year, we went to Maui for Greer's Triathlon. Greer joined the Leukemia Charity to help raise money for them, and they, in turn, would sponsor his entry to some extent. Greer had spent a lot of time training in biking, swimming, and running for the Tri. He also met Angie Gibson at this event.

Gram went with us, and we rented an apartment for the week. Caroline King was in the race as well as Peter Billip, her fiancé. Jason McGlamery was there. He and Greer made many friends in the race for the Leukemia Society. Gram fell asleep in the staging area in a chase lounge such that she was sound asleep when Greer finished the race! He was pleased to see her even though she was fast asleep!

Greer and Jason explored Hana in the dark the next day. The entire trip was a grand adventure with several memorable occurrences. It got pitch dark shortly after meeting Angie and her friends, and the guys were to walk back to their car, but the darkness caused trauma for the guys such that the mountain trail could only be visible by the use of their cell phones as the only source of light. Angie said later that she was concerned about Greer.

The next day, Greer and I played golf on one of Maui's golf courses, and we took Peter and Caroline to dinner at a very fine and fishy restaurant.

One trauma we had was on a highway in Maui when some motorcyclists were involved in a fatal accident that stopped traffic for a long, long time. Susan, Jerry, and Gram had to go to number 1 between the cars involved in the traffic backup. It was very acceptable even among all of the traffic participants. It was a bit out of character for Dainty, but she performed like a champ.

On another day, we flew over to the main island, Hawaii, to view some of Jay's designs at a library or museum.

In the Fall of 2002, Peter Billip married Caroline King in Houston. We flew there for the grand wedding at St Luke's Methodist Church. Linda and Kenny, and Les were so happy.

Later, after he was married, Greer ran in the Dallas Marathon and completed it with pride, for him and all of us.

Chapter 16
Cherry Picking Real Estate Markets

This chapter is written regarding the real estate (homes) that Susan and I owned and lived in periodically.

MERRIMAN PARK ESTATES DALLAS, TEXAS

Circa 1970-2, I was working for Centex as assistant comptroller and was offered stock options in the company before it went public. I cashed in the options, and bingo! It resulted in $9800.00, more money than Susan and I have ever seen. We decided to find our first home and found a foreclosure of a rather large home in Merriman Park Estates, Dallas. I assumed the defaulted payments.

The house had six bedrooms, four complete baths, a swimming pool, and three stories, with a dumb waiter from the garage to the kitchen. Jay's riding train set occupied one of the bedrooms. We bought a shag carpet for the living area, and I tried to wallpaper the kitchen while Susan learned new foul words from me in doing so. I never tried to wall paper again!

I planted 35-40 wax leaf ligustrums around the swimming pool, and LULU, Linda and Kenny's dog, dug them all up, eating their roots. Linda and Kenny were in New York and had asked us to keep LULU until this happened. LULU was being crated up for a New York trip when Susan rescued the damn dog from me and moved it to her mother's.

We hired Betty Robertson to keep Jay while Susan returned to teaching. The salary for teaching was just enough to pay for the hiring of Betty, but it was worth it! Betty was a great cook, Jay loved Betty, and Susan's happiness was restored. Also, Betty made the best chocolate chip cookies for me so she won me over, too.

Betty had four children, Carmen, Silvia, Shaunte, and Tyrone, who came over to swim. Susan gave them swimming lessons as well.

5612 OAK TOP DRIVE COLLEYVILLE, TEXAS

Starting my CPA practice in Grapevine necessitated the need to live out there, so we purchased 5612 Oak Top Drive in Colleyville in 1974 or 1975 when Greer was one, and Jay was four. We had made a good profit, so we built a swimming pool where Wally, Jeff, (Devereaux)and Jay tried to fish out of the hole being dug for the pool.

Greer had his 4-wheeler there on the top of our hilltop, Jay met and established lasting friendships with Ben Utley, and we all grew to know and love our neighbors, including John and Louise Ramey with their son Mike Ramey next door. John helped me with the water well and our swimming pool. And when a copperhead was cornered by Christi, our dachshund, John came over to kill it with a pistol and a hoe.

The Stellmachs lived across the street; and when Greer decided to drive Susan's Toyota station wagon (he was about two or three), he managed to shift the gears on the car. It rolled downhill toward the Stellmach house's bay window when their son Kurt was brave enough to jump into it and stop it! Greer also got the hammer and smashed to headlamp on my car. And took the saw and chased Katy around the yard, thinking if he cut the dog in half, he would then have two dogs.

Water ran in the neighborhood streets, most of it green sewer water, because the City had failed to install a city-wide sewer system.

One summer we sponsored the Hastings Annual reunion that is described elsewhere In these memoirs. The septic system was overloaded that weekend, and our family (My Mother) and others tried the flower beds because the commodes would not flush! It was embarrassing.

We sold Oak Top and moved to Grapevine, but not until Katy, our Weimaraner, did not approve of the buyer who attempted entry while we were gone.

CHOTEAU CIRCLE GRAPEVINE, TEXAS

We purchased a townhome in north Grapevine next door to two delightful gay men, Bob and Alan, a necessity because the home Roy Stewart was building near Cannon Elementary was not completed. This was 1978-79. We lived there less than a year and asked Glynda Kirkland, a realtor, to sell it. She caused the townhome to flood when she showed the house. Fortunately, Alan and Bob's damage, as ours, was covered by our insurance.

346 PEBBLEBOOK GRAPEVINE, TEXAS

Our first constructed home was a four-bedroom home across from Cannon Elementary, about six blocks from my office, and three miles from Grapevine High School, where Susan worked. Roy Stewart built the home after Susan designed it after her grandparents' former home in Sulphur Springs. The center of the home was a dog run down the middle with a view into the backyard. Everything spun off the dog run: kitchen, our bedroom, the stairs, the dining room, the living room, and one-half bath. We moved to Pebblebrook home in 1979 and sold it in 2006. Jay and Greer were raised there and attended elementary, middle, and high school there, including some college at Texas A&M for Jay and Texas Tech for Greer. It had a large back yard for Christi, Katy, Bart, Ebbie and her eight puppies, and the rescue cat Simone.

LAKE HAUS, DILLON COLORADO, APARTMENT B-4

We purchased a 1/3 interest in a townhome at Dillon, Colorado, in 1994 for $25 thousand when Paul Rider and Mike Mariast needed another partner, especially one who could keep the books and pay the bills for a fee simple home (no mortgage) owned by three people. It was a grand experience for our family, who loved to ski, hike, and the out of doors. I was the manager of the money and In charge of the calendar. There were rarely any problems or issues except remodeling the unit periodically. Skiing, family reunions, and charity auctions at CDRI and the church were just some of the activities for Colorado. We sold the townhome in 2018 for a big profit. Paul and Mike were pleased. So were we.

ELBERTA LAKE, SULPHUR SPRINGS, TEXAS

There was an old cabin that Susan's mother owned half and her sister owned the other, which we purchased and razed. Termites! Jay designed a replacement cabin in 2000. Joe Jennings built the cabin. Its slab (30 x 40) was dyed a muted color of red. It had two bedrooms and a bath downstairs with two lofts for two more small bedrooms. It was a lifetime decision since we did not own the real estate that it occupied, but it allowed us to continue a presence that had been in Susan's family since the Elberta Lake Club's inception in the early 1900s.

910 CEMETERY ROAD, FORT DAVIS, TEXAS

My retirement offered the opportunity to purchase seven acres and build a home that Jay and Janann designed in Fort Davis, Texas. We started construction in the summer of 2006 and moved in June 2007, ten months later. We built a summer home since the weather was excellent there in the Davis mountains, with mean humidity averaging 10 to 20 percent— much better than Grapevine's. So it followed for the next 16 -17 years that we would spend our winters in Grapevine and summers in Fort Davis. The home, custom built, included 30 ft ceilings and seven trusses in the great room that had beautiful views of ranch pasture on three sides. While living there, we built a three-car garage (my man cave), a wind turbine, and 30 solar panels. The garage accommodated a pool table in addition to the two cars.

131 GENEVA RUIDOSO, NEW MEXICO

In 2020, with our Colorado gain, we purchased another townhome, this one at Innsbrook Country Club in Ruidoso, New Mexico, with a higher altitude (7400). Ski slopes, horse racing, and lots of people with similar investments that we know or will know in the future. It has two bedrooms and two and one-half baths. We remodeled the unit with new furniture and changed HVAC and outer decks, as it was about thirty years old and needed upgrading. It is solely owned by us to be used by us and never to be rented out nor used as a charity token like Lake Haus.

Chapter 17
Our Two Sons

7/20/09

Jay enrolled in elementary school at Colleyville Elementary, about six blocks from our house in Colleyville. He loved school and looked forward to going every day. He also joined the Cub Scouts that year with Ben Utley. While I do not remember who is den mother was, I do remember the famous pinewood derby with the scouts. Four wheels, two axels, and a block of wood were purchased from the scouts with which to build the pinewood racer. The theory, of course, was founded around the idea that it was a father/son project, one that the cub was to do most of the work in building the racer with the advice and consent of the father. Well, it went fairly well, with the opposite happening. At Jay's age, he was not really ready to work with saws and carving knives, so I assisted a whole bunch, and we produced a racer. That first year was a real learning curve for both of us, but the real racer was built in the second year of scouts, where Jay and I had learned from our previous year's experiences.

We built a real slick racer with lead weights carefully imbedded in the undercarriage of the racer to get the racer's weight up to the maximum five ounces. The axles were engineered perfectly, and the wheels were installed such that we were certain we had a winner! We were nosed out for second place in the big race. It was truly a really frustrating experience for both of us, especially for Jay. I shall never forget the disappointed look on my son's face that day.

The third year for the pinewood derby was coming up, and I proposed an alternative for Jay. I offered, in lieu of the pinewood, that I would take him flying in a private airplane. He accepted. I hired a private pilot to take us for a spin in his Beech craft single engine airplane. We flew over Colleyville, Keller, Grapevine, and the lake. It was a real thrill for both of us and certainly a suitable and better substitute for the pinewood.

Jay's second year teacher was Mrs. Kniffin. Jay was having a lot of trouble with his timed arithmetic drills when Mrs. Kniffin brought it to our attention. A series of math problems, all additions, and subtractions, were to be listed off of the blackboard and then solved in a timed test. Jay was unable to finish the test each time. He did not complete the assignment on time and was materially short on completion. After several different tests, the teacher called us in to discuss the problems he was having.

We had observed that Jay really never crawled as a baby, choosing to swim to get to his destination. His motor skills were not progressing as they should either. Many times, he would kick at the soccer ball but miss it altogether and swing a bat and miss the ball.

Mrs. Kniffin said that he should be tested further for possible dyslectic problems. We Immediately got Gram involved, and she recommended the Slingerland Institute. We enrolled Jay for further testing. The conclusion was that he had severe dyslectic motor skills. He would try to read from right to left, and his motor skills were not up to par. He loved to read, however, and took on every book we presented to him—Hardy Boys, mysteries, and science fiction. He loved Cub Scouts because he would really get involved in building, making, and exploring the unknown that scouting was famous for.

Mrs. Kniffin and Slingerland gave Susan and me great advice. We were to allow Jay to progress at his own pace, to love him, and encourage him in every endeavor. They assured us that there was absolutely nothing wrong with his brain, his IQ was higher than normal, and he was perfectly normal in every way.

Greer Pittman , on the other hand, was into everything. He lived up to the reputation of being a member of the "terrible twos." He got a three-wheeler for his second Christmas, and he adapted to it quite well. He motored all over the house, and when we allowed it, he would motor in the driveway where we had a big hill to climb to the house. He was not ready to motor down the hill yet, but you could see that was to come. He motored around the swimming pool and fell into the pool more than once, but Susan and I were always nearby to pull him out of the water and keep him safe.

Both guys adapted to the swimming pool and swimming quite well. With her Camp Longhorn background, Susan was bound and determined for the boys to swim. They both had formal lessons, and many of their sitters were also swimmers, giving them good pool exercise.

Susan got a call from Sid Pruitt, the principal of Grapevine High, saying that there was an opening in the English department of the High School. We discussed it thoroughly before she accepted. While Betty was no longer available, we needed another "nanny" for Greer Pittman . After putting our feelers out, we found Elsie Blalock to serve as a babysitter while we were at work. Susan took the teaching job at Grapevine High School. Most of her salary was dedicated to paying the babysitter/nannies we hired, as we did not want to use a daycare facility.

We traveled north to Elizabethtown, Kentucky, the home of Fort Knox, where the US gold supply resides. We also had car trouble. The engine had sucked some metal into the cylinder and stopped running. Parts had to be ordered at the local dealership such that we were mired in Elizabethtown for the weekend. So, we toured the Mint and found it quite interesting. We also went to Jack Daniel's distillery in a nearby town. It was also fun, but I am no longer a bourbon drinker after around that stuff while in college.

BC was fixed, so we headed home through as many toll roads as I have fingers. I was convinced that Kentucky owned more toll roads than any other state. And they charged us by the axel. I thought I was going to run out of money before I got out of that state. Jay was beginning to get sick, so we started pushing more to home. We got into Memphis, Tennessee wanting to camp near or on the Mississippi River. We found a campground near the big river only to find out that the mosquitoes there were bigger than grasshoppers! They would bite you and try to carry you off with them, along with a pint of blood, of course. Jay was not feeling good at all, running a fever and a severe sore throat. Susan and I were really worried since he was not keeping any food down either. We bought some mosquito spray and settled down with a very sick little boy for the night.

The next day we departed very early for home. We got to Texas and then to Colleyville by dark. We called Dr. Carlton Pittard on the road, and he was able to diagnose Jay the next day. He was totally dehydrated with a severe case of tonsillitis.

Richard M Nixon was President and in his second term. The term was getting rather rocky since he was involved with spying and conspiring to undermine the opposing party's election efforts. He committed perjury as well. He ultimately resigned from the office of the Presidency, something that was certainly historic and unprecedented. His vice president, Gerald Ford, succeeded him as President.

The Grapevine Rotary Club elected me as their President in June of 1976. I had previously served as their treasurer and sergeant of arms and was honored to be the Rotarian of the Year in 1974. My father was a member of Rotary in Sweetwater, and I was honored to be the student guest of the Lubbock Rotary Club while I was at Texas Tech because I was on the Student Senate at Tech. Rotary has been a great organization for me. Rotary has clubs all over the world, and it is a lot of fun to attend or make up a meeting at other clubs either near your home, in Mexico, or across the ocean.

Rotary's four ways test represents guidelines for daily living:

1. Is the truth?

2. Is it fair to all concerned?

3. Will it develop better friendships?

4. Will it be beneficial to all concerned!

I was the tenth president of the Grapevine Rotary Club, and we celebrated our club's 10"-year birthday at Las Colinas Country Club.

I was unable to hunt much during these years. My practice was calling on a lot of my time, including the City of Grapevine's annual audit being conducted right during deer season, and Jay had started playing soccer for a Colleyville soccer league. I wanted to participate in his soccer, so I enrolled as a soccer referee, became licensed, and bought the uniform, soccer shoes, and red and yellow cards. I attended soccer ref school as well. Every Saturday, I had at least two games to referee as well as attend Jay's game. The under six-year group posted the biggest problems in that the mission of the referee at that age was to get out of the middle and avoid getting kicked. The kids merely wanted to kick the ball or something!

Jay kept having tonsil problems, which they called tonsillitis, fever, and loss of school, which were companions. Dr. Pittard was our doctor and my client, and he scheduled Jay for a tonsillectomy. When Jay came out of the operating room at Grapevine Memorial Hospital (later named Baylor), he was screaming with pain, such that it upset me and Susan because we felt so helpless. He got over it quickly but was confined to the Hospital for a few days. I got him several model airplanes and cars to assemble, which he did in no time. His mother got him a few books. She would come to the hospital during her lunch hour and read him part of the book but purposely have to leave just before the most important part of the book. When she returned that afternoon, Jay had picked up the book and finished that chapter. She purposely teased him into reading more, which he did, and he did not know how his mother had tricked him.

I had built a workbench for my garage where I had various tools, saws, and basic stuff. Greer had his three-wheeler nearby and was almost always out in the garage or near the swimming pool when I was. I liked to have him around and liked having a helper from time to time. We had a garden with tomatoes, potatoes, corn, okra, onions, and radishes. He was labeled 'rattle britches' by Gayle Shumate or Carolyn Frank since he was always on the move, either walking, crawling, or on his three-wheeler in the garage.

He was always into some mischief or trouble. Once, he took my hammer and knocked out the headlight of my station wagon, then on another occasion, he informed me that if he took my saw and worked on Katie, our Weimeriner, cut her in half, he would then have two dogs! On another occasion, he somehow jumped into Susan's Toyota station wagon, slipped it out of gear, and began driving it (so to speak). The car started rolling down the hill from our house, jumped the curb on the Stellmach house, and one of the Stelmach's, seeing what was happening, jumped in the car, put it in gear, and applied the emergency brake. Rattle Britches (Noel Greer Pittman) was into more trouble. Fortunately, he was not hurt, and neither was the car or the Stelmach's tree.

Texas Bi-Centennial celebration was during 1976. Texas declared its independence from Mexico in 1836 and had to prove it at the Alamo in 1845 and later at the Battle of San Jacinto. So, the 150 anniversary was a big deal in Texas. A huge wagon train was conducted all across Texas that year, and the train came through Grapevine. Our city pulled out all stops of hospitality to host the wagon train. It was truly historic, and it was a lot of fun entertaining these faux pioneers and their mode of transportation.

Chapter 18
Living In Grapevine

346 PEBBLEBROOK

Our family had lived at 346 Pebble brook since 1978, when we had hired Roy Stewart to build it for us. I built a basketball goal for Greer and converted a bedroom upstairs into an electric train room for Jay. The garage had a swinging gate for the dog access and where Ebbie delivered her nine puppies, and we had built the whole house around a dark room to accommodate Susan's new hobby, photography.

Susan and I needed a place to live while we were in Grapevine. Fort Davis was to be our summer home from now on, but what about the Winters? We could not financially justify owning a large home in Grapevine or another in Fort Davis. We sold 346 in 2007, realizing that the Fort Davis home was well underway.

Susan was on The Board of Parks and Recreation Department, and in viewing several of their trails, she discovered Linkside Townhomes, which were under construction at the time. These townhomes were across from Grapevine Mills Mall and secluded down a hill through a gated area on the Dallas Cowboy Golf course. They were almost surrounded by apartments. So, I went with her to see them and was impressed. We made a deposit and chose our unit that afternoon with money. Our unit was completed within about 5 months, and we moved in. Our new address is 2627 Eagle Drive. It included three bedrooms and two and one-half baths. It was governed by a homeowner association, so we joined the association, and I was later appointed Treasurer of the HOA, as has always been the case for me.

LINKSIDETOWNHOME

Our townhouse was built by Toll Brothers (2006), and they hired a management company, CMA, to collect the dues and pay the common bills. My job as Treasurer was to help with the budget and review the financials monthly or quarterly as needed. This routine lasted for fifteen years until three board members left or resigned, leaving me and one other with any kind of prior knowledge or experience.

I became President by default of the 39-unit town home addition (2022). Very shortly thereafter, a demand letter was presented to me that intimated a lawsuit would be forthcoming if we did not repair the plaintiffs stucco. I learned quickly why some of the former board members quit, as they thought this complaint would go away. I guess. CMA had hired an attorney, and their fees were mounting.

I met the plaintiff, Phil England, despite CMA and the lawyer advising against it. I assumed that Mr. England was not totally unlike me, and I asked him what it would take to solve this issue. Quickly, Phil England and I addressed and agreed to a solution, including hiring Luis Robledo, a stucco man he had previously found to fix all of the stucco and replaster; and within two weeks, his complaint was mitigated completely. He signed a complete release of the complaint that our attorney drew up, and the threatened lawsuit was dropped and forgotten. We were good friends from then on. But we still had to pay our lawyer, which galled me. I tried to pursue this but met much opposition and dropped my drive.

Luis Robledo was an undocumented immigrant from Durango, Mexico, and a very talented stucco man and carpenter. He spoke broken Ingles (English) that matched my broken Espanola (Spanish). Luis's wife was a Dreamer child who was brought here from Mexico along with hundreds of other babies in years past. They have three boys and live modestly and honestly. I took Luis to a Mexican Insurance Agency in Irving, Texas, and acquired a worker's compensation policy to protect Linkside and their management agents, CMA, I paid to set up monthly payments for him to keep the policy, and he agreed to file income tax returns to stay legal. He had about 10 employees who were all well-dressed when they worked for me. Besides stucco work, they performed carpentry, dry wall, paint, and roofing repair. They were just what Linkside needed after 15 years of ownership. I ended up hiring Luis Robledo to repair about 25 more townhome units. Luis was a good man and eager to conform to our country's laws and culture,

I told my Board of directors that they needed to find a new President. After five months, my successor was elected, and we returned to our summer home in Fort Davis.

Chapter 19
Pneumonia and Melanoma

6/27/09

That spring, Susan was winding down the school year, looking forward to summer. She was experiencing severe allergies with a deep cough and general weakness. She took over-the-counter sinus medicine but did not seem to get any better. She finally went to visit the doctor, Carlton Pittard, who diagnosed her to have pneumonia. He gave her an antibiotic, but she did not improve. He then put her in the hospital, and testing proved she had a severe case of viral pneumonia when one lung collapsed. An oxygen tent was ordered, and intravenous feeding was started. Dr. Pittard tried every antibiotic they made and tested her for Legionnaires disease as she was not getting any better. Susan was feeling ok only a week and requested a beer which was accommodated! In fact, the nurses allowed us to keep a six pack at the nurse's station for her future consumption. Dr. Pittard approved.

Gram and Dede came to the rescue to help me with Jay and, especially during the daytime. I would take Greer over to Grapevine Hospital to see his mother (he was about three or four years old). He was really bitter that she was in the hospital and not able to nurture and take care of him. In the lobby of the hospital, we would wheel his mother out of her bed with an IV bottle in tow, and he would put up a wild eyed fit in front of everyone. He wanted nothing to do with his mother and really expressed his desire/demand to go home, which we did. I felt so sorry for Susan because I knew he had to hurt her feelings while she did not feel that good anyway.

She was in the hospital for about three weeks before her lung got better and could serve her as it should. I took Jay and Greer out sailing one night to occupy all our thoughts and minds. We trolled a fishing line with some sort of spinner lure to see what we might catch. Greer Pittman wanted to eat a fish and was convinced I would cook it for his supper if we did catch one. The only proviso was that he had to catch two keepers before we could take them home and cook. He loved to fish, and damn if he didn't catch two fish! Jay was laughing about the whole affair! So, we went home, and by the time I found the corn meal and the grease and had the fish cooked, Greer had fallen asleep in his highchair! He was exhausted, and so was I—we all missed Susan/mother so much.

Susan and I had talked about selling our home in Colleyville and moving to Grapevine. It appeared to be a good time while she was in the hospital, so I had the house cleaned, appraised, and listed. I listed it with some realtor in Colleyville. I put a price on the house at $10,000 more than the appraisal. It sold in three days! So, I had the dastardly duty to tell Susan while she was in the hospital. My fear was that her other lung might collapse, hearing that I sold the house out from under her while she was ill. We had two months to vacate and find suitable housing in Grapevine.

Actually, I may be exaggerating some of the above since Susan was getting better at the hospital, and we had talked a lot about the boys, the prospect of selling our home, where we would move, and whether we might build a new home. The best time for me to be with Susan was early in the morning after I had deposited Jay at Colleyville Elementary and Greer at 'My School".

We purchased a townhome on Choteau Circle in Grapevine near Dove Elementary. It had three bedrooms and two baths—all upstairs, with the kitchen, living and dining areas downstairs. We had decided to build a new home. We purchased a half-acre lot on Pebble brook in Grapevine and hired Roy Stewart to build the new home. Jerry McClellan, a local pastor, and former draftsman, designed our new home with the specific instructions from Susan because she wanted to model our new home after her grandmother's home in Sulphur Springs.

We were packing and getting ready for the movers to come to move us from Colleyville to Grapevine. Susan was back on her feet and holding her own again. The boys were in school, and we decided to take some lamps and lampshades to the townhouse. We left the two dogs, Christie and Katie, in the backyard. Katie was a beautiful gray Weimaraner, and

Christie, of course, was a Dachshund, ruler of our family and our backyard. We were to pick up the boys before we came back to Colleyville.

The new purchaser of our home stopped by while we were away and went in the front door. She was there illegally and certainly unannounced. She walked into the kitchen, where Katie saw that someone strange was in her house. Katie probably weighed eighty pounds or so. She began barking, and then she bolted through the bay window, shattering glass and all. The buyer ran out of the house with Katie in hot pursuit. Poor Katie, she had glass imbedded in her body at various places and was bleeding profusely. Katie had to have about 60 stitches from the veterinarian. Later that evening, I got a call from the woman who was in our home. That is how I learned exactly what happened. I told her about Katie and the stitches but that she was going to be all right. When she wanted to know if I was going to pay or repair the bay window, I had to remind her that possession of our home had not occurred and she was, in fact, trespassing. She was fortunate that I did not insist on her paying our vet bill.

We lived in the townhome for about eight months, mostly in 1978, while Roy was building our home. I had an interim loan from Roger Cloud at the American Bank of Commerce and a permanent loan from a savings and loan company. We took Katie and Christie on numerous walks while at the townhome. I built the fence in the backyard of the house, and while the fence line was a bit crooked, I still felt the satisfaction of having built it myself the house was to have four bedrooms and three baths with an open area in the middle called the 'dog run' such that you could view the backyard from the front door. A lot of houses of an earlier generation had dog runs, especially those that had difficulty cooling the bedrooms and kitchen areas. The kitchen and the wood-burning stoves would be separated from the bedrooms by the dog run. No, we did not have burning stoves in our new home, but we did design the home as though we did. We had solid tile floors downstairs, and Susan had her very own dark room for her photographic hobby. We had all of the modern conveniences, including central heat and air and an attic fan. We had a two-car garage and a wonderful work room for me to build, tinker, and otherwise get away.

We listed the townhome with a realtor to sell. It was in a good neighborhood across from Dove Elementary School and should sell fairly quickly. It was during the winter of 1978, but our realtor, Glynda Kirkland, accidentally left the French doors unlocked on the north side of the townhome. A blue northern blew in with a 19-degree temperature, causing the French doors to blow open and all the water pipes to freeze.

About two days later, water started flowing down the stairs, out the front door, and over to our neighbors—Bob Dennison and Allan Turnipseed. The water pipes thawed, and water went everywhere! My insurance agent, Mike Davis, told me that since it was unoccupied, more likely the peril and damage might not be covered by his insurance. Mike's new office was next door to mine at 1000 South Main. I told Mike that I was in total disbelief that the damages would not be covered. Further, I told Mike that he needed to tell me that fact face to face—in other words, that we should have a meeting between our office buildings! I told Mike that I was going to bring my baseball bat! Mike called me back only a few minutes later and told me that we were fully covered by insurance!

When everything was fixed, and the townhome was back in shape, we sold it for a small profit.

Chapter 20
Nerf Enterprises 1977-1979

3/16/09

I had two banking relationships but preferred the one with the American Bank of Commerce. The guys at First National Bank of Grapevine were too formal for me. Roger Cloud was the president of ABC, and I enjoyed visiting him. We called it chewing the fat, or swapping lies. Roger was there to loan me money when I needed it, as well as supporting me in pursuing economic and political ideas, mostly local.

I decided to make investments in real estate. I found residential lots for sale in a new area called Trophy Club. These residential lots would be in a neighborhood that had promise–houses being constructed nearby. The land developer was happy to sell me a speculative lot because he was almost always over-extended and glad that I was willing to 'warehouse' his lot for him. Other builders decided the time was right to build on my lot; they offered me a nice profit to sell my lot. I had purchased the lot with ten percent down and financed the balance with Roger. So, I would sell the lot and take my profit and plow it into another lot and effectively borrow less. This process continued for about two years such that I owned three to five lots at a time and merely had a revolving line of credit with ABC and my banker, Roger Cloud.

I purchased the lots in a partnership called Nerf Enterprises. David Harris was my equal partner in Nerf Enterprises and also my partner in the CPA partnership. I needed David to be my partner for two reasons. The first is that since we were CPA partners and his wife Gaye Martin Harris's ranch and oil royalties. Gaye Martin was probably my first girlfriend ever. She and I held hands, and I gave her a neck-lass disc signifying our steady courtship. It was while we were in the fifth grade. What I did not realize in the fifth grade was that while Gaye was raised on a ranch south of Sweetwater, she would be the heir to megabucks of oil property. That interprets into a very attractive balance sheet of wealth—one that bankers like when reviewing the relative creditworthiness of meager borrowers like me. It always helped to have Gaye's financial strength when I had the 'hots' to purchase something with credit involved.

Nerf stood for 'Nest Egg Retirement Fund.' We rarely told anyone for fear that they might not understand. Nerf bought land, hired architects, built office buildings, borrowed interim and permanent money, and entered into office-building leasing. Since I made most of the decisions, David agreed that I should be the managing partner. Nerf still exists today, owning royalty interests in land at 1701 West Northwest Highway and 3651 Wm D Tate in Grapevine and five acres of land on Highway 121, also in Grapevine.

Early on, I found an acre of land on Main Street in Grapevine. It had two houses and a chicken barn on the backside. It was owned by Marvin Thweatt. We paid $55,000 for the land, including the improvements—about one dollar per foot. This was truly a high price, but the future of the site seemed most appealing. Not too long after the purchase, one of the houses burned down early one morning. I had arrived at the office that morning early and had no alibi when the fire marshal, Bill Powers, teasingly asked if I had set the house on fire! The adjacent land in the back was owned by a car dealership, and I negotiated the purchase of that tract as well. Roger Cloud at ABC provided the financing necessary to complete the purchases.

I hired Byron Folse, an architect who had become a client of ours, to design a two-storied office building on the land. Our goal was to have the land note paid off before we started the construction of an office building. The office staff had grown, and so had our practice. We now had about 15 employees besides David and me. We were becoming crowded and needed more room as our practice continued to grow. We had previously divided the firm into three working sections—auditing, tax, and general practice. All professional personnel attended various seminars as 40 hours annually of continued professional education.

We received the Business of the Year award from the Grapevine Chamber of Commerce. The original chamber was named Airport Cities Chamber of Commerce, and over time, Colleyville, Bedford, Southlake, and Keller desired to split out of the Chamber, so Grapevine started its own chamber. We had maintained the books and records at no cost to the chamber, and we had applied for exempt status with the Internal Revenue Service (Section 501 c-2). We were successful. I was also on their board of directors.

Jimmy Carter was the President of the United States. A Democrat from Georgia, Carter was not popular. Our country was not at war, but we were experiencing out-of-control inflation. The prime lending rate was increasing, and money market savings rates were skyrocketing. The price of gasoline went past $2.00 per gallon, with lumber and steel prices spiraling.

With the architects well underway in the design of the building, I needed to find a permanent loan to finance the new building. I found Southern Trust and Mortgage Company, which offered a 10 7/8%-mortgage commitment for $850,000. Certainly, it was more money than any previous loan I was ever involved with. A really big number and a bit scary! We had ten days to sign and agree to this commitment. With uncontrolled inflation and interest rates shooting up every instant, we did not need to let this commitment slip through our hands. David had cold feet. He just was not sure. Perhaps the rate would come down, or something was David's thought. On the day before we were to sign the commitment, I had to remind David that it was now or never. I called his bluff, saying that I would sign this without him if necessary. I was so sure that this was a momentous decision, a truly pivotal career-maker or breaker. I knew my financial strength could not support a loan on a wet noodle, and I also knew I needed Gaye's financial strength to influence the bankers. While it was a bluff, David agreed, and we signed the commitment.

The down payment and collateral was the one acre of land that was paid for, along with the personal guarantees of David, Gaye, Jerry, and Susan.

A few days later, I picked up a new client, Gene Stanford, who had sold his business in New York and moved to Southlake to retire. Mr. Stanford was a Texas Aggie; he had moved to New York some 30 years before, and he had lost much of his Texas speech pattern. In other words, he had a New York-ish speech impediment. We in Texas feel like we are the only people in the entire United States that speak perfectly. He had sold his business for three million dollars and wanted me to calculate and project the taxes he might owe on this sale. His objective was to set aside enough money to pay the income tax, then take the balance of the money and buy municipal tax-free bonds. He said that by buying tax-free bonds, he would "never have another goddamn tax return for the rest of his life!"

He owed about a million dollars of income taxes on the sale of his company, and since it was January of 1979, he had a full year before he would have to pay the tax. He was in the 70% tax bracket, and any money he made during the balance of 1979 would be taxable at 70%! If he invested the one million in the higher than normal money market certificate of deposit, then the IRS would get the lion's share. I was unable to offer much investment advice at the time as he was grasping for some help.

I did suggest that he might consider loaning me the interim money needed to finance the construction of our building, which was backed up with a permanent loan from Southern Trust. I told Gene that we would furnish a first lien deed of trust as collateral, and we could pay him back during the early part of 1980 together with all of the accrued interest in a year of much lower tax brackets. He thought I was self-serving with such a ludicrous suggestion and left. I was embarrassed.

About three days later, Gene wanted to see me again and told me that he had thought about it and would like to do it. We drew up an interim lending agreement. He would loan Nerf Enterprises $850,000 at a fixed rate of 12%, and the loan would come due March 1, 1980. The accrued interest would amount to about $70,000, and it would be taxed in a lower year-1970.

Now having $850,000 in the bank, I was able to purchase certificates of deposit scheduled and staggered to match the construction draws that the builder needed to build the office building. Pete Durant and Durant Construction was the low bidder and awarded the contractor duties to build a 15,383 square-foot office building at 1000 South Main in Grapevine. The certificates of deposits and money market rates were averaging 15 to 16 percent such that I considered it coffee money paying 12 percent to Gene Stanford and receiving 16 percent on money market and certificates of deposits.

Halfway during the construction, I reviewed the documents and specifications of the new building and called a meeting with the architect, Bryon Folse. We met at the building, and I asked him why he had designed a totally electric building when we had a gas line in the easement in front of the building. My thought was that it was cheaper to heat the building with natural gas than electric. Mr. Folse's answer was that he thought that electric prices would parallel gas prices over the short run such that it did not make any difference. I thought his answer was stupid and thoughtless. Historically, gas has been cheaper! So, we had our first construction change order, and that was to convert the electric heaters to gas and to conduct gas lines to the roof of the building as well as to the hot water heater downstairs. I further asked Byron to calculate and tell me the amount of the change and determine the ultimate payout using gas as compared to electricity. I never got the analysis, but I knew it was a good move.

The construction was completed in January of 1980. Pittman, Harris & Co. occupied one-half with my office on the corner looking down Main Street, and it overlooked a huge and beautiful cottonwood tree. Nerf Enterprises completed the construction of the new building, and we moved into our new quarters in November 1980. The Chamber of Commerce had a ribbon cutting, and the whole town came out to celebrate the event. David and Gaye Harris were there, and of course, Jay and Greer. Of course, Greer had to be with his dad when he cut the ribbon and received the key to the city from the mayor.

Chapter 21
Pittman Harris 1980

7/18/09

The CPA practice was doing well as I was beginning to pick up a lot of clients, including my first audit, Plastic Industrial Containers. David Harris was also a CPA working for Middleton and Burns in Dallas. David is a year older and graduated from Newman High School as well. David and I often saw each other at the Texas Society of CPA Education and other functions. We discussed my practice, and he agreed to join me in Grapevine in the fall of 1973. I badly needed him to help me with the growing practice, including the new audit I had acquired. He purchased one-half of the practice so that we would be equal partners in the new firm called Pittman, Harris, and Company CPAs. We also picked up the City of Grapevine's audit that fall.

1980 was the hottest summer Texas had ever experienced—over 100 days of temperature above 100 degrees. We went to Pennsylvania that summer and missed most of Texas's sizzling heat. Thank goodness! The most popular TV show then was "Dallas," the story of JR Ewing and the Empire. Who shot JR was the day's topic, and throughout our trip to Pennsylvania, people back east would ask us this question repeatedly.

The CPA practice was still growing as my new partner. I got him to join the Rotary Club with me, and we continued our involvement with the Chamber of Commerce. One of my first clients was Roy Stewart, formerly employed at General Dynamics in Fort Worth but now a home builder in Grapevine. Roy and I became good friends as well. His bookkeeping method was similar to keeping notes on a big chief tablet, but I could balance cash and make sense of his numbers each year. He incorporated it soon after that, so we had to be more exact with our numbers accordingly. Roy would work long hours managing his subcontractors, and then, on the weekends, he camped out in one of his speculative homes, waiting for a prospective owner to stop in to see his homes.

I found my time devoted more to administrative duties than meeting repeat clients and dealing with their issues. My role was becoming one of finding new clients to feed the firm. At one time, we had three partners and twenty-one staff members; we were the auditors of the City of Grapevine, the City of Colleyville, the City of Sunnyvale, and the City of Keller. We had numerous commercial clients, and our tax practice was expanding. We published quarterly newsletters and mailed clever solicitations to all new homeowners with a $100,000 mortgage or better. It was felt that those with this size of mortgage would more likely than not need a CPA firm to assist them in the transition and move from their "foreign country" (only in jest, meaning from another state). But this solicitation in a folksy newsletter paid off with new clients every year.

Dallas and Fort Worth were growing with new corporations moving to our sunbelt, where we had no state income tax and a generally better climate year-round. American Airlines, Exxon, Braniff Airlines, Fidelity Investments, and Boy Scouts of America were making their world headquarters in the DFW area or making major moves involving our area. Many of their employees lived in Grapevine, Colleyville, or Southlake, our trade area.

I was elected Treasurer of the Rotary Club, and Howard Parsley was the new President. Howard was a banker at First National Bank in Grapevine. Treasurer duties included cleaning up what books of record the club had and determining members' accounts receivable balances. Many good-standing members were not so good standing, and the newly elected board of directors gave me the authority to attempt to collect or serve notice that they were no longer extended members. Some members included Millard Dilg, Dr. Don Ger's chick, Bill Reed, Pearce Horton, and Mike Taylor, D.D. Patteson, Dr. Ed Lancaster, Luther Hillman, Sid Pruitt, Wilbur Goltz, Dennis Hranitzsky, Sid Gilman, and Harold Kaker. Several non-paying members were kicked out of the club. Rotary also had compulsory attendance; you would be automatically expelled if you missed four meetings in a row without making up at some other Rotary club.

Several years earlier, I had the pleasure of getting a new local client named Bill Pirkle. Bill was at least 30 years older, but he needed a CPA. He had owned a dairy in north Grapevine for many years and had some problems reconciling his milk base, not to mention that he and his wife Lorene owned precious land on or near Anderson-Gibson Road in Grapevine. Bill liked to talk; we would spend hours discussing old-time Grapevine, general business, and politics. We became perfect friends, especially when I reconciled his milk base (an accounting term) and amended three prior years' tax returns, getting federal refunds for him each year.

I assisted Bill with the sale of his dairy and land. It was a fair price with a substantial down payment and a receivable mortgage note. It also included a tax-free exchange of land near Prosper, Texas. It was a rather complicated transaction involving simultaneous exchanges of land but no hill for a climber with the capable CPA he had hired—me!

A couple of years went by with the payment of this note, but a default occurred when the acquiring company failed to make an annual installment. The land was repossessed with some tax consequences, but it was a blessing in disguise because Bill could then sell the land again!

Bill and Lorene moved to town after he had built a fine home in a residential area on Dove Loop. His son, Bill Darrell Pirkle, who had assisted his father with the dairy, began a cattle operation on the land near Prosper, Texas. The only problem was that my friend Bill Pirkle died suddenly. This left a real void for me because Bill and I were also friends. It also created numerous tax problems. The negotiations of repossession and resale had not concluded, and an Estate tax return had to be filed nine months after he died; three trusts and a partnership had been created upon his death, and they needed to be set up and started. Sandra Pirkle Foster, their daughter, assumed the business role and responsibility for the family since her brother was involved with the ranching activities at Prosper. The Estate tax return resulted in no federal taxes due because of the unlimited marital deduction. The trusts and partnerships were set up under the will.

His death and related tax issues created much correspondence to and from the Internal Revenue Service. They mainly wrote form letters about the trust, the partnership, the prior amended returns, and the Estate tax return. Lorene Pirkle diligently made trips to my office with these various letters—all addressed to Bill Pirkle, the deceased.

Lorene was getting annoyed with this paperwork, but the icing on the cake was when she received a phone call from an IRS agent asking for Bill Pirkle—two years after his death! Now, we had filed his Estate (now loosely called the Death Tax) return and filed at least two personal tax returns, all disclosing the fact that Bill had died. Lorene was not pleased.

So, I asked her permission, and she permitted me to write a letter. I wrote a letter to the IRS, and it went like this:

Dear Internal Revenue Service,

I am Bill Pirkle. I died two years ago, and I am buried at the Grapevine Texas Cemetery,

> • Lot number 493.

For some reason, my social security number has not died with me as you continue to write letters to me. Today, however, you called me at my home, upsetting my wife, now my widow. What do I need to do? If you want to talk with me, I suggest you bring a shovel to the Grapevine Cemetery.

Please leave my widow alone, as this process is very upsetting to her.

> • Yours truly,

> • Bill Pirkle, deceased

CC: District Director Internal Revenue Service Center, Austin, Texas AND Congressman Jim Wright, United States House of Representatives

I was not trying to be a smart ass; I merely wanted to get my point across to a very insensitive branch of our government. I read the letter (before mailed it) to Lorene, who approved it.

Within a week, Lorene received a phone call from the District Director with his sincere apology. And I received a phone call from Congressman Jim Wright's office telling me that he was starting a congressional investigation into this very important screw-up by our government.

Flowers were sent to Lorene, along with formal letters of apology. There were no more letters addressed to Bill.

All of my employees were special to me. During the 80s, we hired Frank Adams, Dennis Essary, Lynda Munion, Leonora Byrd, Linda Canuteson, Stephanie Baldock, Melinda Moreland, Kaye Shonerstedt, Jean Messinger, Wayne O'Daniel, Max Richardson, Mike Conrad, Ellie Grizzle, Helen Madden, Shirley Elms, Jean Messinger, Barbara McSpadden, Susan Richardson, Tommie Marr, Donna Bustamante, Mike Behren, and Albee Richardson.

Some of these employees had more meaning to me than others. Wayne O'Daniel became my partner when I bought David Harris out in 1983. Max Richardson also became a limited partner at that time as well. Linda Canute son was extremely smart, magna cum laude from Baylor, while Melinda Moreland divorced her husband after having an affair with Max Richardson, my partner. Kaye Schonerstedt gave new meaning to the time needed for a laparoscopic hysterectomy. Jean Messinger had the most enormous mouth of anybody as she saw all, heard all, and told more! Albee Richardson was an Air Force Academy graduate and a CPA but had a personality not unlike a fence post. He typified a bean counter, dull. Albee later became Wayne O'Daniel's partner in 1989 when I decided I needed no more partners or at least those you can't dance or go to bed with! And I already had that partner.

I met Leonora Byrd when I was one of the instructors for the Texas Society of CPA's "Teaching Taxes" program. She enrolled as a student and introduced herself at the break. We continued the conversation when the program concluded. She and her husband, Bill, lived in Fort Worth. She was a CPA and mother of a teenage daughter named Mary Jo and mother of a baby boy named Alan. Leonora worked for me, was very loyal to me, and was a dear friend for the next twenty years until I sold the practice out from under her in 1998.

Leonora, a CPA from Nebraska, was originally from Indiana. She was a bit rusty in the profession, having spent several years raising a family. So, I taught, she learned, and she became my right arm in the practice until I retired.

In January of 1981, I paid Gene Stanford's loan off. He was the one who loaned me the interim money to build 1000 Main. Southern Trust was our permanent mortgage company. I prepared Gene's tax return, and he paid a little less than a million dollars in federal tax and received about $70M of interest income from Nerf Enterprises in a lower tax bracket year, which saved him quite a bit of money. The plan worked beautifully, and we were all happy.

I got involved in teaching other CPAs on various topics. I enrolled as an instructor for the Texas Society of Certified Public Accountants and was later hired by the American Institute of Certified Public Accountants. I traveled across the state for the next three years—to Midland, El Paso, Amarillo, Lubbock, San Antonio, Houston, Brownsville, Corpus, and Tyler. I taught advanced Income Tax Preparation, Community Property taxation upon divorce in Texas, and Oil and Gas personal taxation and accounting. To be a teacher required quite a bit of study because your students were CPAs, and most of them were pretty knowledgeable, if not downright anal. I got high marks on my ratings and considered myself a success at the level of teaching. I had previous teaching experience when I was getting my master's degree, and I taught elementary accounting to first-year students at Tech for two semesters. I worked for the TSCPA for about three years and got tired of being away from my practice and, more importantly, Susan and the boys, so I stopped this process in about 1984.

In the fall of 1983, I was teaching Advanced 1040 preparation for the Texas Society of CPAs, and I flew to College Station and Amarillo for the two-day seminars. Susan and I flew back to Austin on October 29 to see the Texas Tech-Tech game. We had another duck hunt at Fulton that fall, and I attended the Texas School Board Association convention in San Antonio. Rather boring!

My partner, David Harris, and I became increasingly incompatible. His billable hour production was good, but he was not collecting the money. Instead, he would write off forty and fifty percent of our enormous audit fees for the City of Grapevine, Colleyville, Sunnyvale, and The Colony. I was the tax partner collecting almost one hundred percent of my fees (and my staff), but we were not getting anywhere, especially in the profit arena with his substantial write-offs. He had not moved to Grapevine but instead continued to live in Dallas. He managed to be president of the Chamber of Commerce and was a member of the Rotary Club in Grapevine, but we continued having problems with how the practice should be conducted. In June of 1983, after tax season, I proposed that we split the firm, and he would take his clients and related practice to Dallas, and I would keep mine in Grapevine. We would still be partners in Nerf Enterprises, but no longer Pittman Harris and Co. He agreed, and it was an otherwise happy split. I asked Wayne O'Daniel to be my partner, and he accepted. He, too, was dissatisfied with David's performance. David and I remained friends but no longer partners in a CPA practice.

Roger Cloud was the President of the American Bank of Commerce. He was a friend and confidant of mine. We visited often and shared ideas and stories. The bank directors included the doctors at the hospital, including Drs. Carlton Pittard, Mike Simmons, Sam Gladney, and Ed and Minnie Lee Lancaster, to name a few. There were others that I am unable to remember presently. The directors, right or wrong, owned a closely held corporation named Crossroads Development Corp. They used this corporation to acquire repossessed assets held by the bank. One asset in particular included a ten-acre tract of land on Northwest Highway. The tract of land had been held by Crossroads for several years, with the directors contributing money annually to keep the real estate taxes current.

Vic Salvino owned a Kenworth truck dealership in Dallas and was a client of mine. I prepared his and his corporation's annual tax returns, planned his family finances with him, and assisted his secretary/bookkeeper, Lorie Knight, with her accounting and bookkeeping questions regularly. Mr. Salvino was considering expanding his rather large business. The subject of land was discussed many times. I told him of the ten-acre tract in Grapevine owned by Crossroads, an investment of the bank directors. He was intrigued. I received a receptive response when I conveyed the information about Mr. Salvino's interest to Roger Cloud. Roger was happy to sell the land to anybody. Mr. Salvino and his company purchased the land.

But before the purchase, Roger informed me that Crossroads had lost its charter to do business in Texas because the corporation had not filed and paid the Texas Franchise Tax for over ten years. Legally, the corporation did not exist even though it owned this land! Roger hired me to quickly prepare the ten years of delinquent returns, including ten years of federal returns. There were no taxes due to the Federal government since there was no income, but the franchise tax was an annual right to do business in Texas with a small tax due each year. Penalties and interest carried the returns with the numerous delinquencies. Annually, the five shareholders of Crossroads had to contribute money to the corporation to keep the real estate taxes current. Most shareholders were delighted that the land was no longer an albatross around their collective necks.

Roger was pleased that I had brought my client, Mr. Salvino, to the table and wanted to reward me for the brokered relationship. Still, I was not a licensed realtor eligible for a six percent commission. We did agree that the preparation of delinquent ten years of state and federal returns should be $10,000.00, a relatively high fee for such services but not entirely out of line.

But a lawsuit was filed by the shareholders to prevent the sale. The lawsuit said the price was too low, and Roger Cloud acted outside his authority. Lawyer John McBride sent me a subpoena for my deposition in December 1983. The deposition was conducted at lawyer McBride's offices in Fort Worth. One shareholder, the one that instigated the lawsuit, and Roger Cloud attended my deposition. Lawyer McBride smoked Camel cigarettes and blew smoke in my face during the deposition. The lights were dim and primarily trained on my face. The questions were intimidating and involved the fee.

I was charged to prepare the tax returns. It was awful, as I did not have an attorney to represent me—another mistake I made. The facts got twisted; my words were interpreted against me such that I became a defendant in the lawsuit because I was an unlicensed realtor brokering land.

I hired Bill Meyer, former Texas State Senator, to defend me. The plaintiffs wanted to pursue my professional insurance policy and me to recover what they thought was a better price for the land. Practicing real Estate without a license was an offense that should have been reviewed by the Texas State Board of Realtors in Austin; however, the plaintiffs knew that sending the issue to the state board was not in their civil (money) best interest, so they pursued the issue in district court in Fort Worth.

My time sheets to prepare the ten (really twenty) tax returns and my invoices were subpoenaed. My professional insurance carrier got involved, and Bill Meyer worked diligently to defend me. We settled out of court for $10,000, the same fee I had charged to prepare the returns.

I learned a lot in that exercise. I knew I needed to stick with my profession, trust my instincts when dealing with my clients, and be more selective in conducting my CPA practice.

So, Wayne took his clients to a new office across the street and took Max Richardson and one or two employees. It left me with Lynn Bryant and Leonora Byrd. Lynn Bryant stayed six months and ultimately went to start her practice in Hurst. That suited me just fine, as Leonora and I got along quickly. I never doubted her loyalty and her work ethic. She never coveted the practice and always had my best interest at heart.

This was my second CPA partnership, and I decided I needed another CPA partner like another hole in my head. It was abundantly clear that I needed a partner for ONLY two reasons—one to dance with and the other to go to bed with! And I already had my partner, Susan, for those reasons!

After I dissolved the partnership with Wayne O'Daniel in 1989, I hired Welva Lynn Bell. Lynn had an accounting degree and no experience. She had worked for a law firm for two or so years. She had a great attitude, an outgoing personality, and a willingness to learn. Lynn is black. Hiring her opened my eyes, broadened my perspective, and molded my attitude. She worked for me for 14 years until I sold the practice to Randy Powers. She had since gone to work for a CPA firm in Fort Worth. We remain friends to this day.

Litigation support work was continually becoming very popular in my CPA office. Richard Gately, an attorney from Fort Worth, and Richard Green, an attorney from Dallas, called me regularly to hire me for expert testimony for one lawsuit or another. All of them were fun and required a lot of work deciding how and who was harmed, and my job generally involved measuring damages that could be sustained in a court of law.

Richard Green called me in on one of his cases involving the Super Shuttle bus and Dallas Transit Authority, his clients. A periodontic dentist from Allentown, Pennsylvania, was in the Super Shuttle when a large Dallas Transit bus rear-ended the shuttle very slightly. The dentist sued Dallas Transit and Super Shuttle for 5 million dollars, claiming loss of income due to injury and projected loss of revenue over the next 5-10 years. Richard hired me to review the extensive claim work papers that the Austin, Texas, CPA had prepared. The dentist's lawyer was Texas's most notorious plaintiff trial lawyer, Frank Gibbons, the former partner of Dick Grigg, lawyer, loyal Red Raider, and friend of mine and Eddy Windom. The CPA's work papers looked rather extensive and almost intimidating, so I started pursuing another angle.

I called the American Dental Association (ADA) in Chicago to inquire about periodontal specialty for Dentists. Extra college was required, and a certificate was issued for the specialty attained by the dentist. The specialty deals with implants and demands a special fitting and additional costs for the specialty. I inquired further from the ADA and learned that five periodontists were in the Allentown area, and four were certified to practice in the past year. I flew to Allentown and viewed their offices, learning that each was open five days a week and Saturdays were posted as possible. I also visited our dentist's office (the plaintiff), knowing that he was open only four days each week and never on Saturday. This newly created competition would more than likely dilute his earnings and put a significant dent in the "hot dog CPA's extrapolated projection of loss of income as a result of the bus accident." Later, my deposition was taken, and I explained what I did with the DDA research and personal observations in Allentown. I also critiqued the CPA's work papers. I was never put on the stand, and the $5 million lawsuit was settled out of court for $100,000 (legal fees). Richard thought I was the hero!

Chapter 22
Call The Doctor!

3/8/10

UH OH

August 1969

Susan and I returned to Houston for me to resume duties at Arthur Andersen. I completed my Master of Science degree in accounting at Texas Tech. Jay and Pat moved to Dallas or New York—I don't remember which time he was in New York and then Dallas working for First National Bank of Dallas. We were both eager to start/resume our careers with the master's degrees we had earned and hopefully, our price tag had improved with those additional degrees!

Family planning was heavy on our minds now that my master's was completed and my CPA certificate was behind me. Susan was not planning on continuing a teaching career. So, she retired! She had worked for three years, and it was time to retire. We were ready to start our family. We moved into a townhome near Rice University and started looking for a home to purchase.

We cashed in her Teacher Retirement funds after three years of teaching and continuing to contribute to her retirement. We were in our early twenties, and retirement seemed far, far away, and not as important as buying a new Volkswagen Bug. It was beige and air-conditioned, and we named it BC for "baby car" once again. It would be a car that would serve us for many years, and the teacher retirement funds would be available.

Arthur Andersen assigned me a senior audit job in Beaumont. It was a hospital job and a first-time audit for them. I had two assistants working for me. George Appleton was one of the assistants, and I cannot remember the other, and neither one had a lot of experience with a first-time thru audit, and for that matter, neither did I!

Because Beaumont was not too far from Houston, Susan and I could spend time together on the weekends and periodically during the week as the job progressed. By this time, she had been to the doctor to learn she was pregnant! The baby is due in late April or early May. We were so excited! We had no idea what sex the baby would be and did not care— only that the baby would be healthy, and the doctor did not offer it as probably the sonogram machine had not been invented. Birthing techniques and training were generally not attended by the father, and witnessing the birth was all but taboo for the worthless father! Traditionally, the expectant father was relegated to the waiting room only to pace the floor and wait!

Of course, we had to call Jane and Dub and my mother, Jean, as soon as possible for them to celebrate. Of course, the expectant grandparents were giddy. For Jean, it would be the third grandchild, but for Jane and Dub, it is their first! My sister, Carolyn, and her husband, Chuck, had Carl Tanner Selinger and Eric Gavin Selinger, my nephews, a few years earlier.

We located a home in the Memorial area of Houston and issued a contract to purchase it.

I returned to the hospital in Beaumont. We were having trouble balancing the general ledger and reconciling cash. My assistant asked for help, and I also began having trouble with the ledgers. I had a lot on my mind and should not be bothered with the mundane responsibility of balancing the hospital's ledgers. I was working late at night (2 AM) and getting up early (5 AM) to return to work, still having the same problems. I discussed my concerns with Susan over the telephone while I was home with her over the weekends.

Fatigue was getting the best of me as I was getting very few hours of sleep at night. I was worried that I would not be able to complete my assignment, balance the books or whatever—fear of failure got the best of me together with extreme fatigue such that I collapsed on the job!

I do not remember how I got into the hospital in Houston or how Susan was notified. I was so embarrassed and ashamed as I had let Arthur

Andersen down. I was a total failure. I had just finished my Master of Science and completed the CPA exam, my wife was pregnant with our first child, we had a purchase contract on our first home, and I collapsed on the job as fear of failure had set in. I was having a nervous breakdown.

I was in and out of the hospital for thirty days or so under the care of Dr. I.M. Cohen. I had shock treatment to make my mind shift gears from the fear of failure mode and shift more to a forgetful mode such that I was unable to remember what had happened. Dr. Cohen, a psychiatrist, regulated my medicine such that mental therapy followed. Susan was in communication with Dr. Cohen so that she could report my behavior periodically while the sedative medicine was getting adjusted. I learned that any pressure must be put into perspective. I knew that I should not take life so seriously. Inner mental pressures must always be balanced with outer and exterior pressures.

Arthur Andersen gave Susan and me all assurances and support throughout this ordeal. They felt responsible, including taking care of us financially and assisting me with my career continuance. I was feeling perfect and reasonably confident in my abilities. Dr. Cohen and medical treatment were being successful in curing my illness. A relapse is always possible, and caution should be exercised. Identifying pressures inside and outside the mind was the critical lesson I learned that would be useful for the rest of my life.

I needed to avoid high-pressure jobs, and my future employment probably should be away from Arthur Andersen, such that they helped me get a job in Dallas for Centex Corporation.

It was Thanksgiving and Christmas time, and quite a bit of time was available for me and Susan to spend together to plan our future and cure my illness. We played a lot of tennis, and I remember that this was one of the few times I beat Susan at tennis as she was five months pregnant! Otherwise, she was a very good tennis player!

Mental illnesses create stigmas in society. What people think becomes a mental exercise not unlike fear of failure, worries about worries, being fat, and style consciences. A nervous breakdown was a terrible experience for Susan and me at the time, but in the long run, as you can read further in these memoirs, it was a most rewarding experience, making me a stronger person. I learned a lot about myself, my life, and my attitude. My wife told me she would love me no matter what illness would set me back...if for better or for worse and in sickness and in health...I learned she would be as happy with me if I became a manual laborer. It bonded us and made us closer than ever. I was instructed to start slowly, be mindful of my breakpoints, and avoid high-pressure situations.

More importantly, I learned not to take life so seriously!

MELANOMA

One of my early clients was Dr. Russell F. Griffith. Dr. Griffith started his practice in 1972 in Dallas, about the same time I started as a Certified Public Accountant. He was a dermatologist, and I hired him independently to examine me for moles, skin growths, carcinomas, etc. He was most diligent about me as he knew my father had died of melanoma cancer and that it was entirely likely that I could produce melanoma as well. I am fair-complected, and I am a mole producer—one of the worst kinds of skin conditions that could produce melanin.

In the fall of 1979, during one of my periodic six-month visits with Dr. Griffith, I discovered two melanoma growths over my shoulder on my left side. He removed the two growths and sent them to the Parkland Hospital, where a pathologist examined my tissue as he had done over the past six or seven years. Only this time, the tissues contained melanoma cancer cells. They said it constituted Clarks II level cells, which means that they were on the surface of the skin and that they more likely had not penetrated the body or the various nodes.

This was a wake-up call! It put me in a little shock as I recalled the short time my father had lived after his melanoma discovery. Susan got home from school that day, and we both cried and said a prayer.

An oncologist and plastic surgeon made deep cuts on my back, further excising the area of the melanoma. He found nothing and covered his many stitches below the skin, which became a very awkward place for subsurface stitches—rubbing on chairs, pews, etc. They were all later removed! But the best part was this surgeon's waiting room! Through the large wooden and ornate doors was a rather large waiting room full of women—women with small breasts and women with large breasts! It was a wonderful sight! These women were not here for melanomas! I told the surgeon how wonderful I thought his waiting room was just before he put me out for the surgery, and he was not amused. Only, on the follow-up visit, I was immediately ushered into an examination room, which precluded my viewing of the beautiful scenery in the lobby!

The sailing trip to Baja took its toll on me. Two new brown lesions cropped up on my left forearm. Because of my father's death of melanoma and my previous incident of melanoma (1979), I decided to have the two brown spots examined by a dermatologist. They were removed. I visited my dermatologist at least every six months, and he had cut off up to 70 different moles and growths on my neck, back, arms, and legs. These brown spots did not look any other except that they cropped up fairly suddenly. It was September 1992, and we were in the Baja in June! Sure enough, the two lesions were malignant melanoma. Dr. Griffith, my regular dermatologist, removed them and sent them to a lab. Dr. Lieberman was the oncologist surgeon who excised the cuts in a radical way that was more profound into my arm. Dr. Lieberman did not find any melanoma with his deep cuts whatsoever. Once again, I beat melanoma!

ULCERATIVE COLITIS

Sometime in 2003 or 2005, I discovered blood in my stool. I consulted with my general doctor, Brooks Trotter, a general practitioner. He referred me to a colon doctor in Fort Worth, and collectively, they concluded that it was hemorrhoids that should not be a significant problem. They both said that surgery was possible.

A year later, the problem worsened with more blood, and Dr. Trotter recommended a colonoscopy. I visited and had a colonoscopy by Dr. Stephen Lacy, a gastroenterologist. He said that it was not bleeding hemorrhoids but that I had a polyp or two that were releasing blood in my large intestine. His diagnosis was that I had Ulcerative Colitis. He prescribed a medicine that would coat the intestine and stop or otherwise arrest the bleeding. It worked for a while, although the medicine had to be increased periodically.

About ten years later (2014) and fifteen colonoscopies later (some six months apart), the ulcerative colitis increased, the polyps were larger, and Dr. Lacy was recommending that I start a drug called Humira, an intravenous drug that would cost around $18,000 per year. This drug was to coat the intestine again to arrest the bleeding of the now larger polyps.

Before I started this drug, I was fed up with this routine. I called the Mayo Clinic and Hospital in Rochester, Minnesota. Mayo is a renowned hospital that is funded by charity and is known worldwide as being the best hospital for almost any problem. So, I called their toll-free number and gave my name and that I had a severe disease of ulcerative colitis and that I was blowing blood out of my rear periodically. They connected me immediately to the Gastro department of the hospital, and I told them the same story. They asked if I could come to Rochester the following Monday for an appointment at 7 AM.

Susan and I were to be in Lubbock at Texas Tech, attending a banquet honoring older adults like us for serving on the Texas Tech Senate during our college days (50 years ago). From there, I caught an airplane in Lubbock that was indeed a milk run going to Reno, Nevada, Las Vegas, Kansas City, and St. Paul, Minnesota.

A 75-minute bus ride got me to the Days Inn across the street from Mayo on Sunday night.

The lobby was huge, with 81 attending physicians (gastroenterologists) on the board in the front. By noon that day, I had seen three of those doctors, had a lung, stool, and blood test, and was scheduled for a colonoscopy at 7 am the next day! The doctors at Mayo work on a salary, not on how many surgeries or procedures they perform. None of them seemed to be in any hurry, merely that they wanted to interview me and diagnose my issues.

My friend from Elberta, Darla Bennett, and her daughter were at Mayo simultaneously. Darla is from Tyler, Texas, and also owns a cabin at Elberta. She was a great help to me on several occasions, like going to dinner with them in the evenings and escorting my lightheaded person to my hotel room after the medical procedure and colonoscopy on Tuesday morning. More tests followed, and discussions about large polyps. The surgeon who performed the colonoscopy took only 30 minutes to examine my colon. He said they were too large to remove without damaging the colon wall.

More tests were conducted the next day, with a closing conference scheduled that Thursday. My lead doctor and three other doctors were at the closing conference at Mayo Hospital. Their opinion was that cancer of the colon was a real possibility in the future. My recurring medical procedures by Dr. Lacy included a tiny test on the side of the polyps, but that inside or on the back side of the large polyps could already reside. I asked if cancer could develop between annual colonoscopies, and I was assured that it could and possibly infect the bladder, liver, or pancreas.

They recommend that my large intestine be removed.

I left Mayo not necessarily shocked but with many thoughts. But I decided to proceed with the surgery to remove them.

I interviewed two colon surgeons at Baylor Grapevine and chose Dr. Michael Bryan primarily cause he had small hands!

I returned home on another milk run from St. Paul to St. Louis, then to Houston, and finally to Dallas. We spent the summer at Fort Davis, and my surgery was performed on January 4, 2015, successfully. I was in the hospital for a week, then had an ostomy nurse come to my home for sixty days to teach me about ostomy.

Yes, a bag to collect my poop from my small intestine since I no longer had a large intestine and my anal canal was closed. Imagine that I was no longer an asshole cause I didn't have one!

After I arrived home from the hospital, a blood clot developed in my leg, and it traveled to my lung, causing heavy breathing and a very fast heartbeat. The ostomy nurse was attending to me at the time and insisted that I go to the hospital. She called an ambulance with three paramedics on board, one driving, one hooking up an IV, and the other monitoring my heart. We were on the way to the hospital, and I asked if I was entitled to red lights and sirens, and the driver responded, we are only 6 blocks from the hospital, Mr. Pittman, but if you want it, we will comply. They turned them on, especially for me.

The three attending me knew me from my City Council days...

Chapter 23
Family Fun

7/19/09

Bank Robbery - Jerry, Jay, Greer and Floy Pittman

I was on the City of Grapevine's Library Board with Father B, the priest of the Catholic Church. I was still refereeing soccer games on the weekends. Greer had donuts for Dad at Cannon Elementary School—it was his first year at Cannon, across the street from our house. He and I went to school together, as was the tradition for both boys, until they reached the level when they did not want the embarrassment of having their father around on the first day.

Jay walked to Grapevine Middle School daily and had Harlan Jewett as his shop teacher. Greer was finishing up in Cub Scouts, while Jay was heavily involved with Boy Scouts.

We went skiing at Keystone in March and met Jay and Jackie at their rented house. We skied all day together, took many pictures, and did not break, fracture, or sprain anything like we did when we went to Ruidoso while Jay Stanley was married to his previous wife, Pat. Andrew and Decker were not born to Jay and Jackie, and Michael and Chris were about 10 or 12 years old. Greer Pittman was 6, and Jay was 10. The adults stayed up that night while drinking adult beverages and laughing a lot while the kids all went upstairs to bed. It wasn't long after they went to bed that Michael, Chris, and Jay jumped ship and left the room because of Greer's loud snoring.

The annual fall festival was conducted in the Dove Elementary Park area. We had vendors and rides for kids and much fun for all. Buddy Hall was instrumental in closing Main Street, and we had a street dance with an appropriate country band. It was the beginning of Main Street days and later Grapefest Festivals.

I was a speaker before the Northeast Tarrant Board of Realtors. I flew to Houston for the annual Arthur Andersen & Co's alumni party. I saw Bobby Weatherly, Jim Rash, and Harold Cunningham, colleagues who I worked for or with when I was employed there.

David Harris, Max Richardson, and I went to Colorado's Copper Mountain skiing in January of 1982. David and I had decided to bring Max into the CPA partnership as a partner. It was cold, like seven above or below zero, for skiing. That is probably the only thing I remember about the trip. Susan and I had introduced skiing to David and Gaye Harris a few years back, and David fell in love with the sport, so he looked for ways to go.

We went to Sweetwater for Mother's Day. Mother and Eddie were always gracious hosts, cooking great meals for our trips and planning things to do. Eddie loved Jay and Greer so much that he took them fishing or hunting on the farm. Mother entertained Jay by carving windows and doors in a used shoe box. Jay was mesmerized and wanted more.

The Hastings Reunion was in Sweetwater that year. As long as Mother's brothers or sisters were alive, the Hasting Reunion continued annually.

We went skiing in Salt Lake again. Mr. Basketball installed a basketball goalpost in our driveway. This was Greer's birthday present.

Gay Arrington graduated from East Texas State University. Jay had a choir concert, and somehow, we all assumed that it was more likely that he would not make a career singing.

Fahey's restaurant in Grapevine cooked the duck that we brought home from the Rockport trips. We had a big party as almost everyone on the hunt showed. Susan and I learned that we still did not like the taste of duck—it is a lump of dark meat and greasy. I heard, however, about a great recipe for duck. Cook the duck on a pine board slowly at 200 degrees, and stuff the duck with an apple. After cooking the bird for about six hours, throw the duck away and eat the pine board.

3/8/2010

Greer Pittman celebrated his tenth birthday in May. It was about this time and maybe a little earlier that he and I attended an open house at Grapevine Middle School, where I was to meet his teachers. He had told us that Mrs. Biggers was always watching him, and he was invariably in trouble with her. He was convinced that she was after him such that she even had eyes in the back of her head watching him constantly. I am not sure it was much of Greer's idea to go to the open house, but I wanted to do it. We visited each class in order of his schedule, and when we got to Mrs. Bigger's room, Greer sat down in the back of the room, trying not to be seen as I began to ask her to turn around to see the eyes in the back of her head. Greer wanted to crawl under his desk or quickly exit the room. He was embarrassed. He was pretty put out with me after that, but for some reason, her class and his behavior never reappeared.

Roger Cloud moved to Gatesville, Texas, to be a farmer/rancher. He was my banker but now retired. He had a great heart and liked only a few people, and I considered him a friend. New ownership and management entered the bank; somehow, the bank was not the same. He came to

Grapevine in the spring of each year to get his tax return prepared. In 1984, he brought Nedah, his wife, with him. He told me in front of Nedah that he had "drawn the silver bullet" with lung cancer and that he was not going to live much longer. He asked me to look after Nedah and her finances when she needed me. He divulged information on his investments and related financial affairs at that time. Roger lived another six months before he died. The funeral was at Gatesville. I was asked to be his pallbearer along with Bob Burrus, Phil Parker, Mike Taylor, and Roy Stewart. We all gathered at the funeral home for the service. We were all reminiscing about Roger and laughing rather loudly, such that the minister and the funeral director had to hold down our laughter and related loud talking as the people had started gathering and were wondering what was happening. Roger would have loved it and been in the middle of the fun. Roger Cloud was a good man, and I would sincerely miss him.

David Harris was not much of a participant in managing or assisting me in managing Nerf Enterprises. We only had one building at 1000 South Main, and since I was the managing partner, I prepared all of the leases and negotiated all of the lease terms with our lessees. I kept the books, wrote the checks, deposited the money, and negotiated with the bank. I was also involved with the First Methodist Church as their finance chairman, refereed soccer, was on the Grapevine School Board and the Board of Directors of American Bank of Commerce, and was very active with Boy Scout Troop 700, where Jay was now a Star or Life Scout.

I hired Oran Washburn to help me with Nerf Enterprises. Oran was 75-plus years old, retired, and wanted part-time employment. So, he worked half days to be my eyes and ears in the office building. He was in charge of light bulbs, air conditioning, and bathrooms. Commodes constantly had problems, filters had to be changed, and tenants were always hot or cold. It was consuming too much of my time, so I hired Mr. Washburn, or Oran, as he became fondly known by me and everyone he met.

Susan and I planned our official vacation to see her Uncle Jerry in Newport, Oregon. We knew it had to be shortly after we returned from

Philmont before her teaching started in late August. So, on July 27, we loaded up the blue Suburban, which we purchased in Hagerstown, Maryland. We planned to tent camp part of the way and stay in motels in other parts. Our first night was in Cimarron, New Mexico, where we toured Philmont briefly so that Greer and Susan could see it. We stayed in the hotel there in Cimarron. We had a rather ambitious vacation because we only had a week or ten days, so we planned a relatively fast but leisurely trip. We planned on tent camping for most of the journey, but we did have reservations at Reno, Nevada, at the Circus Circus resort, but it was in two days!

The minute we crossed the border into Colorado, the Suburban stopped dead still in a little town named Antonito, Colorado. It was Saturday around noon when everything stopped. It was some transmission problem in that a funny noise had come from the differential. We had joined the AAA automobile club after our last car breakdown, so I called them. After a while, a wrecker showed up. The driver said he would have to tow us to Pueblo to get transmission work before they closed for the weekend. So off we went. Susan, Jay, and Greer were in the Suburban and were being towed backward to Amco Transmission Company in Pueblo, Colorado. They all said that it certainly was a different driving view looking backward. I rode in the truck with the driver.

We got to Amco transmission company just in time, and a small $75.00 part called the governor was all our transmission needed after we grabbed some fast food and got underway and drove until we got to Rifle, Colorado. We arrived at about 1:00 AM. The motel had a swimming pool, so the boys and I had to go swimming that night. Susan went to bed, but we had a good time! We slept as late as we could. Our next stop was Reno, Nevada, at Circus Circus.

Susan and Greer slept, but Jay helped me stay awake, and we arrived in Reno at about 2 AM. We had finally caught up to our agenda. We spent another night there to take in all of the fun at Circus Circus. The boys loved the water activities, and Susan and I tried slot machines, blackjack, and roulette. It was not that thrilling. We went through the desert of

Nevada and California. It was hot. Finally, we arrived on the Pacific and tent camped in the redwood forest. Cool-weather and good campfires, tent camping, and roasting marshmallows were the order of the evening. The redwood trees were giant; one was so big we drove the car through it. The cool Pacific weather was indeed a welcome site after going through the desert of Nevada.

We drove north toward Oregon along Highway 1. A beautiful view of the Pacific and the shore was handed to us. We hiked down to the ocean in some redwood forest. Somehow, Susan dropped her sunglasses beyond some rock that posed a few challenges to climb around the huge rock to retrieve them. Greer and Jay made it down the hill to the ocean without assistance, but going up the hill back to the car was another story for Greer Pittman. "Carry me, Daddy" was his by-line, and I carried him uphill and back to the car.

We arrived at Newport and looked up Susan's Uncle Jerry Waits. He worked for an oyster farm on the Yakina River outside Newport, Oregon. Jerry was Dub's brother and lived with Roy at the oyster farm.

Oysters were better grown in freshwater, which had a minor influence on ocean water. They were grown in 6 x 6-foot vats where a bed of old oyster shells formed the bottom. Screen surrounded the vat, including the trap door on the top. Tiny oyster embryos were placed into the vats and floated out into the river. The tiny embryos would swim to the bottom and attach themselves to an old oyster shell, creating a new oyster. Many vats were floating out in the river, and depending on the size of the oyster they wanted to harvest, they were the criteria for how long to leave the oyster in the vat. Cocktail oysters and petite oysters were the product of the shorter time in the vat, while longer times created oysters to fry or to can or use for oyster soups.

Jay and Greer did not care for oysters or Susan at that time. She did develop a liking for them later in life. Well... I helped myself with hot sauce, beer, and all. Wow, they were great! I scooped them out of the vats, cracked them open, and ate until complete. It was great! Roy and Jerry were wonderful hosts. They took us to their favorite bar and introduced us to the best fish we had ever eaten in Newport. Jerry was good to Greer and Jay and did his best to entertain them throughout our visit. Jerry and Roy were gay and a good couple, and they seemed thrilled.

We left Newport after having fish one more time at a little restaurant or café below a bridge there in town. We drove toward the east, hoping to find a place to camp for the night. Our destination was Jackson Hole before nightfall. We tried to call various campsites only to find they were all full. When we reached the Tetons and Jackson Hole, The Chamber of Commerce saw a campground about twenty miles south of town that was having a Bluebird reunion, but they had room for our tent and related gear. While in Jackson, we purchased food—pork chops, potatoes, and salad material. We made reservations to see the musical being played at their local theatre that evening. The play was Seven Brides and Seven Brothers.

We drove to the campground and set up our tent and bedrolls. We exited the Coleman stove, and Susan began cooking the pork chops. We were surrounded by these vast Bluebird buses with their fancy satellite dishes, televisions, etc. We ate our potatoes, pork chops, and salad, cleaned up our dishes by hand, and packed up our gear to leave to see the play in town. One of the Bluebird owners came over that evening or early the following day and expressed her amazement about how we improvised our campsite with so little, cooked a gourmet meal, cleaned it up, and left. The play Seven Brides and Seven Brothers was excellent, and we all enjoyed the performance.

The Blue Bird buses and their occupants were astonished by our tent camping and Colemans' efficiencies.

We packed up and left pretty early the following day for destinations East. We spent the night in Spokane, Washington, where my mother and I visited when I was a senior in high school. We then went to Yellowstone and saw Old Faithful, the geyser that erupts every 45 minutes. We tent-camped in Pineville, Wyoming, and Trinidad, Colorado, on our way back to Grapevine.

That fall, 1984, Jay took up football in the fall of 1984. I am not sure why. He was a freshman at Grapevine High School and had never played football in his entire life except playing toss with me in the yard. Perhaps it was peer pressure. Anyway, his number was 75, and it was apparent he was not to run downfield to catch a pass or even throw one. His mission was to block and hit someone—which he did well, and he loved doing so! I made almost all of his games, including those in the rain. He stuck it out through the football season and then hung up his cleats to retire permanently from the game of football. But I think he hit enough of his fellow players in practice and did a creditable job at the games that he retired with respect and the satisfaction that he played football for a while.

I went deer hunting in Doss, Texas, along with about five other hunters that year. The most fun of deer hunting was the camaraderie of the hunt with my fellow hunters. We cooked out, drank scotch, and shared hunting experiences. Gary Kirkland, Conrad Heede, and Bob Anding were some hunters, and we hunted Janelle Snowden's ranch.

Chapter 24
The Rio Grande

3/8/10

Tom Powers was my neighbor two doors down. He was politically motivated to run for Mayor and defeated the legendary Bill Tate with the help of several influential town folks, including Jim Glenn and Don Bigbie. He only lasted for one term when Bill Tate mounted a mighty campaign to defeat him, and Tate has been Mayor of Grapevine ever since.

Tom invited me to go canoeing down the Rio Grande on his annual trip. It included the Lower Rio Grande (the wild and scenic part), not to be confused with the Upper Rio Grande, where rafting leisure time and beer drinking are in common. Herb Wright, an IRS estate lawyer from Lubbock, was the straw boss of the canoe trip. He owned numerous waterproof cases in which food could be stored with no risk of getting soaked when and if the rapids dumped you and your canoe. Herb was also a connoisseur of good eats. We always had Grandy's fried chicken on the first day and on other days, sirloin steak, Mexican food, great sandwiches at lunch, lots of cookies, and, of course, eggs and bacon every morning. Beer, not iced down, was stowed in burlap bags so that it would float in the river and move to the various eddies of the river. Ice for the four-day trip was stowed in some of Herb's various waterproof cases and never opened until the ice was needed. Despite the wild river, Herb made sure that we ate well.

The Rio Grande had at least two Class IV rapids and an equal number of Class III and Class II rapids. Class IV rapids were such that a canoe would break into pieces if you were so foolish to venture into them. San Francisco was the name of one, and Panther Canyon was another. The River would flow naturally into a huge rock that was probably thirty feet high and split into two streams at ninety degrees on either side of the rock.

All canoes and gear had to be portaged (carried) around the rapids. Some rapids of lesser volume could be lined, which meant that ropes tied to the bow and stern could be guided through the river, with some of us in the water and some onshore carefully handling the canoe's ropes.

One particular Class II rapid was called Rodeo Rapids. They were always a lot of fun, but invariably a canoe would go over at the completion. It was called Rodeo because the bow of the canoe would rise and dip with the flow of the river over the big rocks near the surface. We would count the dips, and once the fourth dip into the river had occurred, the canoe was so full of water over it went. The landing was soft, with a great shore that we would regroup after a swim and the process of rescuing our gear.

Just past Rodeo was the Hot Springs of the Lower Rio Grande, where we spent the second night in a hot tub of warm water flowing into the river. We always set up our tents and bedrolls before we went to the hot tub area buck naked with a bottle of tequila and Crystal Light. "Jose Cuervo was a friend of mine" was a popular song that got louder and louder on the river as the bottle of tequila emptied.

The Hot Springs was also a great place to bathe and wash your hair. The river's canyons were lower there, so Mexican Caballeros also camped near us on the Mexican side, and we exchanged food and tequila with them. They were always very friendly, especially with my broken Spanish and their broken English.

I made about six trips down the lower canyon over the years. Most of the trips were in the fall, in early November when the hot weather had subsided. We paid a local man in Sanderson to drive the car and the trailer for the canoes to the takeout area on Dudley Harrison's ranch south of Dryden, Texas. The driver took us to the La Linda Bridge, about 30 miles east of the Big Bend National Park boundary. The driver would then double back to Sanderson, pick up a friend with a car, and deliver our vehicle and trailer to Dudley Harrison's ranch south of Dryden, Texas, on the Rio Grande. The ranch road was extremely rough, and it took about four hours to drive from Dryden down to the river. We spent the first night on the green grass behind the post office in Dryden. It was always very comfortable to sleep there since it was really late when we arrived. Little did I know or think of it often, but the grass was, of course, right over the septic tank.

We always had a grand time drinking beer and canoeing down the Rio Grande. On one of the trips, after four full days of canoeing, we were planning on taking out at Dudley Harrison's ranch as planned. We heard many rifles and gunshots as we approached the takeout. A motor boat (the river was wider there, greeted us with more beer, with the driver holstering a pistol. When we arrived, it was like WWIII, with guns shooting across the river (over our heads) and others shooting elsewhere along the river. You see, Dudley Harrison was a member of the State of Texas House of Representatives, and he was having a party for all law enforcement officers in the area and probably beyond the area as well. There were sheriffs, deputies, highway patrol officers, border patrol officers, and constables—all very drunk and shooting their pistols and rifles everywhere. We were all afraid for our lives, so we did not bother to shower, clean up, or otherwise, so we loaded our canoes onto Herb's trailer, packed up our gear, and left for the long four-hour trip back to Dryden. Most of the time, we spent the night and started home the next morning. But not today. On the road home, we came to a vehicle with a flat. It was the sheriff of Terrell County passed out in his Suburban. We stopped and changed his tire for him, and we were not sure he appreciated our disturbing his inebriated state.

The last trip I took with this crew was about 1988 or so. The Rio Grande watershed had received an enormous amount of rain the past few weeks in October. The water supply for the river was not all Juarez's sewer, although we wondered sometimes. The watershed included much of New Mexico all the way past Taos into Colorado, where the headwaters were. The river was full—a "level six" by river standards. The Department of Interior was reluctant to issue us a permit to canoe the wild and scenic, but Herb Wright convinced them to issue the permit. I learned to regret that.

The river was flowing fast and beyond normal. There were no eddies anywhere. When canoes turn over and gear begins to float downstream, one could pick all of it up in some eddy later on. Everything was designed to float and, for the most part, waterproof—beer, ice, food, bedrolls, tents, clothing, etc.

I was the bowman (I really never graduated to the stern man because, I guess, I never provided a canoe), with Mike Luckert as my stern (his canoe). Mike was a CPA from Olney, Texas, a friend of Herb and Tom. We only had two canoes on this trip, with Tom and Herb and Mike and me in the other. We turned over on the second day with a fairly mild rapid. Of course, we both had life vests on, and the training we had included saving your own life first, saving the canoe second and lastly saving your paddle. We accomplished all of the above and tried to move the canoe to the nearest shore to no avail because the river was in control completely. Herb and Tom tried to stay with us while we continued to float downstream. Of course, they rescued all of the beer and ice immediately.

Mike and I floated for at least two miles, holding on to the canoe and a paddle. We kicked and pulled and tried to maneuver the canoe to shore but to no such luck. We went through a shallow area, and Mike hurt his knee on a rock and let go of the canoe. Now, it was up to me to save the canoe. It was our only way out as the canyon walls were fifty feet high on both sides, civilization was at least thirty miles away in most directions, and those 30 miles were known for thorns, stickers, cactuses, and animals that bite, stung, or eat. If ever in my life I had "Seen the Elephant," it was then. I was exhausted and not sure I had too many more kicks left to maneuver this canoe. I saw some river reeds ahead and thought it was my last chance, so I kicked and pulled the canoe over such that my body would hit the reeds first. I stepped on firm soil, perhaps a large rock, and planted my feet there. I then roped the bow line around my arm to pull with all my might such that the canoe came with me into the reeds and stopped. We spent the night there and rested up. Mike was grateful that I had saved his canoe.

Although I have had some desire to go on this trip again, I never went back.

Chapter 25
1985 Eagle Scouts

3/8/2010

We skied Salt Lake again during spring break of 1985. Alan Bristow was head coach of the Denver Nuggets, and we attended a Dallas Maverick/Nugget game. Alan was a tax client of mine, and he gave us the tickets. Alan continued as a client for many years and remained a client of the firm after I retired in 2006.

Gary Kirkland and I toured some property at Roanoke. We had previously purchased three town lots, but this time, we purchased 17 acres on Highway 114 west of Roanoke. About a month later, we traded this land in a simultaneous trade for a small ranch at Caddo, Texas—about 200 acres. We gave the seller a mortgage note for the balance owed. We called the acreage the PK Ranch. It had a ranch house, barn, and several sheds, plus an abundant amount of wildlife—deer, turkey, frogs, and fish, a real paradise for me and the boys.

We spent a lot of time at the ranch. We carried loads of junk to the dumping ground. We cleaned, we painted, we laid new linoleum and carpet, we installed a heating and air conditioner, and we furnished the house with new beds and good used and new furniture throughout. We stocked the kitchen.

On the ranch, we established hunting areas, built blinds, and purchased feeders for the deer and turkey. We started fishing in the two tanks and found we had some fish but more frogs. The frogs were harvested with a .22-caliber rifle. We would shoot their heads off and wait for their little bodies to float to the surface of the water, waded out in the water to pick them up. Frog legs fried in a skillet are a real delicacy. The only thing you have to remember is to remove the black leader cord from the legs; otherwise, they will jump out of the frying pan when you cook them.

Gary's children, Jason and Gary Jr., Greer and Jay, were to enjoy many trips to the PK ranch for much fun. I purchased a 1974 Jeep wagoner with no top that we kept in the garage/barn. The ranch Tom cat took up residence in the back seat of the Jeep. It was a great vehicle for Jay to learn how to drive a stick shift. Greer was a little too young to become a Jeep driver, but he continued to try.

Speaking of learning to drive, Jay and I drove to the PK one Friday evening. We went out there in our GMC black pickup truck. Jay wanted to drive, so once we got to Mineral Wells, where there would be less traffic, he took over. We were cruising quite well until he wanted to try cruise control. He turned it on and somehow did not remember or know how to turn it off when he wanted to. The result was, somehow, we went into the bar ditch and did a complete 180 on the highway. The truck came to a stop, and we decided that we did not want to learn much more about cruise control!

Bill Tate purchased the Tucker White ranch and another ranch south of Sheffield about 20 miles north of Dryden—a total of 38,000 acres. The ranch was huge and spectacular. It had two large ranch houses and windmills throughout, with underground piping conducting water to remote areas of the ranches. The windmills were connected with each other as well. Goat and mohair production and hunting were the primary sources of revenue for the ranch. Bill hired me several times to go to the ranch and help supervise the ranch foreman and related wet backs that were hired. Greer and I went hunting down there several times. The game was plentiful, with lots of deer and turkey. We witnessed several illegals walking across the ranch, especially when we were quiet and settled in a deer blind.

We took Gary and Chris Fickes down to the Tate ranch once, and Gary shot a Havalena hog and insisted on carrying it back to Grapevine. It smelled like high heaven, and I have never forgiven Gary for the smell it left in my suburban!

One of the highlights of the PK ranch was the deer hunting season. We all looked forward to it. The camaraderie, the stories, the anticipation of the hunt, and the enjoyment of nature made it a special time each year. Greer became an excellent marksman and enjoyed the hunt as much as I did.

Our trips to the ranch were not just about hunting; they were about spending quality time together as a family and with friends. We made countless memories at the PK ranch that we still cherish today.

As I look back on these times, I realize how fortunate we were to have such experiences and how they have shaped us. Greer, Gary, and the others have grown into fine men, each with their own families and careers. The lessons learned and the bonds formed at the PK ranch have lasted a lifetime.

In June of 1985, Jay went to Europe with Maurine LeBeau, his Latin teacher. It was between his freshman and sophomore year at Grapevine High School. They toured Greece and Italy. The scout troop committee approved his Eagle Scout project the previous month of May. His project included painting all of the bollards at Heritage Park with metallic silver paint. The project was planned by Jay, and it would occur sometime in August of that year.

Mother and Eddie had won a boat cruise from Nassau, Bahamas, and they gave it to me and Susan, so we departed on a big boat trip where food was served at all levels and every hour day and night. We left Miami and went to Nassau, Freeport, and Dolphin Island. Susan and I walked around the boat from bow to stern many times to work off the multiple food consumptions.

Greer went to Camp Summer Life in Odessa when we got back from Miami. Then he went to New Mexico with the scout troop—Camp Wheenapay, I think. It was weeklong in the mountains of New Mexico.

Gary Kirkland, I purchased 32 acres of land near Rome, Texas, on Highway 114. At the time, I thought it was a good investment and at least a place to hunt dove in September! Little did I know how valuable this piece of property would be later in life. Dove hunting was not that good, but the chiggeres were outstanding!

Page 146

Greer's s Eagle project was a few years later, but the time is now to talk about it. Greer did a great job of planning and engineering the project. It dealt with recycling for Grapevine. Recycling was a new concept in those days, but its appeal was catching on. Edith Butterworth and Joe Moore were instrumental in helping Greer plan and establish schedules to man the central collection bin in downtown Grapevine. In those days, we operated from a small site, and the central bin was emptied once a week. Now, Grapevine has a huge recycling facility and program. Greer's contribution was significant in the initial stages of this program.

Separated glass, aluminum, paper, and newsprint. We opened the collection every Saturday, and Greer got other members of his troop to build the bins and arrange for the delivery of the recycled goods each week. This was the true beginning of recycling in our town, and as time went on, recycling picked up today from door to door with huge trucks. Hooray for Greer!

Greer was now in line for the highest award in Boy Scouts, the Eagle.

Chapter 26
Carolyn And Starr Frank

6/13/2010

Susan was the sponsor of the Academic Decathlon team at Grapevine High School. Six team members with three alternates would compete with other high schools on academic subjects, with the final state competition concluding in late January each year. She would recruit juniors and seniors to join in the competition. The Super Quiz had a different subject each year, with a super bowl of questions offered to the students to compete live with each other. Subjects included (the best I can remember) Flight, the American Indian, etc. Jay competed during his Junior and Senior years. He was dating Jean Fulmer at the time. They had a lot in common with the competing nature involving academics.

We had these kids over to our house often, and I always enjoyed them. Some were like eggheads; others had more outgoing personalities. We cooked hamburgers often as they always liked to eat!

The team won district more than once and competed in the state finals as well, all a result of Susan's outstanding ability to recruit, teach, and inspire those kids.

I purchased season tickets for the Dallas Cowboys, and we attended several games. This investment did not last long when we both got bored with the Cowboys. It was especially boring when I noted that Susan was falling asleep in the stands, waiting for the commercial to end and for the Cowboys to start playing again.

On January 9, 1986, I took Greer to the dentist to have his braces removed. He was in the seventh grade, I think. Throughout the process of wearing braces, his discipline excluded a lot of foods that would foul up the braces, like apples, meat, pecans, beef, etc. We had to stop at Luby's cafeteria on the way home for him to order everything that he had missed during the past six months. He made up for lost time—he had two entrées and two desserts!

I was still on the Grapevine Colleyville School Board, finance chairman at the Methodist Church, member of the board of trustees of the Church, member of the board of directors at American Bank of Commerce, and investor with Teleprompters (the cable TV operator in Grapevine), member of the board of directors of the Longhorn Council of the Boy Scouts of America, and committee chairman of Troop 700. With the CPA practice, I was keeping busy with many meetings.

Susan mostly taught English classes at Grapevine High School. She graded papers seem like all night long, almost every night. I know that for each word that every student wrote, she read and generally commented on each person's paper. She was a good teacher. We had season tickets to attend the football games and attended some volleyball and basketball games as well. After school, Susan picked up Greer at Children's Academy (he called it "my school") and headed over to Carolyn and Starr's house for a beer. Carolyn and Starr Frank lived in this old house on Wall. It was probably built in the late 1800s. Starr was at least 80 years old, and she was born in this old house. Starr taught piano, and Carolyn, her old maid daughter, was secretary to Sid Pruitt, the principal of Grapevine High School. The house was so decrepit. The floors were uneven, there was no hot water in the kitchen, the electric wires were bare, and the water in the commodes froze in the wintertime. It was a good place to gather after a hard day at school and drink a beer or two. That's where Greer got his nickname "Rattle Britches" with his otherwise noisy diapers.

Commercial development was extremely popular during my three terms on the City Council. One event really was special involving Luby's Cafeteria. Our senior citizens were frequently asked when Grapevine was going to have a cafeteria. We knew that the famous Luby's Cafeteria had purchased land to build a new cafeteria a few years earlier, but nothing had been started. So, several council members and members of the

Grapevine Chamber of Commerce went to their corporate headquarters in San Antonio. We heard their corporate mish-mash about location, proximity to their other stores, demographics, and population issues. We listened in boredom for over an hour, and then we finally got fed up. Bill Tate, our mayor, stood up and told their Chairman, "If you don't build a cafeteria in Grapevine, then we will find a competing cafeteria to build one for us." We all stood up from the conference table and went back to Grapevine. They took out a building permit the following week and commenced construction.

Carolyn lived on Wall Street with her mother, Starr, 80 years young. The house where they lived was older than Starr's since she was born in that old house. The floors were not level, the house's electrical wires were all bare, and there was no hot water in the kitchen. The back of the commodes froze in the wintertime. They lived with at least seventeen cats in the house.

Carolyn Frank was the secretary at the high school. Sid Pruitt was the principal who hired Susan to teach at Grapevine High School in 1976. Jay was enrolled in Cannon Elementary, and Greer was enrolled in a day school that he called "My School." Every day, or almost every day, Susan picked up Greer and trekked over to Carolyn Frank's for a cold beer or two. Gayle Shumate, a journalism teacher at the High School, joined them. Greer was still in diapers during many of these visits, such that Gayle named him "Rattle Britches."

Everyone knew and loved Carolyn. She lined up the seniors at graduation and was in charge of every graduation celebration for probably thirty years. She was an "old maid"—never married. She lived at home with her mother, Starr Frank. They lived in the duplex that I bought for them with proceeds from their old circa 1890 house. Carolyn owned a 1959 Chevrolet two-door car that she drove only to purchase groceries and beer. She taught dance in her earlier years and was always involved with Grapevine High in one way or another. Carolyn rooted for Greer on the football field; she supported Jay in all of his efforts at the school, including being editor of the Main Stream. She helped change his diapers in his early years, and she and Gayle Shumate named Greer "Rattle Britches."

Carolyn smoked camel cigarettes and loved her beer. She and her mother, Starr, entertained every afternoon from 4 to 6 at their home. Starr would drink her Old Weller whiskey, and we all had to have a beer. We discussed everything about Grapevine, the city council, the school board, and politics in general, and just about every person that ever crossed their paths was fair game.

Carolyn Frank

Carolyn neglected her health. She never went to the doctor or dentist. Her teeth were awful. When she started feeling bad, she declined rapidly. She developed jaundice and went to bed. One day, Michelle, their caregiver, called me, and I went immediately to the home—she told me Carolyn had taken a turn for the worse. Susan and Gayle were still at school, and Stormy Withers, her nephew, and Starr's grown grandson were visiting the house. Not long after I got to the house, Carolyn died.

Stormy Withers lived in New England and just happened to be in Grapevine when all of this was happening. He was married to Freckles, and they had two or so kids living at home. He was what I call a "space cadet," as he loved trains better than life itself. He is a stamp collector and graduated from the University of South Carolina with, I am sure, a liberal arts degree. His sister, Connie Grote, was the most responsible one of the family, the one whom I looked to whenever a family matter arose.

I called the funeral home and was in the process of calling Johnny Withers and Connie when Stormy interrupted several times, wanting to know what he could do. He was running around like a banty rooster with his head cut off! I told Stormy that the front grass needed mowing since we were going to be having guests in the near future. And that is exactly what Stormy did. He mowed the front yard with his tie on, but he did leave his suit coat in the house. We buried Carolyn in the Withers plot at Grapevine, where Minnie Ursula was buried a few years back. She was Carolyn's older sister and mother of Stormy, Connie, and two other children that I really never got to know very well.

Starr Frank was a living icon of our city. She was the daughter of one of Grapevine's first physicians. She was divorced from Max, whom I never met. She had three children: Minnie Ursula, Tommy, and Carolyn. She had lots of stories to tell everyone, especially about the history of Grapevine. The front porch of her home was in real disrepair and looked as though it was about to fall down. I asked her more than once if she shouldn't consider selling the house and moving into something a little more up-to-date. She would not hear of it and dismissed my discussion on the matter rather quickly. One of the stories that Starr told was about how Dr. Colley performed abortions at the end of Wall Street, mostly of African American women. Colleyville was named after that physician many years later.

Starr and Carolyn Frank

We celebrated Starr's 80th birthday in that old house, and almost everyone from Grapevine came to the party. Starr had a Chickering grand piano. She taught piano, and she played for the Lions Club, the Rotary Club, the Bayview Club, and for whoever asked from time to time. Carolyn drove a 1959 Chevrolet coupe only when she had to. Alice Harrell picked her up on most mornings for the daily trip to the high school. The car was used principally to purchase staples, like beer, for all the friends who came over daily. Starr drank Old Weller bourbon whiskey and smoked Camel cigarettes. She mixed a little whiskey with a lot of water using a clean Kraft cheese glass for her daily Weller and water. She loved to play the piano, and I loved hearing it! She was so good at it she could turn completely around and play songs backward—now think about that. Everything reversed! Her father had been the postmaster of Grapevine, and Starr wrote the music for the alma mater at Grapevine High School— "On the Thresholds of Tomorrow.".... She also had numerous stories to tell—one for almost every time I visited. Carolyn and Starr were proud that I was elected to the school board, so much of the discussions over at their home involved school personnel, especially the superintendent, Bob Fair.

Starr and Carolyn lived as paupers. They lived on Carolyn's secretarial salary mostly. Starr's social security check each month was less than $50 per month. She had some income from piano teaching as well. The house and land on Wall Street had value in that it backed up to a commercial area on Northwest Highway. It was obvious to me that Starr could sell the land and purchase a new/used home that had hot/cold running water etc. The old house was in such bad shape that it was the topic of my conversation with Starr periodically. One day I noticed that the front porch was listing and falling apart. I told Starr that the porch might fall down on her some morning while she was retrieving the paper, resulting in an early death for the 80-plus-year-old. She acted like she didn't hear, or rather, she flipped her wrist at me and the suggestion such that she did not want to hear about it again. Somehow, I am unable to put in writing here the sound uttered by Starr when she "flipped her wrist" at me. That was not the first time she flipped me off in her very special way.

Later, when I returned from a hunting trip that fall, I knew Susan would probably be over at Starr and Carolyn's house, so I stopped at 322 Wall. I was drinking a beer with Gayle, Susan, and Starr when suddenly Starr asked me what I had done regarding her house. I said, "Excuse me?" She said she wanted to sell her home and wanted to know what, if anything, I had done to that end!

The next day, I called Doyle Dickerson, the Exxon jobber who owned connecting real estate that fronted Northwest Highway. He wanted to buy it; we settled on a price and prepared a contract for Starr to sign. Real estate was selling for great prices, and it was good to sell during this period.

Moving Starr and her junk required several decisions. Her grand piano had to be moved, and it had to fit in her new home. We needed a garage/estate sale to sell a lot of her music, furniture, jewelry, and other stuff. Carolyn had a closet full of unopened gifts. Being the secretary of the high school, she got lots of gifts and tossed them into this closet. We opened most of them with her permission. Jewelry was the principal gift, so we put those items into the estate sale as well.

Starr was supportive of everything I suggested except that I needed to choose carefully the company/person that moved her Chickering Grand Piano. And the seventeen cats were not moving into the new home. They had to be either given away or abandoned! Neither of them said anything about the cats.

We purchased a new duplex on Crestview, and I found a qualified mover who took the piano apart very carefully for the move. Starr supervised and approved the mover's abilities. She had her coat on, sat in her chair (that was the very last item to be moved), and watched every move involving her piano. Once the piano had been moved and reassembled, I went to pick up Starr. She got in my Suburban and traveled the six blocks to the Crestview duplex. I carried her over the threshold of the new house, and she immediately went to the piano and played a waltz (my favorites) for me. That was her way of saying thanks, Jerry.

Starr Frank lived in her duplex on Dogwood with a caregiver, Michelle Falateau, and her daughter. I paid Michelle a weekly wage and gave her money to buy groceries for Starr and Michelle. Starr was convinced that Michelle was trying to poison her, and accordingly, Starr would fire Michelle almost daily. Of course, I hired Michelle back each time Starr would get off some kind of binge. Fortunately, when Carolyn Frank died, she left enough money for Starr to live on for the rest of Starr's, or at least I hoped. Starr was now 98 years old and still wanted her Old Weller whiskey to drink every evening. She had quit smoking a few years earlier, sometime after her daughter Carolyn died.

One day, Michelle called to tell me that Starr had tripped over her ottoman and fallen. I drove over to find Starr in some pain and lying on the floor. I called Dr. Minnie Lee Lancaster, and she instructed me to take Starr to the hospital. Starr was watching a funeral on television. It was George Burns's funeral, and he was 105. On the way to the hospital, Starr asked when it would be her time…to die. I assured her that it would be any time she was ready.

She had broken her hip, and the hospital replaced it with another. She was doing better after about three days in the hospital. She wanted to play her piano, but I assured her that we were unable to bring her grand piano to the hospital room. Susan had a grand idea to rent a laptop piano, and we wheeled her to the Baylor Hospital lobby for her to play. She did. And played for almost an hour. When she was complete, she asked her audience in the lobby… "Aren't you going to applaud?"

They did. We returned her to her room and went home. We got a call about an hour later that she had died.

Starr had played her last recital.

Starr gave her home to Connie Grote, who was the only grandchild who cared for her. The other grandchildren were bitter, but there was nothing I could do for them. Starr was sure of her intentions. She gave me her 1947 Chickering Grand Piano, and I had it restored and donated it to the Lancaster Theatre in Grapevine, where it now resides.

Chapter 27
1986 PK Ranch And Elwood P Dowd

6/12/12

Lyndon Johnson did not seek reelection as President of the United States. He felt that Vietnam was his demise and that it was a war that could not be won. Richard Nixon, a Republican, was elected President. He later resigned because he was involved in a voter conspiracy (Watergate) and cover-up that was unacceptable to the public. Gerald Ford followed. He pardoned Nixon and served one term until Jimmy Carter was elected. Jimmy Carter and the Democrats were in office until the conservative savior Ronald Reagan was elected in 1980. Reagan served two terms and ushered in lower tax rates (from 70% to 50%) for all of his rich friends. Even lower tax rates were ushered in by the Republicans during Reagan's second term. With this legislation, many other modifications were made to the tax law, mostly bad ones.

Contributions to IRA and retirement accounts (401k) had new and more restrictive definitions. Interest expense was redefined into six categories further, restricting the deductibility. Because customers could no longer receive a tax benefit for the deduction of interest expense, they began to default on their loans. Savings and loans then had to repossess the real estate investment or mortgage at the same time. The source of income for the S&L was dried up with the limitation of new money and IRA funds also created by this new tax act of 1986.

I hired Oran Washburn during the spring of 1987. Oran was a senior citizen, about 75 years old. He was a cowboy and had a good heart. I needed someone to help me daily with the management of our office building. There were issues involving light bulbs, commodes, air conditioning, etc. Oran would be my eyes and ears, always protecting me in the eyes of the various tenants. He took a real burden off my back.

With Savings and Loans going out of business, the federal government established a government-controlled entity to acquire the repossessed assets of the failing banks and savings and loans. Thus, the Resolution Equity Trust Corporation (RETC) was created. The market for repossessed mortgages and real estate went crazy. Following this enactment, my practice really grew, and we were all extremely occupied staying abreast of the new laws.

We called our ranch at Caddo the PK Ranch (short for Possum Kingdom). We made many trips there. Some were better than others.

We got to know Quincy and Johnny Corbett, nearby ranchers. They owned and managed 10,000 acres of ranch land and produced handsome profits raising cattle. Quincy was contemplating retirement, and I introduced him to Joe Ziegler to design a defined benefit pension plan where Quincy could make substantial deposits over a relatively short period and accordingly provide for his retirement. Joe was a charter life underwriter and owned a pension development company in Fort Worth. He represented Aetna Life Insurance Company.

About a year later, Quincy called me one morning very early to tell me that something was wrong with Joe Ziegler and his investments. I called Joe and could not locate him. I called Tim Evans, my fraternity brother and assistant district attorney in Fort Worth. Joe Ziegler was in jail for fraud. Most of Quincy Corbett's money was never delivered to Aetna. Joe Ziegler had stolen Quincy's money along with many other surprised victims.

Since Joe Ziegler was acting as an agent of Aetna Life Insurance, they would ultimately be liable to make good all of Quincy's contributions to his defined benefit plan. This took numerous telephone calls and several letters over several months.

I felt so bad that this happened to my client and friend. He had relied on me and my advice. Ultimately, Quincy Corbett's money was restored, and he was happy. He called Susan and arranged with her to have me fitted for a new men's suit at Culwell, a great young men's clothing store near SMU.

In the Summer of 1985, the Dooley community theatre was auditioning for Harvey. The play is about an invisible six-foot-tall rabbit. I auditioned for the role of Elwood P. Dowd, the lunatic who could see the pooka, and got the part. The play was to run for a week in July and was held for another week because the play was a sell-out every night. I had a ball playing Elwood again (the prior time was in high school). Well, in high school, I was in that play as well as "Little Women," HMS Pinafore, "On the Journey from Trenton to Camden," or something like that. Well, "Harvey" was about a man named Elwood P. Dowd who imagined that his best friend was a big white rabbit—the size of a man. His sister, Veta, tried to have Elwood committed to a nut farm, only to find out that Veta had imagined seeing Harvey herself. The Play was staged here in Grapevine and ran for two weeks. It was even extended for one extra week to sell out audiences each night. I received the Dooley Award for the best actor of the year. It was a lot of fun!

Susan and I were inspired by the Sierra Club's summer work sessions, so we inquired and signed up for a two-week work session at Lost Mine Trail in Colorado. The work involved building and repairing trails at the Continental Divide in Colorado near Aspen, at 11,000 feet of altitude. We met at the trailhead along with about 20 other volunteers in August of 1986, as I recall. We hiked up the trail about 7 miles to the campsite. We took our tents, bedrolls, clothing, and personal items, including a portable shower, in our backpacks.

Food and water were to be provided by the Sierra Club, as well as cooking gear. A cook and two Sierra Club guides were also provided. We were to work on trails for three days, then have a day off, then three again, etc.

The trails and campground were at about 11,500 feet altitude. The work concentrated on all of the trails almost up to the top of the divide at about 12,000 feet. Yes, it was cool, if not cold, at night at that level, and taking a solar shower was definitely a challenge because there was not enough sun to heat up the water. Showers had to be taken no later than 4:30 if then because the temperature would drop dramatically thereafter, and it would be too cold to shower.

The melting snow off the mountain made a real mess of the trails. Many of them washed out with mud bog replacing them where hikers would walk any place to avoid the mud. We repaired these trails by bringing in rocks and supporting the trail with water bars leading across the trail to conduct the melting snow and water. There was lots of water! We also built two major bridges over more distinct and extensive lengths of mud bogs. Building a bridge required rather large rocks (like boulders), the successive smaller rocks to support an elevated trail that would be the final product of the building. We learned quickly that these support boulders and rocks were best found up above the trail since getting those rocks to the work site took substantially less effort to roll them downhill to the trail rather than trying to bring them up to the trail! That is what we call engineering genius! The work meant wet hiking boots and wet clothes because each rock had to be positioned correctly to support a three-foot-wide trail and strong enough to support hikers and their pack animals.

The guide was Doug from Salt Lake. He was a great leader. He also learned that Susan and I were probably the hardest workers he had. The food was fairly good, but generally, there was not enough of it after working so hard during the day. We only had one dessert during the entire trek, and Susan and I were starved for sweets such that we had a sweet overdose on the trip home.

Hikers continued to use the trail while we were repairing them. They walked anywhere around the mud bogs that they could, trying to avoid the water and mud. We called them "Mushroom Pickers." It really made Susan and me appreciate and avoid unnecessary deviations from any trail thereafter because of the terrible deviations caused to the trail. One of our more famous Mushroom Pickers was Ed Bradley of 60 Minutes!

The trip lasted nine days, and we felt quite fulfilled with our accomplishments—about a half mile to a mile of major repairs to the trail, including two elevated bridges that extended 50 feet and 3 feet wide that supported hikers and pack animals (horses and mules).

Susan and I signed up for a two-week Sierra Club work trip to Colorado in June. The Sierra Club offered these treks to members, and this one appealed to us. We were to repair mountain trails at Independence Pass, Colorado, which was between Aspen and Leadville at about 10,000 feet in altitude. The trail was/is called The Lost Man Trail. We backpacked our personal gear (bedroll, tent, clothing, shower, and personal items), and the Sierra Club had all of our food and cooking gear delivered to the work site by mule train. The campsite was about nine miles up the trail, and the working areas were further up the trail. The melting snow caused all kinds of mud bogs across the popular Independence Pass trail, and it was our job to repair the bogs. We created water bars across the trail and supported the trail with rocks, lots of rocks. Of more importance were the larger bogs that required us to build bridges across the running water. The bridges were made of rocks and sand; only large rocks started the process, and they had to be rolled to the site. Then, smaller rocks and even smaller rocks supported the bridge until it was built up high enough to support a sand base. The bridges had to be wide and strong enough to support pack animals (mules and horses). We built two of those bridges. Susan and I wonder whether they will stand today.

We worked three days and then were off for a day. We would go hiking and fishing on our day off. We also would clean our clothes and our bodies. We had a sun shower; yes, filled it with creek water, and hung it on a tree for the sun (hopefully) to heat the water. Then, using the water sparingly, we would take shower baths.

The food was ok and certainly not stellar. When they served Tofu, I balked and deferred to the jerky that I had brought in my backpack. Perhaps Jack and Noah will now understand why I hate tofu and did not appreciate it being offered to me as any kind of food! Desserts were nonexistent, and we craved sweets. On the way home, we ate Snickers, ice cream, and anything sweet we could find.

We were proud of our accomplishments. The two weeks there was time well spent.

Chapter 28
1988 Texas A & M

7/25/10

Tommy Golf was the Chairman of the board of the American Bank of Commerce and was involved in making several questionable loans, including to people who were borrowing money to finance the purchase of the bank's holding company—probably very close to being illegal. The loan listing that was reviewed by the loan committee never included any of these types. So, I asked the bank staff to prepare a separate list for me. When Golf objected to my actions, I changed the name of the listing to "Pittman's Smell List" for the next month and brought it to the loan committee meeting. Golf asked me to resign from the Board of Directors, and I gladly obliged. Within six months later, the bank was in financial trouble and merged with another bank. Tommy Golf was not rehired by the new bank.

Jay took an art course taught by Janie Sanders at Grapevine High. It was an elective, and he loved it! Janie Sanders told us several years later what a stellar student Jay was. He had a real knack for art and creative design. The course was truly down his alley. Probably, this helped his decision-making progress in his pursuit of architecture.

Jay did not want Susan to be his English teacher. Neither did Greer. Both boys felt that if their mom was their teacher, then they would be served English 24/7 at breakfast, dinner, and supper! This is not unlike the world globe, which was always on the breakfast table for further discussion! So, for his senior English teacher, he had Nancy Wilson. Now, that did not go well either. It seems that Nancy had a love affair with all Grapevine High football players, which Jay was not. Jay was the editor of the Mane.

The National School Board convention was held in San Francisco in April of that year. Susan and I flew out later than most of the other school board members, and when we arrived at the Fairmont Hotel, they did not have a room for us except for a suite of rooms above the main entrance to the hotel. It was a great suite with all the beautiful flags outside our many windows. It was so large we had to throw a party for all the school board members and their wives/husbands. Penny Bigbie, Jack Dortch, Jeannie Hrnatsky, Walt Milner, Joe Deupre, and Steve Humphrey were some of the school board members who served with me during the six years I was on the School Board. Don Bigbie (Penny's husband) took all the spouses on a Napa Valley wine tour while we attended school board professional education seminars. Boring!

Stream, GHS's school newspaper. When she ripped up the Mane Stream in her class and called it a rag...Jay begged to differ and told her so. She promptly retaliated with a D on his recent paper and suggested that his successful completion of her course was in serious doubt.

It was rather awkward for Susan since they were in the same department at the high school, and it was further awkward for me since I was still on the school board. He changed teachers in mid-semester.

His graduation was special as I was able to give him his diploma (school board privilege). Steve Jacoby was the goofball principal who could not pronounce "epitome," and every expression had the word "super" in it.

So, the graduates bought buckets of super Double Bubble Gum, and when they shook his hand in the graduating line, Mr. Jacoby got his share of "super" Double Bubble. At least it was better than condoms at a wedding! A huge pile of Double Bubble was by Jacoby's feet. He dropped them as soon as he got them.

The little boy I had called Big Boy all his life had grown up and was going to college! I had taken him to school every day for many years and, especially on the first day of school for most of his grade school experience. He was to live at 1201 Harvey, Apartment 57, College Station. He left home with his shoes untied—a trademark that he carried all his life. While he knew better, I think he left home that day with them untied just for me—not to harass me but in celebration of our lives together. His mother and I had a few tears that day!

His grades in high school had not been that stellar, as I am fairly certain he either barely made or barely missed the top ten percent of his class, but he scored well on the SAT exam, and accordingly, Texas A&M accepted him hands down! He really never gave Texas Tech the time of day, as he had his heart set on being an Aggie. I started researching scholarships and grants in order to determine how to finance his education. Susan purchased a book on how to finance college, including how to apply for scholarships. The only problem was that we were not minorities and not divorced, and both of us worked. This eliminated 99 percent of the scholarships. I did note an opportunity to apply for an interest-free loan at The United States Bank of Galveston. So, I called Judith Whelton there and asked for an application. The Abe and Annie Seibel Foundation was being administrated by Judy Whelton at the bank! The Seibel Foundation would provide $1,500 per semester loans to worthy college students who maintained a 3.0 or better grade point. At the end of each semester and after proving the grade qualification, a new loan of $1,500 would be provided. Loan repayment would not start until he graduated, and then it would be amortized over a 10-year period, interest-free! It was a good deal and the best deal we could find. Jay maintained a 3.0 average every semester while at Texas A&M and qualified each semester for fresh money! In fact, he continued drawing on the loan while at Rice for his postgraduate master's degree at a higher rate, I believe at $2,250 per semester. Susan and I paid off the loan after he graduated. We were so proud of his grades and accomplishments.

During the summer, Greer and Jay were at home painting my office building. They painted all of the exterior wood with oil-based paint. I think they got as much paint on themselves as they did on the building did on the building. But they really did a good job, and the paint job lasted a long time.

We went to A & M to see Big Boy in April of 1991. He was now a junior majoring in Environmental Design and doing quite well. He continued to excel in his grades, averaging above 3 points each semester, and Ann and Abe Siebel Foundation was equally proud as they continued to fund non-bearing loans to him each semester. He achieved above 3 points. He was taking an elective history course this semester. He always liked history, but this was, I think, a military history taught by a Colonel of the Army there at Texas A&M. The vast majority of the students were members of the Corps, with Jay being the exception. He got a B in the course and was most disappointed. He thought he earned an A. It was fairly obvious that the non-Corp member would earn a B in military history with the Colonel and all Corps students!

It was not long after he arrived that he changed his major to Environmental Design and began Architecture objectives. After the first semester, he qualified for the honors college and continued on the honors rolls at the University. A normal five-year program was completed in four years, with him also completing his portfolio of selected drawings for graduation presentations. He received acceptances and scholarship offers from the University of Urbana in Illinois, Columbia in New York, and Rice University in Houston. (It seems like there was one more, but my memory faded).

Jay left for Italy in August of 1990. He was majoring in Environmental Design, which was basically architecture. He had an opportunity to study architecture for a semester in Castiglione, Florentine, Italy, at an affiliate of Texas A & M. It was a great opportunity for him. He had a little trouble keeping a camera while he was in Rome, such that he was stolen while he was busy with his drawings. Susan and Gram visited Jay in Italy in October. I was able to talk with Jay over there every Sunday night. That was important. When he came home, his plane was to land at Houston Intercontinental Airport, and I almost had a wreck trying to get to him at his deplaning area. I did jump a curb and went the wrong way on a one-way street to get there. BUT BIG BOY WAS HOME, and I did not care. I think Susan was fit to be tied over my driving at the airport.

He chose Rice since it was the least expensive (full ride) and offered an $1800 stipend per semester on a two-year program because his little brother was to start at Texas Tech that fall, and the financial burden on Susan and me was considered. He did well at Rice. They even doubled his stipend in the second year.

Chapter 29
Scouts And Scouting

Baldy Mountain at Pilmont – Greer, Jerry, and Jay

I loved the Boy Scouts. It was a great place to develop friendships and learn values that otherwise would be difficult to build. I never attended the National Jamboree, while my friends, Tommy Leonard and Richard Green, enjoyed the trip to Valley Forge, Pennsylvania. But I did make the 50-mile hiking trek at Philmont in 1958. I had a wooden pack and carried my bedroll and gear in it. We alternated carrying a Dutch oven. There were about fifteen of us on this high adventure—Tommy Leonard, Richard Green, and Mike Guy, among others. We learned that if our clothes were dirty, rather than carry them home, we merely burned them in the fire, thereby making our packs lighter. "Remember Rayado, remember Beaubien and ice-cold coke, ice-cold coke" were many of our chants as we hiked all the trails. Recently, I read Waite Phillip's biography. He donated his ranch in Cimarron, New Mexico—a beautiful 18,000-acre mountainous paradise to the Boy Scouts of America. He made the donation in 1951, I think, and it makes me proud that I was able to attend and experience the place some seven years later.

Summer camp was always at Camp Tonkawa near Buffalo Gap, Texas. I never served as a staff member, but I learned how to swim well there, earning my swimming and lifesaving merit badges. Mike Guy was also a friend who went to camp with me. His brother, Jan Guy, was the first Eagle Scout I knew, and I thought he was really special in that he helped me earn several merit badges. I guess you could say that he was a mini-hero of mine, along with Mickey Mantle of the New York Yankees.

I earned my God and Country award in 1957 with my pastor, Marshal Rhew, at the Methodist Church in Sweetwater. Richard Earl Green and I were in Boy Scouts together. We went to Philmont and were awarded the Eagle Award together in the fall of 1959. This ranking is something I have cherished all my life and something that has had meaning to me in almost everything I have done. I had to memorize the Beatitudes, the Ten Commandments, and a couple of verses in Psalms. A scout is trustworthy and loyal...

It was even a bigger thrill for me as an adult to assist and share the joy with Jay and Greer, our two sons, for them to attain the rank of Eagle Scout as well. In 2020, my twin grandsons, Noah Waits Pittman and John Caulder Pittman, attained the Eagle rank in Houston, where they live.

Boy Scout Troop 700, under the leadership of Earl Stuart, was primed to go to Philmont Scout Ranch in the summer of 1984. We had prepared earlier with a backpacking trip to Pecos Wilderness, and the boys were ready. I volunteered to take them. Dennis Jordan, Kirk Howard, Mark Ganus, Jay Pittman, and Rusty Morrison were among the guys going. James Morrison was going to be my assistant scout leader. We prepared for the trip. Philmont provided guides on what to bring and what not to bring. Plastic baggies were needed to store almost everything, as rain was a sure thing on the trail. Our trip was agreed to by Philmont. It was going to be a sixty-mile hike in the southern part of Philmont, Scout Haven, if not a heaven, for boys to experience. Waite Phillips gave his ranch to the Boy Scouts of America in 1951. It was comprised of 18,000 acres and was located at Cimarron, New Mexico. It had six base stations throughout the ranch where food, gear, and program were provided. I attended Philmont when I was a boy in 1959. The mountains of New Mexico offered cool air, campfires, singing, fishing, and all kinds of programs, like rock climbing, skeet shooting, root beer bars, and freeze-dried food.

During the summer of 1986, Gary Fickes and I decided to take the Boy Scout Troop to the Arkansas River—a scout ranch that offered swimming and other high ventures. We loaded about 30 Scouts (Greer and his other Scout members) onto the First Methodist church bus, and off we went to Arkansas. Merit badge production was the number one objective of most of the Scouts attending. The river was pretty, but the place was HOT. It was hot at night, hot during the day, hot all of the time. I took a shower about every time I went by the boys' shower.

Our trip home was truly eventful. Gary took his pickup, and on the first leg, he and I were driving it when the bus called on the CB, stating that the bus had stopped due to engine problems. We went back to learn that the truck had thrown three rods through the side of the engine. That bus was going nowhere! Gary and I drove down the road to the nearest town—Ozone, Arkansas. We found Mary at the general store at Ozone and told her that we had 30 or so boys on the side of the road a few miles back with a broken-down bus. Mary was truly a take-charge woman who took charge! She immediately went out to the road and started shouting at her neighbors (Ozone was a very small community). "Fred, Tom, Bill, get your pickup trucks and go up the road and pick those stranded boys up off of the highway!" They did. Mary then called the superintendent of schools at the nearest school district, asking (sounded more like she was telling him) to send a bus and bus driver to Ozone to take these boys back to Grapevine.

Mary was having a flea market next to her store, so the boys were fully occupied when they arrived. About thirty minutes later, the school bus arrived, and we were underway back to Grapevine. The school district had our bus towed to the Chevrolet dealership. The dealership was owned by a Methodist. They put a new motor on the bus. We stopped for burgers at McDonald's and were home about one hour later than we had originally thought.

We had found an angel. Her name was Mary. She did not know us, but she took charge, knowing that all of the mothers and daddies involved would do the same for her.

Jay turned 13 that year—our new teenager! In June, we went to the Pecos Wilderness in New Mexico and backpacked for 25 miles. Earl Stuart, our scoutmaster, Jim Morrison, and I were the other adults, while the Boy Scouts included Rusty and James Morrison, Dennis Jordan, Jay, Kurt Howard, and others, all of whom were preparing for our Philmont High Adventure trip later.

Jay's eagle project was very eventful—he assembled about twelve of his fellow scouts, and they painted the bollards at Heritage Park. Some of the scouts got more paint on themselves than they did on the bollards. Toward the end of the project, the summer wind gusted, and some dust blew around the park. At the same time, an airplane was landing at DFW airport, and the same wind gust caused a wind shear, causing the plane to crash just past HWY 114 on its final approach to the runway, except the pilot did not make it. It was a real tragedy. However, the Eagle Project was completed, and Jay was in line to get the highest award in scouting.

Jay received the highest award in scouting in 1986—an eagle scout. I was especially proud since I earned the award in 1958. Susan's father, Dub Waits, was also an eagle scout, and he was equally proud.

Our Scout troop was to have a week of scouting in Colorado. I was to conduct the High Adventure portion of this week because I had previous experience with backpacking at Philmont. Because Harvey was held over, I had to fly up to Colorado to join the group a day later. George Richey and Gary Fickes picked me up at the Colorado Springs Airport. The next day started the High Adventure backpacking fun.

Greer was a sophomore at Grapevine High School, while Jay was a sophomore at Texas A & M. Having earned about 21 merit badges and completed his Eagle project (recycle), Greer successfully completed his board of review. His Eagle Court of Honor followed shortly after that. Susan and I were proud of our son. Greer and I went to PK Ranch as often as we could.

Hunting season included dove in September, turkey and deer from November to January, and fish, frogs, and rabbits year-round. There were all kinds of things we needed to do together. We shot frogs in the head with a .22 caliber rifle. After a while, the dead frog would float to the surface of the water, and we would harvest our hunt for frog legs at supper!

Greer turned 16 on his birthday, May 13. He got his driver's license, so when he got home from school, we went down to the Grapevine Police Department. I wanted to introduce him to the chief of police and every cop there. I wanted them to know that another 16-year-old was on the streets, and his name was Greer. Further that they had my full blessing and permission to book him for any offense that may remotely apply to him while driving on the streets of Grapevine! Greer was not impressed.

It was 1989, and recycling was coming of age. Recycling newspapers, magazines, plastic, glass, aluminum cans, and tin cans was becoming more important across the country. We met Coleen Butterfield in Grapevine, who had already stirred up substantial interest in Grapevine. Greer got involved and decided that this would be a great Eagle Scout project. With Ms. Butterfield's help, they met with the city, found a location to gather the recycling material, and planned the opening weekend. He organized his scout troop, planned the publicity, and organized the eventful first day. Many people came with their recycling material, and the scouts assisted in the drive-through collecting and sorting the material. Every week thereafter, for some time, Greer and some scouts were involved on Saturdays, assisting in collecting and sorting the recycled materials. It was Grapevine's beginning that later evolved into curbside collection throughout the city. It was a very successful Eagle Scout project! I was so proud of my son.

One of three trips to Philmont Scout Ranch

Troop 700 sold yard fertilizer as a fundraiser, and Greer was a great salesman. We delivered the fertilizer on the weekends. The troop was raising money for the planned trip to Philmont Scout Ranch in Cimarron, New Mexico, and Camp Wehnapae, also in New Mexico, all in the summer of 1988. Greer was inducted into the Order of the Arrow, and we began preparing for the 70-mile trek at Philmont.

It was 1988 and my third trek to Philmont Scout Ranch. I was the scout leader for Philmont. Since Jay had turned 19, he would be my assistant scout leader. I was to take the older scouts with me for a longer trek, while Phil Perry was to take the younger scouts on a shorter trek. Greer was the youngest scout that I had, but I would not have it any other way. Chris Fickes was to be my Senior Patrol Leader. Dennis Jordan, Kirk Howard, Chris Ganus, Rob Ganus, and Greer. Greer Pittman's backpack was a little heavy for a 14-year-old, but he was not to be told anything of the sort. He also had been given a tetanus shot at base camp that made him sick for a few days. Plus, his father was the adult leader, and his brother was the other adult leader. In other words, I was stupid dumb, and Jay did not count! Thank goodness Greer got better, the fever went away, and he started fraternizing with his fellow scouts. It helped matters a lot when Greer won, hands down, the skeet shooting contest over all others!

Rob Ganus was also 14 or maybe 15 when he decided to hike ahead of the other scouts out of sight and possibly a mile ahead of me and the rest of the scouts. He had been a counselor at Camp Tonkawa, near Abilene, for a few weeks before Philmont and washomesick with a log or chip on his shoulder! Chris Ganus, his brother, volunteered to run ahead and find Rob.

When we finally found our wayward scout, he was emotionally upset. He informed me that he did not like Philmont, his fellow scouts, me, or anyone else. He said he wanted to go home. I told Rob that I did like him as well, that he should not have left me and the other guys under any circumstances, that this stunt scared me and, that I found his actions totally unacceptable, that he was setting a bad example for the others! I told him that we were to reach Beaubien, an outlying base camp, the next night and that I would arrange to have one of the Suburbans that carries supplies to take him home with the understanding that his parents come and take him home. I told him also that I would try to reach Philmont's base to arrange a helicopter to expedite his trip home.

He cleared up his attitude and was a real prince for the remainder of the trek. He finished our 70 miles with flying colors!

Greer was a ranger at Philmont Scout Ranch for the summers of 1995 and 1996. We visited him one of the summers. He was going to teach wilderness training at Philmont that summer to the recruits at the Air Force Academy! We left him and Philmont and toured the Trans Pecos area on the way. We went on to the West Coast to visit Jerry Waits and the oyster farm on the Yakina River in Oregon. Jerry lived with Roy on the oyster farm. The oysters were great, and Roy and Jerry were good hosts.

We purchased season football tickets at Tech, which gave us more opportunities to see Greer and support our college. Texas Tech had just joined the Big 12 football league, and watching the Red Raiders was always more fun for us than perennially listening to them on the radio.

Chapter 30
Grenna And Eddie

8/14/2010

Delaware Punch was the drink of the day when we went to Sweetwater to visit Mother and Eddie. The boys called her Grenna and Eddie by his name. Mother was a great cook and applied her skills dutifully when we went to visit. Barbeque brisket, potato salad, creamed buttered quash, and peach cobbler were some of her delicacies, and certainly, we learned to love them dearly as well.

Pittman Floor Covering Inc. in Sweetwater was not doing well as the drought produced poor cotton crops, and business was generally bad. Mother and Eddie decided to close out the store and liquidate the inventory. The store had operated since the end of World War II by my father and his brother Floy Pittman. When my dad died in 1962, my mother continued the business, and when she married Eddie in 1970, Eddie bought into the store by adding a new injection of cash and inventory. For almost twenty years, they were successful until the drought in West Texas got the best of them. So, retirement was in order for both of them. Of course, Eddie had his cows and made some money buying, feeding, and selling cattle. They owned 500 acres north of town. The place had two tanks that were great for dove and quail hunting, and there were some occasional fishing opportunities. Eddie built a couple of barns and a workroom out there as well. Mother had bought a travel trailer and needed a barn to store it. Mother and Eddie took one trip in their trailer. They went to California to look up Eddie's son, Eddie Junior. They found him, and he later came to Sweetwater to look for work. He had alcohol and drug problems and wanted money from his Mother and Eddie to support his habits. He did not stay long in Sweetwater, and I never met him—my step-half-brother.

Eddie had married mother in 1970, the year Jay was born, and he was truly the only grandfather the boys ever knew, at least from my family. Since the store (Pittman, Floor Covering and Furniture Store) had ceased operations in 1985, Eddie had plenty of time on his hands. He owned about 500 acres north of Sweetwater, where he raised cattle. Susie, Ida, Marylou, and Ralphie were some of the names he gave to the cattle. He had cattle shoots and stalls to vaccinate them. He was a master welder and could make almost anything. I always had something to help him with regarding the cattle. We vaccinated them, penned the ornery ones, and put some in the trailer to haul to the vet or market. It was this experience that made me never want a cattle operation. They were a lot of trouble, and the market for beef was extremely volatile, with the price fluctuating up and down with demand and other market conditions.

He was convinced that Coronado, the Spanish explorer, had buried gold on his 500 acres. He even had some sort of map of the property that described the general location of the gold. So, he began to dig all over his land. He hired backhoes and bulldozers to move dirt in search of Coronado's gold. Not having a whole lot of money, he pledged a portion of the gold to many people in exchange for their efforts, labor, and equipment to search for the gold. We all never believed Coronado left any gold anywhere in Texas, but we all held back because we believed that if Eddie thought there was gold there, then that was good enough for us.

He never found gold but discovered a great source of water. It was like an artesian well that flowed and filled up a large area that became a pond for fish and a great source for dove hunting in September. We spent many good times there fishing for catfish and getting our limits in dove. The area oil companies learned of his great source of water and purchased the water from him in order to service their area wells. The pond never depleted and remained at a constant level even though the surrounding area was affected by drought. The oil trucks were pumping thousands of gallons out of it daily. We all agreed (all except Eddie) that the water was really the GOLD, and it was being proven by the dollars they made by selling it.

Eddie told Jay and Greer stories, and mostly the same stories each time we visited. They included his Navy experience, his growing up, his football fun, and cattle raising. He was full of life and joked and laughed at almost everything. When Jay or Greer, who were very adventuresome, would do anything with peril, Eddie would warn them that they were going to "break an egg." Eddie played football for Texas A&M during the late '30s. He was the quarterback at Sweetwater High School during his high school days. A bad knee kept him from true stardom at Texas A&M, according to his account.

Greer was only about three years old when he had his first jalapeno pepper. We were in Sweetwater, and Greer came in the house screaming his lungs out. Susan, Mother, and I could not figure out what had happened. We thought could it be a spider bite, snake bite, or a severe fall? He could not communicate very well at that age, but he could cry with a loud bellow! I went into the backyard and found a jalapeno pepper with two tiny teeth marks on it. I knew then that Greer had experienced his first!

One Labor Day, we met Mother and Eddie in Ruidoso, New Mexico. Carolyn and Chuck Selinger joined us there. We must have left Jay and Greer with Jane and Dub. It was the American Futurity Classic at Ruidoso Downs (horse racing), and Mother had arranged with Nita Brooks (a rancher friend) to get us into the jockey club. Eddie had mixed up a gallon of Bloody Mary's with adequate vodka that we mostly drank in their Cadillac on the way to the horse race. There were ten races, and we all had to place bets on each race after studying the racing forms, jockey history, and odds maker predictions. We won some and lost some, not losing too much money but having fun yelling for this horse or another.

Susan was wild about betting on a horse owned by someone from Colleyville, so she did. She won a place ticket when she invested $2.00 and got back $6.00, as I recall. We could not find Eddie at the end of the races. He had disappeared. We thought he might be in the parking lot where we had left Mother's Cadillac. Sure enough! He was there and had consumed the remaining gallon of Bloody Mary drinks. Needless to say, Eddie was extremely happy, if not completely drunk. We put him to bed when we got back to the trailers.

I had agonized with Susan that I did not have an organ in our home in Grapevine, and I wanted one. I asked Mother if I could have hers; it was a B-1 Hammond, but she refused, saying that she still played it. A story that I suspected was untrue. Later, I offered to purchase the organ. I offered her $1,400.00 for it, which was the price she paid originally. She refused once again. So, I found a Hammond C-1 in Keller for sale for $2,300.00, complete with a Wurlitzer amplifier. I just wanted to play the mounds of music that I had acquired over the years from Professor Summerlin and from music stores. It was a great outlet for me to relax and play. Christmas was always fun when we gathered and sang Christmas carols together. I told Mother, and she was pleased.

Eddie had worked with machinery during most of his productive years in Los Angeles. Welding, woodworking, lathe, and drill presses were just some of the tools for which Eddie was most proficient. He built him a workshop out at the farm to house these tools he had collected over the years. The workshop was also a good outlet to give him personal time away from Grenna. She had a phone installed out at the shop so she could keep tabs on him, tell him that dinner or supper was ready, etc.

When he located a Profiler machine in the heart of Los Angeles that he wanted to buy, he planned on taking his Chevy S-10 with a cattle flatbed trailer out there to pick it up, but Grenna was not sure he should go out there alone. So, I agreed to go with him. It might be fun to see Los Angeles and the surrounding area, plus it was a good time for bonding with Eddie.

He picked me up at the Midland airport, and off we went towing that cattle flatbed. We alternated drivers periodically and spent the night in Phoenix going out and Tucson coming back, driving 12 hours daily. Eddie needed to do some negotiating during the day, so he let me out at the Universal Studios for a tour where simulated scenery was used in various movies and television shows. I saw Colombo's broken-down Studebaker and simulated rivers and waterfalls. I saw the television sets used for the shows Bonanza and Gun Smoke. I was impressed.

Page 178

On the outskirts of Phoenix, we had a blowout on the trailer while I was driving. Rubber from the tamed tire was thrown all over the Interstate before we stopped to investigate. We limped into Phoenix and, purchased a new tire, and straightened the wheel. When we stopped for the blowout, we discovered that the trailer axle was bent slightly. Apparently, the Profiler was heavier than the capacity of the flatbed trailer. Eddie insisted that we should proceed, and that is what we did. We made it back to Sweetwater, bent axle and all, and unloaded the Profiler for his workshop. He let me out at the Midland airport, and I flew home. It was a good time to spend with Eddie as I learned a lot about his values and ideas. He was dedicated to my mother, as he loved her and was always faithful.

The Profiler could trace and reproduce metal art and other objects. Locking in the picture or wood model of, say, an Indian head and the Profiler could copy it onto hard or sheet metal. Eddie made wind vanes, door stops, mud scrapers, windmills, and plant hangers, to name a few. He loved working with his Profiler and various tools out at the shop.

In their retirement years, each of them had a lazy boy recliner aimed at the television set. They were in their early 70s and were slowing down. Eddie spent most of his day out at the shop, while Mother was involved with at least two bridge clubs that met weekly. The Texas Rangers and the Houston Astros were popular with them such that when we did visit, we were not to interrupt their "games." But Jay and Greer could! Mother worshipped her grandchildren, Tanner, Suzanne, Eric, Richard, Jay, and Greer. She always had something for them to play with, tinker with, or read. She arranged for everyone to go swimming at the country club, and Eddie always had a field trip to the farm to hunt doves and quail or to take pictures of his prize cows. He was experimenting with a special breed of cattle called the Murray Gray, an especially high-back, broad shoulder cow with apple cheeks for a rear end. It was fascinating that he was involved in developing this breed, including artificial insemination and all that was involved with that. Jay was totally consumed when Mother got an old shoe box out, and together, they carved doors and windows with an exacto knife and otherwise made a house out of it. During the winter and fall months, we harvested pecans from one of the two quite large pecan trees in her yard. We also made snowmen during the many snows afforded West Texas.

While I was on the Los Angeles trip with Eddie, I purchased a beautiful cherry wood cane for Mother. She was getting up there in age and increasingly getting a bit feeble, and I thought this might be helpful in her ability to be mobile. I left it in the truck and in Eddie's trusty hands to deliver the cane, which he did. About two weeks later, I got a scathing letter from Mother that she did not approve of the gift. She was not an invalid; she was quite mobile, and she was insulted that I would have been so presumptive to give her such an awful gift! She said she planned on burning the cane in the fireplace! I was crushed. To hurt her really hurt me, and apparently, I did.

Eddie developed prostate cancer. He had some surgery to remove it, and radiation followed. Increasingly, he was having much difficulty in getting around. His groin and legs were weakened by the radiation that he received at Hendricks Hospital in Abilene. He sold all of his cattle and stayed mostly at home every day with Mother. He was hospitalized several times at Hendricks Memorial Hospital and later moved to the hospital in Sweetwater.

I stayed in Sweetwater and traveled back and forth to Abilene to look after Eddie. Mother was not able to drive to Abilene, but she was worried about him. His daughter or son could not be located. They probably would not come to assist, either. One morning in Sweetwater, Mother insisted that I eat a bowl of cereal before I left for Abilene. So, I did. Then, on the way out of the door, she inquired what cereal I had eaten. I told her that it was the last of the Granola Crunch. She immediately got upset and informed me that it was her favorite cereal, that she could not believe that I had consumed the last of her favorite cereal and that she was very upset. Of course, she had given me no instruction regarding what cereal I should consume. So, I apologized and left. I went straight to Village Supermarket, purchased ten boxes of Granola Crunch, and took them to the house to give to her. She wanted to know why I did that and wanted to pay me for them. I went to Abilene.

I made many trips to Sweetwater to help where needed. When he was in the hospital in Abilene, I visited him several times. He was having difficulty walking, saying that the doctors burned him with the radiation. When he was transferred back to Sweetwater, we all decided to move him into a rest home. He lasted two months there before he died. When he lost his ability to walk, drive his truck, and be otherwise a man, he lost his desire to live. I took him milkshakes and sirloin steaks, but he did not want to eat them. He wanted to die since he was no longer a productive man.

In January 1992, he died. We had a Masonic funeral for him, and he was buried in the Garden of Memories Cemetery east of town. There was no church service, only gravesite rites. It was a cold winter day, and we drove Mother to the Cemetery and insisted that she stay in the car with the door open so she could hear the preacher and Masons. The two old Masons had blue jeans and light sports jackets and shivered with their Masonic recitals. Mother had lost her second husband, and she was not in the best shape either. Her emphysema crippled her lung capacity, and she was using a walker to maneuver around the house. I knew she could have used her cane now, but I was not about to raise that subject again!

Mother gave me the safety deposit box key with strict instructions to look for the honorable discharge papers that Eddie received when he finished his Navy tour. Such papers would qualify Eddie for a veteran's allowance for burial, together with a US flag to drape across his casket. When I returned from the bank with the papers, I was drilled with twenty questions from Mother. What else did I see or get out of her safety deposit box? Did I get any of her gold coins? Where is the key? I expected this question; it was her style.

Sharon, Eddie's daughter, came for the Chevy S-10 pickup and several of Eddie's keepsakes. She asked for money from Mother but went back to California without it. If she had come to see Eddie while he was living or at least made his funeral, Mother would have been more sympathetic.

Chapter 31
1989 GCISD Board

/20/2010

My tenure on the Grapevine Colleyville School board lasted six years or two terms. I never had an opponent during the two times I ran for election. I might have been a formidable candidate, or perhaps no one else wanted the job. I suspect the latter. It truly was a thankless job calling for monthly meetings and a multitude of committee assignments. The job did not enhance my practice of accounting. There was no compensation either, only a good meal prepared by the school cooks before every meeting. We also went to the annual school board conventions at various places. Some of that was fun. Most of the complaints were of a nonacademic nature. I received many telephone calls dealing with the football team, band uniforms, gaudy earrings worn by the cheerleaders, and bus routes.

We were at a middle school football game one afternoon when I overheard a dissatisfied Colleyville resident complain about the cheerleaders. I initially paid no attention until he came up and asked the direct question, realizing I was a school board member: Why are there more Grapevine cheerleaders out there than Colleyville cheerleaders? I replied that I did not know that this was not an issue of the GCISD board. He continued to complain and was all but in my face with the issue that there were six cheerleaders from Grapevine and only two from Colleyville. He was getting to become a pest, so I replied that perhaps the Grapevine cheerleaders were better looking in Grapevine than in Colleyville!

One particular convention we attended was in San Francisco, California, where we were to stay in the luxurious Fairmont Hotel. I paid for Susan to accompany me, but we had to leave a day later than the other board members, so we arrived late on a Friday night to learn that the Fairmont did not have a room for us. They were accommodating and put us up in a swanky two-bedroom suite overlooking the multi-flagged entry of the Fairmont. We promptly had a party for all of our fellow school board members (Penny Bigbie, Jack Dortch, Jeannie Hartsaky, Walt Milner, Joe Deupree, and Steve Humphry, and their spouses. The next day, Susan took a wine tour of Napa Valley with Don Bigbie and all of their spouses, and I attended all of the convention's boring meetings. I just about walked Jack Dortch's legs off on a walk that weekend. His cowboy boots were not so accommodating to those San Francisco hills!

Greer was a sophomore at Grapevine High School. He loved sports and was especially good at football, playing tight end. Susan and I had season tickets at the same place at Mustang Stadium for over twenty years. We enjoyed watching Greer play, and I got frustrated with the coaches for not throwing the ball to Greer more often. Instead, the quarterback would throw passes to the wide receiver Chris Williams, who could not catch. I kept saying, "Chris can't catch, throw it to Greer," to no avail. Chris got a football scholarship to Rice—for always mysterious reasons. I knew that Chris's father was very involved in the recruiting politics.

Another event at Mustang Stadium happened around 1975, and I almost forgot about it. Susan and I were new at the season ticket business and went religiously to the Grapevine High School football games. While sitting in our seats for one of the first games we saw, we kept hearing from a couple that was sitting a few rows behind us. The chant was "Give it to Timmy", "Give it to Timmy". Obviously, it was another frustrated father who wanted the quarterback to give the ball to his son, Timmy. Later, I inquired about who these people were and who Timmy was. The couple was Dr. Ed and Minnie Lee Lancaster—medical doctors and respected pioneers in Grapevine. Timmy was their son Tim Lancaster, whose number on his jersey was 75, and he played offensive tackle! It was not totally out of the realm of possibility but fairly preposterous that the quarterback would/should give the ball to an offensive Tackle, but after I got to know what a space cadet Dr. Lancaster was, I realized that he really did not know the difference.

Dr. Ed, as well as his son Tim in Grapevine, was bald-headed and wore a toupee—many times backward, not necessarily on purpose, but because he just did not know. Once, word got out about his diagnosis of a local woman with soreness in her stomach as being a tumor. She later went to another doctor to find out she was pregnant! He drove his convertible Cadillac on Northwest Highway in Grapevine during an ice/snow storm doing "wheelies."

We (the school board) had decided to build a new elementary school in south /west Grapevine. I suggested that we name the school after the Yellow Rose of Texas, Emily Morgan. In fact, I made the motion before the GCISD school board. Emily Morgan was a woman who was one of Santa Anna's mistresses. Santa Anna and his Mexican army had in 1836 defeated the Texans at the Alamo (killing 186), then about a month later, also defeated the Texans in the battle of Goliad (killing 400). Emily Morgan became the yellow rose of Texas when she, disgusted with Santa Anna's tactics, joined General Sam Houston and divulged the locations of the Mexican troops. Houston defeated Santa Anna and took him prisoner at the Battle of Jacinto. My motion to name the elementary school The Emily Morgan failed for the lack of a second. Emily Morgan was a true hero in Texas history, but no one wanted to name the school after a mulatta prostitute!

My nephew, Eric Selinger, got married in June, right before we left to join the Navy Seabees. Eric was almost always in trouble with the law while growing up, and it was my understanding that upon graduation from High School, a judge gave him two choices: join the armed forces or go to jail. So, Eric joined the Navy Seabees. After the wedding, Susan and I drove to Albuquerque, New Mexico, drank beer in a saloon in Madres, New Mexico, and generally took a few days off. I took Shane Wilbanks to Rotary on October 11, 1989. Shane and I had a lot in common. He and Paula, his wife, had great children that matched ages generally with our children. Paula worked at Grapevine High School with Susan. I introduced Shane as a prospective member of the Rotary. Shane was a very good Rotarian, as he held every office in the Rotary, including the Presidency. Shane is still a great friend.

Christmas 1989 was special. Actually, all Christmases were special for many reasons. Mostly because we were all healthy and happy. We flew to Jackson Hole, Wyoming, to ski. We had been there sometime back, tent camping on our return from Jerry Waits home, and we all wanted to go back. We did not want Gram to spend Christmas alone, especially since Dub had died the previous Christmas. Probably the most spectacular part of the trip was the dynamic landing American Airlines performed by flying down in the Jackson Hole valley. The plane just dropped as soon as the mountains cleared the valley. Greer had the flu and was sick the entire time. That was another reason we were glad to have Gram with us, as she stayed in the room while we went skiing. The ski slopes of the Grand Teton Mountains were great, but nothing stood out. Jay skied mostly with us since Greer was sick. We were not bad skiers, and all of us had a lot of experience—Utah, Colorado, New Mexico, and not Wyoming.

Chapter 32
The Waits

8/12/10

I never met Daddy Mike or Mr. Sanders, Susan's grandfather, as he died long before Susan and I met and married. I did get to know his wife, Nanny Sanders, whom Susan called Granada. Mr. and Mrs. Sanders were the parents of Jane Elizabeth, Susan's mother, as well as Susan Riddell, her aunt.

Granada told me that she tried to teach Susan how to play the piano early in life but failed because Susan was not interested. Granada was small and very opinionated, especially in her narrowed view of life and things in general. I tried to keep my distance from her when she began a tirade regarding whether we should allow our sons to taste beer. There were other discussions involving politics for which we also disagreed. She was a yellow dog Democrat, and I was a Republican at that time. She would not listen to any reason. She was very much a principled woman, so I still respected her rights and her overall well-being.

Susan's paternal grandparents were Rufus and Leila Waits. They also lived in Sulphur Springs same as Granada. Rufus died early in our marriage, while Mrs. Waits lived several years thereafter. Grandmother was what Susan and Linda called her, and she lived in her home, and we visited her periodically. She was a good cook and always had a great spread of food for us when we came. She had much pride in the fruit cake that she made every Christmas, and since I did enjoy a good fruit cake, I made the mistake of bragging about hers. That is when she went into a long discussion of how she made it and further how proud she liked hers. By the time she finished discussing the intricacies of her fruit cake in her living room, Susan and Linda were nowhere to be found!

William Thomas Waits (Dub), Susan's father, had two brothers, Buddy and Jerry. Buddy Waits lived mostly in New Orleans with his significant other, another male, and then later in Como, Texas, with his aunt. Buddy had been married and divorced. He had two children that I really never met or knew much about. Jerry Waits lived in Newport, Oregon, with his significant other, Roy.

We visited Buddy in New Orleans on one of our vacations. They were involved in restoring an old home in New Orleans. We stayed with them one night and admired their truly artistic and creative abilities in restoring this old two-story home.

We also went to Oregon on a vacation to visit Jerry. He was the accountant of an oyster farm on the Yaquina River not far from Portland. Roy was the manager of the oyster farm, which was owned by a restaurant in Portland. We drank beer, ate well, and consumed my share of oysters while we visited Jerry. The oyster farm was fascinating, to say the least. Numerous large screened containers (say 5-foot square) floated in the river where the oysters grew and developed. Inside these containers were numerous broken and spent empty oyster shells. Embryonic oyster eggs were put into the container, and they would attach to the old spent shells. The containers were then labeled and moored out in the river. At any time, there would be as many as 100 of those containers floating out in the river.

The Yaquina River fed into the Pacific Ocean, only a few miles from the oyster farm. Oysters are best developed and grown in fresh water, a fact that I learned on this trip. Each container had been labeled with inception dates. They were then divided into categories: oysters, cocktail oysters, canning oysters, and soup (rather large) oysters, depending on the age of each container. Depending on the demand of the restaurant, these oysters would be harvested in their shells and sent for consumption.

Susan, Jay, and Greer had no desire to eat an oyster, BUT I DID! Jerry set up a chair, made some oyster cocktail sauce, provided a tool to crack them, and turned me loose to spend an hour or so at the waterfront eating oysters. They were great!

Dub (he was also called Dumpy Dub) was an FAA controller at Love Field when Susan and I married. Jane (Susan called her Dainty Jane) was an elementary school teacher at Bradfield Elementary and then McCullough in Highland Park, Dallas. They lived at 4114 San Carlos in the University Park area.

Linda Grace Waits, Susan's sister, went to Texas Tech as well. She pledged Pi Phi the year that Susan was Rush Captain of the sorority. Linda was a freshman when Susan was a senior at Tech. Linda had dropped her high school boyfriend, Mark True, and begun dating Kenny King, a graduate of Bellaire High School in Houston. Kenny liked to party and joined the Phi Delta Theta fraternity at Tech. Susan and I did not have a lot in common with them because our interests were so diverse. Susan was teaching back when Susan and I met and ran around with Jay and Pat Stanley.

One summer, while Kenny and Linda were dating, he was employed by Brown and Root, an oil drilling company in Houston. He worked on the Brown and Root yacht. Executive boat trips with fishing, good eating, and drinking were stalwarts of the yacht trips, right down Kenny's thought patterns. Kenny sent Dainty Jane and Dumpy Dub some fish from the yacht. However, somehow, the shipping got mixed up, and bait fish was sent instead of red snapper or other delicacies. Dainty Jane was so pleased with Kenny's thoughtfulness. Unfamiliar with any fish that looked or smelled like this, she discreetly asked us how to cook it. I told her it was not a delicacy of the ocean; instead, it looked like bait fish and for toss it. She never said anything to Kenny, but Kenny found out that the wrong package had been sent! Needless to say, Kenny was a bit embarrassed!

Linda married Kenny King before they graduated from Tech. They both worked at the Brookshire Inn, a restaurant while in Lubbock.

Kenny was not your stellar scholar at Tech and managed to flunk out with bad grades during the year that Susan and I returned to Lubbock for me to work on my Master's degree. He had to wait a year before he could be readmitted. Linda and Kenny were both seniors, but this was a major setback in their careers, causing a delay in the completion of their undergraduate degrees. Linda would end up graduating a year or so before Kenny since he would have to lay out a semester before he could be admitted again at Tech.

I was a teaching assistant at Tech, teaching elementary accounting level I and level II, and since I was on the faculty, Kenny asked if I could do anything to get him back in school. Susan, Linda, and I collaborated with Dainty Jane, their mother, and concluded that I should discuss Kenny's dilemma with the Dean of Admissions, Dean Floyd Boze. Liz intimated that Dean Boze had attended and graduated from East Texas State University with her and Dub. Further, she knew and remembered him well. So, when we returned to Lubbock, Kenny and I went to see Dean Boze. We explained that Kenny was a good student and could turn things around. Further, he was working too much at the restaurant and would cut back on his work schedule to devote more time to his studies. We gave him all good reasons to readmit him, but the real reason was yet to come. We explained to Dean Boze that we were the sons-in-law of Jane Elizabeth Sanders Waits, who attended East Texas with him. Dean Boze paused and said her name two or three times---Elizabeth Sanders, Elizabeth Sanders... what a beautiful woman! He wanted to know all about her and reminisced thoroughly of his time at East Texas and repeated her name again. That was all we needed. He readmitted Kenny immediately!

Dub and Jane sold their home at 4114 San Carlos in 1985 or 1986. They had purchased this home in the heart of University Park for $12,500 with a 3 % mortgage rate in 1960. That was the year they moved from Sulpher Springs. Jane began teaching in the Highland Park School district, and Dub went to work for the FAA at Love Field.

They sold the house for $325,000—a very nice return on the investment! They had a great CPA (me) who figured out a way to buy another home and keep a bundle for themselves without paying any income taxes.

Periodically, Susan and I traveled to Sulphur Springs to visit relatives. Some of those included Grandmother Waits' sisters, Mary Evelyn and Grace. Mary Evelyn lived in Como, and Susan's Uncle Buddy lived with her for a while. Mary Evelyn was handicapped (Polio) in a wheelchair, but that did not deter her as she cooked and kept house. Her delicacies always pleased our two sons. Aunt Grace lived with her husband, Uncle Hob, in Mineola, Texas. Aunt Grace wore her lipstick twice, once on her lips and the other around her lips. She always chased me and the boys around her house, both inside and outside, to plant kisses on us. We (the boys, I, and even Susan) ran from her all of the time and dreaded our visits!

Jane retired from teaching after a career at it, which must have been around 1980 or so. She must have been a grand teacher because she was always receiving kudos, letters, and gifts from her former students. She spent much of her time thereafter pursuing her grandchildren's interests. Jay and Greer called her Gram, and Dub, they called Dede. It was fitting because they loved Jay and Greer as much as life itself. They read to them and were always buying them books, toys, and learning things. The Airstream camping trailer was employed regularly on some trip or another with Jay and Greer right in the middle of the venture. This was always a joy for Susan and me since it allowed us some independence periodically, and that was important.

Lake Elberta is a small 75-acre lake south of Sulphur Springs on Farm Road 2305. Lake Elberta had about 25 cabins around the lake and was originally a "hunting and fishing club." The Waits had a cabin out there originally (perhaps more than one). Grandmother Waits was accustomed to fishing and fishing a lot and mostly at Lake Elberta. Susan loved Elberta as a child as a source for swimming and creek exploring. Dub and Jane acquired the old cabin, and joint ventured it with Jane's sister, Susan and her husband Bill. The cabin was efficient, with one large room and a bath and kitchen attached. It had a large porch out front with twin beds—a great place for an afternoon nap. The cabin was heated by a wood stove and had no air conditioning. The walls were merely wood with no insulation, and the roof leaked a bit. It had two TVs, and neither one of them worked. The wood stove leaked smoke, and we all smelled smoky after staying there. Elberta was a source of much fun. It had a canoe, so we could use it on the lake. Elberta was also a midway stop during Christmas on our family's annual trek to cut down a live Christmas tree.

In 1999, I purchased Susan Riddell's one-half interests in the cabin. Jane gave us the other one half, and in the year 2000, we tore the old cabin down and built another, with our architect's son's help.

Dub was a pilot and pilot instructor. He really loved airplanes, especially the propeller type. He was never licensed to fly jets, and they were coming of age at Love Field, where he worked. He could talk forever about flying and the times he flew. He was a World War II US Air Force Flying Instructor at Bryan, Texas, where Susan was born. He flew his private single engine plane in and around Sulphur Springs. Susan recalls many fond memories of his flying adventures.

Dub retired from the FAA with a medical retirement. He had many emotional setbacks during his last days at the FAA, including a severe bout with alcohol. Susan and I concluded that the age of the Jet and the intricacies of automation (computers) got the best of him. The FAA kept Dub on medical leave until they decided that he should retire. It was like night and day for Dub immediately. He was relieved! Retirement was what he needed. He quit alcohol, and the old Dede was back! He purchased another Airstream travel trailer, and he and Jane began to travel again.

They took that Airstream and traveled with their retired buddies all over the United States. They spent many of their winters at Trailer Village near Brownsville. They loved to trailer down to Lake Whitney and Lake Texoma. Many times, they took Jay and Greer with them, and the boys loved the opportunity to go. One time when we joined them on a campout and pitched our tent beside the trailer when it started raining. Jay and Greer tried to sleep in the tent with us, but when they realized that water was flowing through the tent, they abandoned us in favor of joining Gram and Dede in the dry trailer.

Dub drove Jane everywhere. He allowed Jane to be a well-kept woman without expecting her to lift a finger in looking after the trailer. But Jane had her duties as well—two distinct roles for two great people. They both had their own idiosyncrasies as well. Susan and I purchased a new 1968 Oldsmobile Cutlass while we were visiting Dallas, which was not ready to be picked up at the time. So, Jane and Dub drove it down to Houston, where we lived. They arrived in Houston at 4:30 AM. Why we could never figure it out, except Dub was excited about it and left Dallas about midnight! Jane slept the entire trip. We got up that morning at our usual time to find Jane and Dub in our apartment's parking lot, sitting in our new car.

Sometime in November of 1988, Dub and Jane flew to Hawaii (I believe) for a vacation of sorts. My calendar told me to pick them up at the Pan American baggage area at DFW airport on November 30, 1988.

On December 12, 1988, Dub had a massive stroke at home and died. He was buried in Sulphur Springs with two services—one at Highland Park Methodist Church and one at First Methodist Church in Sulphur Springs. Jay was a freshman at Texas A&M, and Greer was a freshman at Grapevine High School when they lost their grandfather, whom they called Dede.

Susan's mother died in the Fall of 2006. Jane Elizabeth Sanders Waits was 86, I believe. She was truly an inspiration to anyone whom she met. I loved to tease her about the dirty top of her fridge or, how her husband Dub gave her a hard time about losing her purse, or how she hoped that the game would be interesting when Susan and both wanted Tech to win. Her burial was certainly interesting when Jack, our grandson, and her great-grandson wanted to know if the funeral van that carried her casket was "Big Grandma's truck?"

I called her Gram mostly because that was what Jay and Greer called her. She called me Kenny many times--Linda's husband. Gram got me, and Kenny confused. She would be so embarrassed when Susan corrected her. Linda and Susan called her Dainty, as in Dainty Jane. She had a fairly stubborn streak, and she, like her mother, Mrs. Sanders, whom we called Granada, was truly Yellow Dog Democrat when politics were involved. In 2002 she joined us to watch Greer and Caroline in Hawaii for a triathlon event. We were going through security at the airport before we left, and she got screened for taking her home security remote control, which was bigger than my shoe and residing in her purse. Susan and I were convinced that she would lose this remote, but she somehow convinced the security that she knew what she was doing and that she did not even remotely understand what their concern might be.

She loved me, and I know she did as she trusted me for any of her financial decisions and honored the manner in which we raised our sons. She was a great lady, and I am proud to have had a great mother-in-law.

After her death, Susan was able to spend more time with me at Fort Davis while we built our home, living as it were in that 25-foot trailer and listening while I called and kept our contractors and subcontractors in line.

Chapter 33
Garner, Aaron, Skiing and Pk Ranch

We went to Garner State Park in June. The Frio River there was a lot of fun enjoying the water and tubing a couple of miles. This was the second time we had gone to Garner. Garner had jute box music every night when all the campers would gather around a pavilion where everyone danced until ten o'clock. In August, we all went to Hot Springs Village in Arkansas, where we stayed in a free townhome if we agreed to a 90-minute presentation about purchasing a lot in Hot Springs Village. Well, I purchased a residential lot. By being a nonresident owner, you could play golf on any of their seven golf courses for next to nothing. I liked the idea, but Susan, Jay, and Greer were not sure of the wisdom!

We went to Ruidoso, New Mexico, to ski in December. Greer asked Chad Paris and Aaron Lineweaver to go skiing at Ski Apache with us. Chad took lessons while Aaron said he did not need lessons because he had been skiing before, although we never could determine what or where he developed such experience. He and Greer skied together, and Susan and I skied together. Chad was busy with his skiing lesson. Within the first hour of that first day, I was being paged by the paging system so that I could come to the emergency medical hut. Aaron had run into a tree and was out cold! Greer told me that Aaron was skiing out of control, just as we suspected; he had no experience.

Aaron was an all-star athlete. He was a pitcher on the Southlake Baseball team and already had pitched his first no-hitter. However, he did have somewhat of a deficiency in his cranium capacity; I think he was a resource student, representing his less-than-stellar academic ability. The emergency room doctor at the hospital declared that Aaron had experienced a mild concussion. Part of the testing was to ask Aaron multiple questions involving the math of 7's, i.e., 7 x 2 is, 7 x 6 is, and so forth. We seriously doubted that Aaron knew the math of 7's irrespective of the concussion! When we went skiing the next day, we left Aaron in the hospital for observation.

We had harvested our own Christmas tree every year since the boys were very young. We found them in East Texas, generally around Quitman, Texas. Greer had to make the decision each and every year as to which tree we were to harvest! It was HIS decision, as he made that abundantly clear to all of us. I always enjoyed going to the First National Bank of Grapevine's annual Christmas party. It was the only time you could go to the teller and get a beer. Normally, one would only deposit money or make payments there. One year, the bank invited Jay and Greer to be the doormen for the annual Christmas Party. Their mother and I were so proud to see our sons in tuxedos greeting Grapevine for the bank at Christmas.

PK RANCH

Gary Kirkland, my partner with the ranch near Caddo, Texas, was beginning to have financial difficulties and was unable to fulfill his share of the monthly mortgage payment. Gary was in the real estate business, and that industry was having trouble during 1990 and 1991.

I carried Gary's share for about a year until it became obvious in late 1991 that I, too, would be heading to financial pinches with both boys in college at the same time. So, we advertised the ranch for sale. I made several trips out to the ranch to show it and keep it mowed and otherwise clean. I killed a rather large rattlesnake near the back door one day and decided we needed a cat or two to ward off such creatures. The Caddo general store owners let it be known around the various ranches that we needed a cat or two for our ranch. Suddenly, we had cats roaming around the house. Various people came and left the cats, mostly kittens, to survive the rustics of our house and grounds. I purchased a big bag of cat food and left them a water trough outside the back door.

I was unable to sell the PK ranch. Very few people were even interested.

Raw land and ranches were not selling. So, I decided to default on the mortgage. Mr. Earnest Wright was the holder of our mortgage note and the original owner, or at least the owner from whom we purchased the ranch. Mr. Wright could look only to the land as collateral, as Gary Kirkland and I were never personally liable in the note. During our ownership, we generally cleaned up the house and the ranch. We installed central heat and air conditioning, washer and dryers, carpet and wallpaper, and satellite television. We cleaned and sowed the pastures and left three hunting blinds on the ranch. We also made a $40,000 down payment and made monthly payments religiously for four years. Accordingly, I was not going to give the ranch back without something in return.

I started my negotiations when Mr. Wright hired an attorney to start foreclosure. I wanted to keep the mineral rights on the ranch and told the attorney. I informed the attorney that these various improvements might or might not be possible if we could not keep the mineral rights. The attorney consulted with Mr. Wright, and they relented and let us keep the mineral rights. I still hold those mineral rights in my name if they ever drill for oil or gas on or near the ranch in Stephens County, Texas.

It was a great ranch—one that we all have fond memories of. We hunted, fished, learned how to drive a stick shift jeep, cooked, ate frog legs, got limits in the dove, and harvested quail. It was fun and a great experience.

Chapter 34
Lakeview

Ronald Reagan gave up his cowboy hat and spurs and got elected President of the United States in 1980. He replaced Jimmy Carter, who was far too liberal for me. Interest rates were around 18 to 20 percent, and our tax rate was 70% on income more than $200,000! Reagan ushered in a maximum tax rate of 50% and got inflation under control by lowering the Fed interest rates. When Reagan was reelected to a second term in 1984, he lowered the maximum tax rate further to 28%. Many other changes were made to the tax code, including the redefinition of interest expense. Prepaid interest was no longer allowed, and interest expense on investments could only be deducted if you had an equal amount of interest and dividend income. This modification caused the default of many real estate investments; the owners could not deduct their interest expense! Reagan also redefined rules for funding Individual Retirement Accounts and created new 401K plans. This step dried up a major source of income for banks and savings and loans.

When banks and savings and loans had to repossess real estate investments, and at the same time, sources of income dried up, they, too, started to go under. The middle and late 80s witnessed the default, closing, and mergers of hundreds of banks and savings and loans. First National Bank of Dallas and Republic National Bank both closed their doors. All mergers by savings and loan associations went away. The government created the Resolution Trust Company (RTC) to acquire the real estate repossessed by these defaulting banks and marshal them out to the highest bidder in an open marketplace.

Real estate lending was being redefined, and rules were changing dramatically with the intervention of the Federal government. The large mortgages were being reevaluated to assess adequate collateral. In the middle to late months of 1991, my mortgage on our office building was reevaluated. First National Bank called to inform me that the fair market value of my 15,000-square-foot building was upside down when they compared their newly revised fair market value analysis to the outstanding mortgage. Further, they wanted me to make an immediate $100,000 reduction in the mortgage to get it in line.

Wow, First, I did not have that kind of money. Second, I had never missed a monthly payment since 1980, when the mortgage was created. And third, the building was fully occupied by current paying lessees. I went to the bank to see the President (Harold Kaker). I showed him my rent roll, and I reminded him that we had made all payments on time since the inception of the mortgage. I told him I did not have the money, and further, if he and his gurus were sincere, they would have to repossess the building. I put the master key to the building on his desk. The bank did not want any more repossessed real estate and realized that they were barking up the wrong tree! They backed off, saying that they were wrong and that they had no intention of collecting a lump sum payment on the mortgage. I had called his bluff. I never heard from them again!

The real estate repossessions were happening everywhere, all over the Dallas-Fort Worth area. Every day, the newspapers covered issues of banks and savings and loans going under with the RTC taking possession of their mortgages and related secured real estate. Sun America was a savings and loan company that was going under, and they had a mortgage on another office building in Grapevine called Lakeview.

I inquired about the particulars and contacted Darlene Freed, a local real estate broker. She contacted Sun America about the office building. It was built about three years earlier by a developer who had defaulted, and Sun America was in the process of turning their mortgages over to the RTC because Sun was going under as well. The building had 40,000 square feet, and it was on 3 acres of land which included a lake that was on the west side of the building. Only the downstairs was occupied by an executive suite company. The RTC wanted two million for the building, which I thought was too much money.

So, Darlene and I started our negotiations to purchase the building. We offered one million dollars for the building and land; they countered with a higher number, and we offered an even lower number than their original offer. We played back and forth for about four months, offer then counter, offer then counter. But each time I made an offer, I lowered my next offer. My first offer back was nine hundred thousand, and then I changed it the next time to eight hundred fifty thousand. Then on the final round, I made an offer of eight hundred thousand. They apparently got the message and accepted the last offer. David and I had good experience in owning and managing office buildings with the 1000 Main Building, and David's wife had very impressive ranch properties in Nolan County that had producing oil and gas wells on them. Susan and I offered our good looks on paper, but we had the resolve to get this done. Apparently, the RTC recognized that we were bona fide buyers and allowed us to purchase the building.

We arranged financing at First National Bank in Grapevine. The loan-to-value ratio was great in that the building was appraised for almost three million dollars. The work, however, was just to begin. We had to get the building suitable for lease and then lease it as soon as possible.

Jay was finishing his studies at Texas A&M, and this was one of his first projects for a prospective architect. We mapped out the downstairs and realized that the air conditioning ducts were not completed. So, we hired and spent a lot of money installing ductwork to complete the air conditioning. Tenants were happy for a change once cool air had been provided downstairs.

Within a year, we had secured tenants for the upstairs and renegotiated the executive suite downstairs. The building was cash-flowing and operating successfully. We reached 100 percent of occupancy within two years. Jay was a great help in that he provided drawings for each lease space on CAD suitable to be attached to the respective lease agreements.

The building was located at 1701 West Northwest Highway in Grapevine called Lakeview. There were an additional three acres behind Lakeview that the original developers had also defaulted on with another bank, this time in Coppell, Texas. This acreage was land locked in, so the only access to the land was through my parking lot at Lakeview.

I contacted the bank to purchase the three acres. They wanted two hundred thousand dollars. I reminded them that they were landlocked and that anything built on that property had to tie into my sewer line. I negotiated and bought the property for $50,000. The bank was really happy to get rid of their repossessed real estate, even though not at the price they wanted.

For the next four years after 1994, Nerf Enterprises owned the Lakeview office building as well as 1000 South Main and then contemplated the building of a third office building on the three acres acquired. We hired Speed Fab-Crete to design and build an office building. They provided the architects and the building experts with the necessary skills to build. They designed another 40,000-square-foot building that would overlook to the north of the lake. We called the building Lakeview II, and its address is 1705 West Northwest Highway. They used a concept of poured-in-place concrete with a granite rock embedded in the concrete. When finished, the building would be red in color and well-built. We poured concrete in piers to support the structure and discovered water as shallow as seven feet in 19 of the piers. Accordingly, while we were drilling the piers, I had the driller drill one more for Lakeview's water well. This well-provided water for all of the five acres (grass) was free of charge. Lakeview II was completed in 1998 and fully occupied by the end of 1999. Mike Lease and Grady Herzog successfully bid for all of the tenants to finish out on the second floor. Darlene Freed and I decided how we wanted the second prebuilt and suitable to occupy. They did a great job, and Darlene and I ended up having suitable footage for at least 12 tenants. They were all occupied within a year.

Nerf Enterprises is now the owner of three office buildings comprising over 100,000 square feet of professional rental space. I was the general manager of the buildings. David Harris was really a silent partner in Nerf Enterprises. My job included leasing each space, paying all of the bills, and hiring the right kind of talent to maintain, protect, and operate each building. I took the philosophy that each tenant had the right to expect good air conditioning, clean restrooms, and a pleasant place to work—

green shrubs, grass, beautiful trees, etc. On the other hand, I assumed a tough role regarding the rent due on the first of each month. I was a mean SOB. If my tenant did not pay the rent timely, I exercised the right to change the locks and lock my tenant out after 10 days and proper notice. Once the routine was established and the tenants knew my attitude and knew they were getting good and clean office buildings, we had no problems. At any given time, we had as many as fifty total tenants, not counting the 30 or so who individually occupied executive spaces.

I purchased and installed a software package that would monitor all of the air conditioning units for all three buildings. It could control thermostats, set holiday and off-peak hours, and detect failures almost as soon as they occurred. I could call my HVAC contractor many times before a tenant would complain.

I hired Jose Torres to work full time to be my eyes and ears regarding tenant concerns. Oran Washburn was instrumental in training Jose. Oran had been working for me now for about five years, and he was slowing down a bit. He was approaching 80 and already had a bypass heart procedure.

Oran was an old cowboy who loved horses and ranching in general. He had his own jargon in that he called his heart "his ticker" and used "that thingamajig or over yonder, or next to the thing," thinking we surely knew exactly what he was saying. His choice of words was not exactly complete. When I called him while I was on vacation, he reported that we had some air conditioning problems at Lakeview I and that the HVAC repair may have "electrocuted himself." I panicked! I soon found out that the repairman was merely shocked.

When Oran had Jose Torres adequately trained, we all concluded that it was time for Oran to retire. About a year later, Oran's heart gave out, and he died. He had a horse-drawn casket at his burial. It was really neat. Oran was a good man. He always had my best interest at heart.

Later, when operating the rental aspects, I learned that I could replace my 4 x 4 light fixtures in my office building with 2 x 2 light bulbs and have

85 % of the lumens afterward, and then I would save money! Kevin Hannah told me that he could install a reflector, cut my bulb purchase in half, and reduce my electric bill proportionally. We agreed, and he installed them one night so my tenants in the Lakeview Office Building would not know the difference. He did, and they didn't, except one person complained that there was dust on her desk the next day.

I hired Kevin to retrofit our building at 1000 S Main as well. Kevin and I became good friends and ultimately formed a partnership named Sont Enterprises. We purchased land and built mini-warehouses in Commerce, Texas. I was to be the investor, and he was to manage the construction and rental of the warehouse units.

Chapter 35
Greer And Graduation

On October 3, we went down to College Station to see the Texas Tech game with Texas A&M. Nancy Jo Dyer, an old friend of Susan's and a professor, arranged our lodging at the MSC—an on-campus hotel there at A&M. We were there to see Big Boy, who was finishing up his work before going to Rice. We also secretly wanted to see our Texas Tech Red Raiders beat the Aggies. But just in case, I went off campus early that day, and long before the game was to start, I purchased a case of beer and iced it down. Since the Aggies stood up for the entire ball game, and, if by chance, Texas Tech did not show up to play, I had to have Plan B ready to go. Far be it for me to stand up an entire ball game while getting my butt beat on the field. The Aggies beat Tech 47 to something low, and I spent the entire second half in the car drinking beer (Plan B).

Greer enrolled at Texas Tech with a desire to major in environmental engineering. He had always loved Tech and rooted for them every time they played. Of course, he was highly influenced by Susan and me, as was Jay, but with Jay, it never registered! Oh, well, we were proud of our Aggie. The Fiji fraternity put a mad rush on Greer . He pledged Phi Gamma Delta (Fijis) along with about 26 other freshmen. He was happy with his choice despite the legacy issue. Actually, I had gotten a lot smarter, and so had his mom, once he surpassed his 17th birthday! Accordingly, his respect for us both had improved immensely.

One evening later, I got a call from Greer telling me that he had hit a deer on the highway. After I determined that he was all right, as were his other passengers, I asked him where he was. He responded that the deer was hit outside of Sterling City. Sterling City! I exclaimed, realizing that I was at least 100 miles away from Lubbock. What are you doing in Sterling City? He replied that he and a few of his pledge brothers were taking a "pledge cut" to...... Cuidad Acuna. I responded, "Cuna!?" I realized after I said it that Susan was finely tuned in. Acuna was the town in Mexico that had a "Boys Town" where high school and college guys frequented for beer and whatever. I remember it well from my high school days in Sweetwater.

I called George Nelson, the Purple Legionnaire of the fraternity and also a lawyer in Lubbock. He immediately took charge and somehow got the DUI charge dropped, suspended, and put aside. He and Greer arranged for the car to be repaired. This, too, passed.

Greer was taking 16 hours, as I recalled, including calculus. His mid-semester grades looked bad, really bad, for Calculus, History, and English. Susan and I went out to Lubbock for a football game in the Fall to see him and discuss the semester. We found Wonder Woman (Greer) at a fraternity party in downtown Lubbock. He was dressed as Wonder Woman for this fraternity party. He was taken aback by his grades and was without a solution, as we discussed then and later that weekend. We all concluded that he should hire a tutor to assist his learning curves and consider dropping calculus until he could get his feet on the ground. He did both thereafter and dug out passing grades for the semester, so he completed his pledge-ship of the fraternity. The next semester, he changed his major to business and never had any grade issues thereafter.

Actually, almost the very same thing happened to me in 1962 when I pledged to Fiji. I graduated in the top 10 percent of my class at Sweetwater High School (there were only 110 of us). I was hot stuff—going to take college by storm. I got an F on my first English paper, failed my first history exam, and Economics was going South for sure. My mother had never attended college, and she did not know what to do to turn my program around. So, she made an appointment with Dr. Frank Barker in Abilene one Saturday when I was home. Dr. Barker concluded that I was probably not college material after all and that I should put college on hold and join the Army. It did not take me long to realize that meant Vietnam, as our country was at war with them. I went back to Lubbock, dropped two courses, and ended up passing the semester with a 2.9 grade average—I made my grades, pledged the fraternity, and never had another grade issue thereafter.

Page 204

I guess it was reverse psychology on Dr. Barker's part, such that I had seen the Elephant and came to the reality that college was not a bad deal after all, but it was certainly attainable with a little determination, resolve, and hard work.

Greer and I had another thing in common in our college days. Greer got to witness the Texas Tech Lady Raiders win the National Championship with Cheryl Schoops, their all-American ball player. This happened during the mid-90s. I witnessed the Texas Tech men's basketball team almost win the Southwest Conference basketball championship but was disqualified as a result of Norman Reuther's grades.

Prior to the time, Greer pledged to my fraternity (the Fijis or Phi Gamma Delta), and he noted that they did not have a very good lodge to hold their meetings. The alums claimed that they had intentions of building a new lodge, especially by the sign on the proposed real estate lot. I found out later that the alums merely slapped fresh paint on the sign and talked a good game of building a new lodge, further that they had gathered some money toward that end but not enough to get started.

Greer's pledge class was noted as being the strongest and best in many years. Paul Rider's nephew, Tim, also pledged Fiji with Greer.

Paul had pledged to Fiji a year or so after I did. He was from Stanford, Texas, and later had a very good career as a stockbroker, specializing in bond underwriting and related sales. Paul was a bit eccentric in that he had never married, considering himself a playboy, traveling all over the world with a different woman with each trip. He had a big, beautiful home in north Dallas with three or four cars in the garages. He had his own chauffeur, M.T., to drive him around the Dallas area at Paul's pleasure. They drove out to Grapevine to deliver some of Paul's tax information, and M.T. would stay in Paul's car (Rolls Royce) while Paul and I would go get some BBQ for lunch. Several years later, when MT got cancer, Paul ended up driving his Rolls out to Grapevine himself with MT riding in the back seat! I got to know and love M.T., and he consulted with me a couple of times, so I arranged to have his will modified. It was a sad day when MT died for Paul.

Paul and I flew out to Lubbock to investigate the circumstances of the failure to build a lodge. Terry Grantham and Donnie Baker were those good old boys who had the fresh paint for the sign each year. We reviewed the proposed plans to build the lodge and went to Lamesa, Texas, where Bob Brown was the president and part owner of the First National Bank of Lamesa. Bob was also a Fiji a few years before me. We needed to borrow a half million to construct the lodge. The lot on which the lodge was to be built was a 99-year leased lot. The land on Greek Circle II was granted by the Texas Legislature to the Greek community for Greek lodges but not sold. Since there was no fee simple collateral for the lodge, there could be no bona fide collateral for a bank for a loan. We offered the guarantees of about five to seven alumni, and I offered a jumbo CD of Paul's as additional collateral. I told Paul on the airplane home that I had pledged one of his $100,000 CDs on the borrowed funds. Paul's biggest concern was whether he would continue drawing interest in the CD. Bob, the banker, accepted the collateral and guarantees, and construction was to begin. It took us about a year to build the new lodge. It had a large meeting room, formal and informal parlors, three apartments for resident caretakers to occupy, a complete kitchen, a study hall, restrooms, and a chapter room. Meeting room. My best friend, Rick Stacy, sold me the furniture for the new lodge at his cost or below.

We asked for the resignations of the existing so-called (do nothing) board members. We named Larry Lowe as President, with me assuming the role of Treasurer and Paul as Vice something. We needed to raise money fast to build the lodge and pay off this new debt! I created The White Owl Housing Foundation, Inc. The name had a nice ring to it, as it sounded official. George Nelson, the Fiji alum Purple Legionnaire, was very helpful in everything we did. When George was not writing newsletters to the graduates, I was. We sold engraved brick pavers for $500.00 each and instituted naming opportunities throughout the lodge. We sold many bricks and received large contributions of bricks. And with each contribution, George and I wrote personal letters thanking them for their generous gift.

The Lodge cost us about $850,000 to build. We raised a lot of money but still owed $225,000 on the loan. The bank was pleased, but I was running out of sources of money. George Nelson and I wrote letters and newsletters asking our fellow FIJIs to contribute, but we gained little for our efforts. The undergraduates were to pay rent out of their monthly dues to help service the debt and related maintenance, but the numbers were staggering for them and me, too. The rent would have to be more than the undergraduates could pay.

As the house was nearing completion, I wrote a bleeding heart newsletter describing one last appeal for money to the alum graduates of Phi Gamma Delta. I told them of the dire straits we were under, that the rent would have to service the debt and maintenance, and that we needed their help desperately!

I got a call from Van Hubbard, who had already given $50,000 and a beautiful bronze statue of a White Owl, asking me to come to his office in North Richland Hills, Texas—only about 30 miles from my office, he had something to give me. He was the CEO and Chairman of the Board of Technol Corporation, a publicly traded corporation of paper products. I arrived at his office mid-morning and waited in his beautiful lobby for him. After a few minutes, he came to the lobby and presented me with a sealed envelope. He told me not to raise the rent on the lodge as he hurried off and returned to the meeting he was having at his office. I went back to my pickup truck and opened the envelope. In it was a stock certificate of Technol Corporation worth $200,000!

It was truly an answer to a prayer. I immediately called George Nelson, and we cried in happiness together. The new lodge was paid for, and our worries were over!

Chapter 36
The Windoms

Barbara and Eddy Windom

We returned to Lubbock to complete my Masters degree at Tech in 1969. I applied to teach elementary accounting to Sophomores at the Business college while I pursued the 300 hours, including a thesis at Tech. Susan applied to teach at MacKensie Junior High. We rented a duplex from Hugh, and our first dog, Virginia, was with us. Since I was on the faculty at Tech, the Fijis and the Pi Phis were quick to get us assigned to be their faculty advisors and liaisons. I met Eddy Windom then as he had pledged Fijis while his new wife Barbara, a twirler, pledged Pi Beta Phi (Susan's sorority). Eddy and I had golf in West Texas, we had two sons, and they had three sons, not to forget the Fiji brotherhood in common, and, of course, we became fast friends. After graduation and a couple of years later, we met the Windoms again in Grapevine, especially when Eddy started EJ Sports, a sporting store when he needed a CPA or a good bookkeeper to guide his hand. We would meet at my office at 1000 Main in Grapevine, mainly at night, to post his records onto his general ledger, etc. His undying humor kept me in stitches constantly.

The Texas heat and our desire to play golf caused us to travel to Cloud Croft, New Mexico, to stay at the world-famous The Lodge, which had a nine-hole golf course. We left Grapevine with 100+ heat, flew to El Paso, and drove to Cloud Croft, where there was a fire in the fireplace and a 65-degree temperature. The trip was over Labor Day, and we managed to go there two or three more Labor Days thereafter. At night, we played hearts or spades and enjoyed a glass or two of wine after dinner.

We were intrigued and fascinated by the Viking tours and enlisted in their Grand European river tour from Amsterdam to Budapest. We flew to Paris, France, and took several tours of the city, including hard rain, the Eiffel Tower, and the Louvre. We also took their lovely train system to Normandy. Where we met Eddy and Barbara Windom at Normandy and hired a full-time guide through Normandy. We were in awe at the beautiful cemeteries, which brought reverence and respect from us, a reminiscence of the history of this place. It was inconceivable that so many of our soldiers, pilots, paratroopers, and allies lay their lives down to save France and turn Hitler around during WWII.

We took another train from there to Amsterdam and caught a 10-day boat ride to Budapest via the Sein and Danube Rivers through water dams, vineyards, castles, wineries, and beautiful countryside. We were on the boat with a total of 10 Texans and all sorts of other English-speaking travelers. On board, they had a great dance floor where we congregated every evening after dinner. Eddy and I were the only men among the ten Texans, so we were in high demand to dance with the remaining eight women! The piano was great, with lots of speakers, woofers, and built-in rhythms and tunes. Filardi was a Romanian piano player who could play almost anything that we could imagine. I stumped Filardi with a request of 'Fraulein,' thinking that it would be a well-known song due to its relevance to Europe. He said he did not know it but that he would research it on the web and play it tomorrow. He did, and we all sang and danced to 'Fraulein.' That prompted me to ask Filardi if he knew or could play 'Waltz Across Texas.' He did not know it but would research it and play it tomorrow night, and that is exactly what he did!

Imagine a Romanian piano player adapting to country music requests in the middle of Europe on the Danube River!

We went to Ireland in 2005 or so with Barb and Eddy Windom and played a lot of golf, saw some beautiful sites, and ate delicious food. Each night, we drank wine and played spades and hearts. We have traveled a lot with the Windoms, and we share a lot in common, and we always enjoy their company. Other trips with them include river tours with Viking in Europe, another tour boat down the St. Lawrence, Labor Day in Cloud Croft, and trips enjoying our Texas Tech Red Raiders! In Ireland, we had dinner at the Smuggler's Inn, and the reader of this memoir must ask Eddy, Barb, or Susan about my behavior at the restaurant.

I continued teaching continuing education courses for the American Institute of Certified Public Accountants. This year, I traveled to Amarillo, El Paso, and Corpus Christi. Susan, Greer went, and I stayed at The Lodge and ate at Rebecca's, their restaurant. It was always fun to go, especially to fly to El Paso and drive to Cloudcroft in the summer. The weather was so cool that a fire was needed in the lobby of The Lodge. We went there with Eddy and Barbara Windom for several Labor Day weekends. Eddy and I were in the fraternity together (although he was about three years younger). He and Barbara also lived in Grapevine, and we were involved socially with them frequently, and we loved our visits together.

Chapter 37
Don't Put My Age In The Paper!

But this summer, Jay and Greer decided to do a little hiking of their own. At Jay's graduation in May of 1994, they decided to hike the Rocky Mountain National Forest near Estes Park, Colorado. Greer was enrolled in the first semester of summer school at Texas Tech, while Jay was busy helping his friend Tim with the finishing touches of his master's at Rice. They left for Colorado around the 18th of July. We met them in Colorado, and we were up there, staying at our condo in Dillon at the time.

Susan and I were busy at the condo painting the living area when I got a phone call from Chuck Selinger in Odessa (he married my sister, Carolyn). My mother had had a stroke in Sweetwater. She was at the Sweetwater hospital.

Susan and I packed our bags and left immediately for Sweetwater. Susan had cooked a great roast beef, and that was our sandwich on the way back to Texas. We had a cell phone (my first), so I called and left word at an Estes Park ranger station for the boys to call me as soon as they could. While in transit to Sweetwater, Chuck called again to tell me they were moving Mother to the Midland Memorial Hospital and for us to come on to Midland.

When we met at the Midland Hospital, we found Mother unconscious and on feeding tubes. Carolyn said that she was not responding to anything. I took her hand, squeezed it, and told her that this was Jerry and that I loved her. She squeezed my hand back. I was encouraged. Realizing there was nothing I could do, Susan and I drove on to Sweetwater to spend the night. Susan drove on to Grapevine the next day, and I took Mother's car back to Midland to check on her.

While at Mother's home in Sweetwater, I found her will. Fortunately, she had changed it pursuant to her previous plans. It was a simple will and did not set up a trust for Carolyn as long as she was married to Chuck, something I vehemently objected to. She required Carolyn to pay back the $24,000 that Chuck owed her with interest before Carolyn could share the balance of her estate.

What was interesting, if not fascinating, was that there were two post-it notes (yellow stickies) on the will. One said, "Jerry, I want each of my grandchildren to have $10,000 each," she named each Tanner, Suzanne, Eric, Richard, Jay, and Greer.

And the other post-it note said: "Jerry, do not put my age in the newspaper!"

I also found the cherry wood cane that I gave Mother when I returned from Los Angeles with Eddie to pick up his profiler. As you may recall, she was insulted that I would think that she should need a cane to walk and told me she burned it in the fireplace. It was in the furnace closet behind some chairs.

I flew home from Abilene Airport, leaving her car there.

Mother died a few days after that, never regaining consciousness. She was buried at the Sweetwater Cemetery next to my father, Roy Calvert, on July 26, 1994. Her grandsons were her pallbearers: Tanner Selinger, Eric Selinger, Richard Selinger, Jay, and Greer. Bryan Hargis, Suzanne Selinger's husband, joined. Leonora Byrd, Lynn Bell, and Peggy Curry from my office came to the service, as did Rick and Diane Stacy.

Mother had willed her Hammond Organ to me. By then, I had already bought my own (and that is another story where I tried to buy hers, but she would not sell it to me). Besides the note that Chuck owed, there was nothing else left to do except sell the house and the furnishings. We divided up her furniture, gave her clothes to Goodwill, and sold the house and the remaining furniture in rather short order. Susan and I got a wall-hanging clock, some of her great recipes, and a few fireplace mantel items.

My sister cooperated and did not dispute any part of the settling of Mother's estate. Tanner, Suzanne, Eric, Richard, Jay, and Greer were most helpful in cleaning up and helping with the stuff!

The most important idea that developed from this ordeal was that Carolyn and I decided to start having a biannual reunion of the s and Selingers. Each reunion would be chaired by a different member of the family, and the event would be held over the 4th of July every other year.

The mother's obituary clearly did not disclose her age.

Mother made the best pecan pie ever. And her peach cobbler, creamed squash, potato salad, and Boston Baked beans were the best. Once, Susan was cooking something in her kitchen, using one of her famous recipes, and while the potato salad or whatever she was cooking was really good, it was not up to mother's standards or expectations, so she suggested that perhaps Susan did not stir with her left hand!

Mother was left-handed!

She loved the Texas Rangers on television. Nothing got in her way when they were playing. She acknowledged our arrival and insisted that we get food out of the fridge and sit and watch the game with her. She had a passion for gin rummy and played anyone for a quarter of a cent per point. She loved to play bridge with her friends until she was unable to.

I opened accounts at Edward Jones and Company for me and my sister in Marble Falls, Texas, where my good friend, Hugh D. Reed, a broker, handled her money transfers.

Chapter 38
City Council Grapevine 1989-1998

1/8/12

I learned that the Palace Theatre was for sale. The Palace was an old movie house that was built in the 1940s. It was the home of the Grapevine Opry, with Chasia Childs and Johnny High as the leading entertainers. Bill Tate appointed a committee of me, Linda Oliver, and Mike McKinney to investigate whether the city should buy the venue. What a wonderful auditorium this would be, a place for meetings, seminars, children's theatre, and movies. Unfortunately, my committee members, Mike and Linda, were not as enthusiastic about the city hall's acquisition of the Palace as I was, and the idea, when presented to the city council, died with a lack of interest. Susan and I could not afford it either, even though the purchase price was only $680,000! Ha!

After six years on the GCISD school board, I decided I could do better on the Grapevine City Council, so I filed for Place 4, and Charles Nunn decided to run against me. It would be difficult for me to be elected in early May, shortly after my major tax deadline of the 15th of April every year. So, with my soccer parents and my client base, I asked selected friends to post signs throughout our city in early April and stand ready to speak in my support. More importantly, I walked several neighborhoods from door to door wearing more than one pair of shoes. I started in Mr. Nunn's neighborhood. I talked with the people and left my brochures, and I asked them to call me if they had questions or problems. Will Wickman, an old friend of mine, ran for Place 5 in the same race and teamed up with Nunn in my race against me. I called many people and had lots of help. I beat Charles Nunn by twenty-five percent, and Will Wickman became my friend again. He was elected to Place 5 and would be my fellow council member in the next few years. My initial fellow city council members were Ted Ware, Sharon Spencer, Will Wickman, Gil Traverse, Clydene Parker, Bill Tate (mayor), and me. I was immediately assigned to the utility, golf course, finance, and convention visitor committees. The airport was busy trying to decide to build another north/south runway that would parallel Main Street in Grapevine such that the very loud airplanes would be less than 800 feet high when flying over the downtown area.

We, along with some other City of Grapevine officials, went to New York to meet with Moody's and Standard and Poor's regarding the investment rating of the City of Grapevine's general obligation and revenue bonds. Favorable ratings by these two companies would result in lower interest costs and attractiveness to sell. The rating agencies knew more about Grapevine than I ever thought. I think that is why the City wanted me to go since my expertise was in finance and accounting. One of the meetings was in the top few stories of the World Trade Center—yes, the one that a hijacked airplane destroyed in 2002. The rating agencies were concerned that Grapevine's revenue was too heavily concentrated on DFW airport-related businesses.

This trip to New York included an opportunity to see the New York Knicks play the Chicago Bulls (Michael Jordan) in Madison Square Gardens. Broadway plays and delicious meals were also included in these trips.

I was also on the utility committee as a City Council member. This included cable TV, water, telephone, and, to some extent, gas and electric utilities. General Telephone (now Verizon) had a new proposal for the city to join their Centranet group since we were so close to their switching station at the airport. This was a no-brainer, except one of our choices in the conversion was to add or not add VOICEMAIL. We had a knockdown drag-out at the Council level because there were at least two members who never wanted customers of City Hall to experience something as cold as a voice message. Only personal conversations were acceptable. Voicemail passed with a 4-3 split, and now (twenty years later) the dissenters think that was the best decision they ever made!

I was serving on the advisory board of the Grapevine Golf Course. The 18-hole course behind the Grapevine Dam was really a cash cow, generating 70,000 rounds of golf annually. The course was built in 1978 with City bond money. It was constructed behind Lake Grapevine's water dam. The course was run by Jim Smith, the golf pro, along with a committee appointed by the City Council. And since I was the only golfer on the Council, I got to be the liaison member—it was also a nine-year job, but quite enjoyable.

But, Jim Smith and I did not agree on all facets of the golf course. There were no restrooms on the course. Jim said the women could use trees as men do. Credit cards were not allowed to be used to charge course fees, buy clothing, or hire instruction. Jim claimed that it took too much time and cost too much money! The golf scorecard had printed on it "GOLF IS A FOUR-HOUR GAME" in bold print—a rather offensive statement. Also, in the beginning, the Grapevine High golf team was not allowed to play or practice at no charge due to the fact that the course was built on federal land. Jim assured me that the Corps of Engineers of the Federal Government would insist that ALL high school golf teams would have equal and fair opportunities to play on the course if Grapevine were allowed to play.

If the Grapevine High golf team paid the greens, there would be no discrimination with other area high schools. The equivalent green fees, which is the amount of green fees for a year for the team to play and practice, was about $8,000, according to Jim Smith and Jim Galbraith, the high school golf instructor. I called Trent Petty, the City Manager, and asked him to write a check out of the City's general fund for $8,000 and buy the equivalent amount of green fees at the golf course. Then, the golf course, which is also owned by the City, writes a dividend check back to the General Fund as a dividend in the same amount of $8,000! The Corps was happy, Jim Smith was happy, and the kids at Grapevine High were delighted. And I was happy since we were not taking advantage of other area high schools.

During the City's budget workshops, I put $30,000 in the golf course budget, and when Jim Smith asked, I told him it was for men's and women's restrooms on the front and back nine holes, respectively. He thought men could hike a leg up against a tree but had no ideas for women golfers.

After hearing numerous customers complain that we needed to allow credit cards to be used at the Golf Course to pay for green fees, purchase green fees, buy golf clothing, etc., I called Trent Petty again and assured him that I had four other council members' votes that said we should allow credit cards on the golf course. Trent informed Jim Smith that credit cards were allowed the next day! When we put a picture on the scorecard to replace "Golf is a Four-Hour Game," Jim did not speak to me for a month!

Greer had been hired the previous two summers to be a Ranger at Philmont Scout Ranch. He was mobile as he was driving one of my older pickups. He took new treks out for their three-day orientations at the Ranch and enjoyed the staff comradery that Philmont afforded.

We bought a steer at the Texas State Fair. We purchased a pig or a steer every year from the State Fair. It has always been a help to the young boys with the FFA (Future Farmers of America). The price was fair—actually more than the fair market value and certainly less than if I had purchased meat at the grocery store. Besides, we had a freezer to accommodate large quantities of meat.

Lone Star Gas invited me and other council members to join them on a deer hunt outside of Sonora. We flew down in their Lear jet and landed on the ranch; we were picked up there to join others for a great meal already prepared, and then we were off to hunt. The guide merely circled the feeding area, scattered corn, and let me out in the blind. Within minutes after the guide left, I had deer and turkey everywhere. We slept in a great bunkhouse only to hunt again in the morning after a big breakfast. I shot a buck and a turkey—more meat for the freezer. On Sunday, they drove us to the runway, and we watched the jet circle and land. The trip took 45 minutes. It was a first-rate hunting trip. I guess it was an attempt to bribe a public official by the City's gas franchise, but it was a very popular and vogue thing in those days. The pay was not so good as a City Council member, and I never knew how Lone Star Gas could have bribed me since rates were regulated by the State and they were the only gas company.

The Wallis Hotel was dedicated in December. The original Wallis Hotel was built in Grapevine around the turn of the 1900s down by the railroad track in Grapevine. It was torn down some twenty-nine years later. Legend and old stories said that the Wallis was a red-light hotel, the home of prostitutes serving the railroad men, and the uppity town folk were aghast over the business and insisted that the hotel be torn down. Well, we rebuilt the Wallis using Convention Visitor money. We built it on Main Street across from the snow cone stand, which is now the City Hall. The Wallis is not used as a hotel. Instead, it is used as the office of the Convention Visitors Bureau.

The EIS study was completed, and DFW airport and their intentions were clear (early 1992). A new runway would be aimed north, with airplanes flying directly over the downtown area of Grapevine. We had joint meetings with council members from Irving and Euless. We decided to file a lawsuit.

I decided to run for a third term (3 years) in 1995. It would also be my last as there were a number of boring days as a City Council member. I had already served six years on the school board, and now this would be a total of nine years. I felt those 15 years of public service were quite satisfying enough.

The airport decided that it would attempt to lobby with the Texas Legislature to strip Grapevine of all of its revenues from the airport.

Since two-thirds of Grapevine was used to build the DFW airport, we were entitled to sales, liquor, and property taxes generated under Grapevine's jurisdiction. Grapevine hired moneyed lobbyists, and the fight started.

Previously, many legal issues, zoning cases, and environmental studies had delayed the construction of a new runway parallel to Main Street.

DFW became rather frustrated that their muscle was unable to overpower Grapevine, especially when the National Historic Trust got involved regarding the protection of the old historic buildings in downtown Grapevine.

We on the Council made a major decision to protect the history of Grapevine. We created a historic zone—a large area around the downtown area. The historic zones were modeled after Santa Fe, New Mexico, and Charlotte, North Carolina ordinances. A Historic Protection Commission was established that required direct supervision and approval for any type of change to any structure in this zone. The Grapevine Heritage Foundation was created to foster and promote historic restoration, including the purchase of the old Palace Theatre and the old Buckner Cash Grocery Store. These efforts were all designed to protect and promote the history of Grapevine. After all, Grapevine is the oldest town in Tarrant County—including Fort Worth.

On another front, several of us went to New York to visit our bond rating agencies—Moody's and Standard & Poor's. As a city issues bonds, they must be rated by these agencies to validate the investment quality of the bonds and establish a rating—AAA, AA, A, B, etc. The bond's rate of interest is also established, and the better the rate, the more interest expense for the city, and the lower the rate, a converse relationship. I was thrilled to go to New York, and it was about my third or fourth time to visit with the agencies.

The agencies asked a very pivotal question. They commented that Grapevine was overloaded with revenues from the airport, such that if these revenues went away, Grapevine's financial picture would be in peril. Grapevine's rating was affected accordingly.

The major decision and this pivotal question created a desire for our city to seek other sources of revenue besides those from the airport. Our city manager, Trent Petty, and our community development manager, Tommy Hardy, sought and secured a commitment from The Mills Corporation to build a huge mall in the Northeast section of Grapevine. Bass Pro was hustled, and they committed to come to town. Many other developments followed, including various restaurants, hotels, and related services. The Gaylord Hotel and The Great Wolf Lodge were mega hotels that came as well—most every new development was in the Northeast quadrant of the city, thereby protecting the Historic Zone and keeping sacred the National Trust concepts.

The National Historic Trust and the FAA locked horns, so to speak, on the issue of building a new runway to the east of Main Street Grapevine—it was truly an impasse. Lt Governor Bill Clayton took a rather dim view of Dallas and Fort Worth trying to strip Grapevine of its jurisdictional rights. He ended this the last fight between Grapevine and the airport. The airport gave up on its expansion plans.

The Convention Visitors Board was established by the City with a 9-member appointed board. I was the City's Council and Liaison member. The CVB collected the "Bed Tax" from the various hotels. The State allowed the assessment of what they called "The Occupancy Tax," which was 8% of hotel and motel revenues. Its purpose was to promote tourist and convention facilities, promotions, and advertising to lure guests to stay in Grapevine Hotels. Promotions were held annually in Los Angeles and New York, including parties entertaining the convention decision-makers of large corporations. Susan and I attended several of these parties in New York, and they were timed with St. Patrick's Day with the huge parade and all related festivities. Our party was at the Alamo or Texas Bar or at a hotel on 5th Avenue, where we hosted one hundred or so guests.

The CVB built the "Wallis Hotel," a two-story building across the street from City Hall. While it was a replica of the old Wallis that was built around 1900 on the railroad tracks, its purpose changed when it was reconstructed. The first Wallis was truly a hotel that provided lodging for railroad personnel, but after 25 or so years, it was torn down. It was the home for prostitutes and a real red-light district, and the men and women of Grapevine would not tolerate it! The restored Wallis was built to be the CVB's office and staff.

Under the leadership of the CVB and their director, PW McCallum, a sister city committee was established. A city in Mexico was first targeted to be a sister city to Grapevine. It was Parras de la Fuente in Coahuila, Mexico. Located two hours west of Monterrey, Parras was the home of the oldest winery in the Americas—Casa Madera. The Germans, in late 1800, in search of silver and gold, discovered a tremendous source of water for Parras; thus, pecans and vineyards flourished. Casa Madera was 400 years old and was established and still owned by the Madera family. The vineyards constituted several hundred hectares (like acres) and had their own landing strip for the Madera jets.

Chapter 39
Wheaton, Maryland

1/9/12

It was May of 1992 and graduation for both boys. Greer was one of the Senior Class Favorites, and he had been the Homecoming King at Grapevine High School. His grades were good, and he finished with a high standing in his class. His graduation celebration went off without a hitch, and he was very responsible. Part of that may be because we were among sponsors at his all-night party.

Jay finished his senior year at Texas A&M with a degree in Environmental Design. He graduated very high in his graduating class; I think they called it "with honors." His intentions were to complete his architectural work by getting his Masters. In order to do that, he had to prepare a "Portfolio of his Work." His portfolio was completed before he graduated, which in itself was the exception rather than the rule for this study. Most students took an additional semester or even a year to complete their portfolios.

The portfolio was published and furnished to several universities. Jay had offers to complete his Masters at Columbia in New York, the University of Illinois at Urbana, and Rice University. He chose Rice for several reasons. First, it offered the best financial package, while the others only offered tuition. Secondly, the travel would not be a burden, and lastly, he knew that his brother was entering college that fall and was well aware of the financial strain of having two guys in college at the same time on me and his mom.

I bought a new Ford Ranger for Jay's graduation and gave Greer my 1991 Chevrolet pickup for his graduation.

We celebrated their graduation by flying to Sorento to sail the Baja peninsula by bareboat. The four of us had sailed the British Virgin Islands a few years earlier and really wanted to enjoy the Baja. We ate well, drank beer, snorkeled, and fished. The wind was not good for the trip, with only a couple of days to enjoy true sailing. Greer caught a Bonita fish while we were sailing. It was fairly big, feisty, and slick in feel. Huge sailfish were seen off the bow of the boat regularly. One spectacular event was watching two natives catch a sailfish in a rather small johnboat. The fish was almost as long as the boat, and watching them was hilarious. The fish actually was pulling the boat around in the water for the longest time.

That year, Jay finished up at Rice University with his Masters of Architecture. We were so proud of him as he completed his master's work in two years and graduated with honors from Rice. Rice paid his tuition fully, and the University gave him a stipend for each of the four or six semesters he attended. The stipend helped all of us financially, together with the Abe and Annie Siebel Foundation, which provided a loan each semester he made a 3.0 or better. So basically, we paid only for Jay's room and board.

The graduation was on the Rice Campus in, I guess, what they called the Commons. Susan and I arrived in Houston the day or so before so she could visit with Jay. She had another event that weekend that conflicted, but she wanted her first priority to be with her son. She was the coach of Grapevine High School's Interscholastic Literary Criticism Team. This particular year, the team advanced through district and regional competitions to state competitions. Well, the state meet was in Austin on the same day as Big Boy's graduation. So, she was with the team, and after winning the state championship, she flew to Houston in time for the Rice graduation. Yes, with the satisfaction that the team that she coached won the State Championship in 5A Literary Criticism! She was so proud, as we all were, of her efforts.

It was October 1994 when Jay decided to take his first architectural job—in Washington, DC, with George Sexton & Associates. They were architectural lighting experts, and he was thrilled with the unfolding world and opportunities.

He had accumulated some furniture, books, and clothing over his college years. He had his Ford Ranger truck, stereo equipment, etc. He had inherited some tools, band saw, and other larger tools from Eddie Freeze that I had stored in a mini-warehouse, along with some more furniture.

He leased a bobtailed rental truck along with a tow trailer for the Ford Ranger. I wanted to go with him to help him unload and get settled in his apartment. He welcomed the help and really (I think) wanted me to come too. He was to drive the truck towing the Ford Ranger to Grapevine, spend the night, and we were to embark eastward the next day. He and Tim loaded the truck and hitched the trailer and Ranger to the rear. The rental truck was full, but what about mattresses and all?

At about 7 pm, Jay called me. He was at Corsicana, Texas, at a service station headed for Grapevine. He said that the Ford Ranger truck was no longer attached to the big truck and was missing! He had no clue as to where the Ranger might be. The Bob Tailed truck had a high and wide carriage holding his furniture with a large hydraulic lift at the rear. It was so wide that while driving, Jay could not see directly behind him—no, he could not see the Ford Ranger and had no knowledge that it was or was not there until he stopped to refuel the truck in Corsicana. He said, "Dad, I do not know where it is as I could not see it—it could be anywhere between here (Corsicana) and Houston!"

I told Jay to drive on to Grapevine and that I would contact the appropriate police to notify them. I could not imagine where the Ranger was or how it had broken loose from the big truck's tow. I called the Texas Highway Patrol to report a missing truck. I really think they thought I was crazy or something. Because the dispatcher with the HP wanted to know how the truck became "missing"—was I sure it wasn't stolen? I then called the Grapevine Police, and they sent out a squad car and an officer to write up a report. I am really not sure what they could or might do other than write some kind of report that probably would go nowhere. They were probably patronizing me with my bizarre story because I was still on the City Council at the time. I also called the Houston Police about the missing truck. Somehow, this must be routine for all of the police departments, and they have some sort of computer program that requires routine info like license, color, make, model, markings, wrecked, stolen, owner, addresses, and telephone number, but not the word "Missing"!

When Jay arrived, I finally understood how the truck could be missing. The towing trailer had canvas straps that wrapped around the front wheels, and the rear wheels would ride on the ground as the vehicle was towed. A steel safety chain attached to the frame secured the towed vehicle to the trailer.

Except, Jay did not connect the steel safety chain, and thus, the truck was missing!

We had given the Ford Ranger to Jay as a partial graduation present from Texas A&M and Rice University. I had sent the title to the truck for him to transfer the title and get it insured sometime earlier, but he told me that he had not transferred the title but that he had gotten it insured. I questioned myself as to how one might insure a vehicle that one does not own.

It was a rather long night. I could not imagine where the truck might be. Houston to Dallas was every bit of 300 miles, and the truck could be anywhere along Interstate 45. It could be in some bar ditch, smashed off of a bridge, or head on with another car. I could see the car careening off of the highway, running across the freeway, and ramming head on with a carload of Hispanics, and the driver was pregnant—obviously a bad dream during what little sleep I got.

The phone rang at about 6 am. It was a call from the Houston City Police Department saying they had located the Ford Ranger in a vacant lot on Fannin in Houston. They said it looked in good shape and was not wrecked and unlocked—they wanted to know whether I wanted them to impound the truck in their lot or leave it there until I came for it. I told them I could be there within two hours via Southwest Airlines and to leave it in the lot on Fannin.

I told Jay we could probably meet somewhere in Arkansas if he took the bobtail truck and headed East. I would drive the Ford Ranger straight up Highway 59, so we agreed to meet in Hope, Arkansas, at Wally World

(Wal-Mart).

Susan took me to Love Field in Dallas, and I took the next hourly flight to Houston. I was so relieved! The car had been located. It had not run over anybody or anything. But taking a cab ride from Hobby Airport in Houston was certainly eventful. Most cabs were driven by Africans, and my cab was no different. and explained to him that I wanted him to drive me down Fannin looking for a blue Ford Ranger mired in a vacant lot. You want to do what?

It was located across the street from a Whataburger where Jay had gotten his dinner the night before and made a turn back on to Fannin to head North, and without the chains affixed to the truck, it merely slipped off of the canvas girders and kept going. The truck hit the curb and jumped all four wheels onto the vacant lot.

I got into the truck and started it. The computer, music, and dirty clothes were all intact. It may have been the smell of the clothes in the back seat that warded off any theft of the truck or the personal items in it. I started the truck, backed it out and off of the curb, and headed north down Highway 59 to meet Big Boy in Hope, Arkansas.

I arrived at the Wally World parking lot, and there was Jay in the bobtailed truck with the tow trailer, which we hooked up the Ford Ranger with the canvas around the wheels and, of course, the chain to the frame and the trailer. After we drove a few miles or so, we stopped to check everything out with the tow. The Ford Ranger was leaking fluid and was orange in color. We both concluded that it must be transmission fluid, so we dropped the drive train out of the Ranger and put it in the bed.

We had no other incidents the rest of the way to Washington. We put the drive shaft back onto the Ranger and tried to drive it, but we found out that it had no steering. The steering wheel would not turn the wheels. The steering fluid was empty, which we originally thought was transmission fluid. We asked the Exxon station mechanic to examine the Ranger, only to find out that the steering column was broken!

Apparently, when the Ranger hit and jumped the curb in Houston, the steering column cracked or broke partially. The Ranger allowed me to drive it (rather fast) up Highway 59 to Hope, Arkansas. But the steering column went ahead and broke shortly after we hooked it up to the tow.

I guess I used one of my nine lives on that trip! I flew home after we moved everything into Jay's apartment.

Jay was working for George Sexton, an architectural lighting consultant, in Georgetown, Maryland. His experience there reaped many rewards, including museum designs in Denver and the Modern Art Museum in Fort Worth. Tadao Ando, the famous Japanese architect who designed the Modern, was impressed with Jay's conceptual model, which showed how sunlight would glance off of concrete walls and finally come to rest on valuable art inside. So, George Sexton got the nod to be the lighting consultant for the Modern Art Museum in Fort Worth.

Jay came home a couple of times to supervise the lighting at the Modern, and Susan applied and became a Docent at the Modern when it was completed.

Chapter 40
CPA And Investments 95, 96, 97

Blessed are those
Who arrange diverse elements
Into masterful
Works of fiction
For they shall be called
Certified Public Accountants

Bessie Mitchell was a client of mine, and I prepared her tax return every year. Her daughters were Betty Harwell, and her sons were C.D. Mitchell and Billy Mitchell. Bessie walked every morning around our neighborhood, as did Susan and I, along with Tootsie Roll, our brown Labrador. Bessie lived in a house on Ball Street next to the City's Heritage Park. When Bessie died (old age), I asked Betty Harwell and her brothers if they might consider selling Bessie's house to the City of Grapevine. I convinced my fellow City Council Members that we needed a small meeting place for various reasons. So, the city purchased the house and agreed to rename the house "The Bessie Mitchell Meeting

Facility." The city remodeled the place, installed adequate parking, conformed to ADA compliance, and the meeting facility became a reality. Bessie would have been proud!

Another widow woman who was also a client of mine was Florine Williamson, who was in her 80s and worked as a hostess at Lucas Funeral Home. She lived in the old farmhouse at the corner of Wall and College Streets in Grapevine. The farm included all of the land stretching to the south to Highway 114 and all of the land to the West along the Cotton Belt railroad to the hospital (now Baylor Medical Center). She lived in this old farmhouse under a marital survivor agreement created by the will of her deceased husband (Mr. Williamson) upon his death several earlier years. Florine had married Mr. Williamson sometime in the 50s, and when he died, a marital survivor rights agreement existed in his will. In other words, the land was bequeathed to his heirs—children of his from an earlier marriage.

But Florine, his widow, had the right to live in the house and on the land as long as she lived, and the heirs could not dispose of the land so long as she occupied the property.

Florine was living like a pauper in that old farmhouse with a penance of income as a hostess in a funeral home, so she came to me for advice. She said her husband's children were putting her under some pressure to release her marital rights in order for them to sell a portion of her land. Walmart and Fina Oil seemed to want to purchase the land south of the farmhouse to Highway 114.

I suggested to the heirs that they purchase an annuity to pay Florine $1,500 per month in exchange for her releasing her marital rights on the land. Her marital rights exempted her from paying the real estate tax, which also had to be discussed with the heirs.

They agreed. Florine was in the money—more than she had seen for some time. She bought a new car and continued as a hostess at the funeral home. Walmart built their new store, and so did Fina. About a year after that, the property to the west of the Farm House was negotiated, and Florine got another annuity for $1,200 per month. That was when Florine retired from the funeral home.

When Florine died, the City of Grapevine purchased the farmhouse in 1997 and named it The Nash Farm for the Nash family that owned the farm prior to Mr. Williamson. No mention or history has ever been given to Mr. Williamson and Florine, my client.

I had practiced as a sole practitioner CPA now for almost ten years after I bought Wayne O'Daniel out, or at least when we separated the firm clients. I was now 48 years old; Jay and Greer were officially off of our payroll and on their own. My dream and objective were to "reclassify" at age 55. By that, I meant that at age 55, I would seek a new direction aimed at slowing down and ultimately retiring or doing something radically different. Susan was also nearing full retirement status with the school system.

We walked every day around the hospital near our home in Grapevine with Toots, our brown Labrador, and we had much time to think about my (our) future—retirement or whatever. Susan had about five more years to attain full retirement on a teacher pension with the Teachers Retirement System of Texas.

I began actively looking for a purchaser of my practice. I was the first CPA Grapevine ever had when I started my practice in 1972, and it had developed into a premier practice with the cream of the crop of clients throughout the years. The two larger firms in Tarrant County wanted to purchase the practice but wanted me to continue to work and manage the firm while paying for their purchase price. I figured it differently because I wanted to slow down, play golf, and begin a different pace. I turned down both of their offers. Randy Powers, CPA, had leased office space at my Lakeview office building, and I started discussing the practice with him. I wanted him to pay a substantial down payment, pay my purchase price over five years, and continue my employment during the payment period.

He agreed, and on January 1, 1999, we completed the transaction. I notified my clients but assured them all that I was not leaving them as their CPA—or at least not then, implying that it may happen someday. For the next six years, as I collected my notes, Randy Powers paid me a salary, and I continued serving "our" clients. I regularly took up golf by joining a country club (Trophy Club) and blocked my calendar off three afternoons each week. I stopped Saturday appointments. My employees were happy with the new regime. They included Welva Lynn Bell, Diane Glenz, and Leonora Byrd. They all were the most loyal and responsive employees one could ever have, and I loved and cherished each.

About three years later, in 2002, I received a call from one of my clients, Ann Parsons, telling me that her son, Michael, needed to come to see me as soon as possible. He had won the Texas Lottery, amounting to nine million dollars! Mike and Ann came to see me the next day, and we visited at length about what he wanted to do with the winnings. He had already agreed to 24 annual payments for the nine million—as an option made when purchasing the ticket. I called the lottery commission in Austin to verify that I had the winning ticket, but I did not disclose the winner's name. Mike wanted to share his winnings with his parents and two brothers. We formed a partnership (Coolio Enterprises) as the ticket owner, with the five being the partners (Mike, of course, would receive 60 percent of the annuity each year). Larry Flynn, the attorney, authored the agreement and agreed to receive the money in Austin on behalf of the partnership, keeping the Parsons and Mike, in particular, incognito.

SOME OF MY INVESTMENTS

I made several mistakes and bad investments in my lifetime. I will briefly enumerate those now. When we were first married, we purchased a Horizon City lot near El Paso. We later realized that it was in the desert and had no interest in pursuing it further, so we defaulted. During the growing trend of Grapevine, I purchased the Office Supply Company (about 1970). Jay Stanley and Neal Young joined me in the purchase. We hired Neal's uncle to start a printing company, and I hired Dub Waits (Susan's father) to help. After about two years, we 'lost our shirt' and closed the store down. We sold the remaining supplies and printing presses. Somehow, the remaining partners (Neal, Jay and me) ended up getting the uncle's motorboat which we traded off with the manager of the local marina discussed below. I did not finish my story. Neal's uncle Bud gave us his 40-hp motorboat that we tried to enjoy. However, we had a near disaster the first and only time we went water skiing. Neal and Trisha, Jay and Pat, and Susan and I pulled the motorboat to shore in a rocky area at Lake Buchanan, and somehow a piece of the propeller sheared off and flew right over Susan's head. She heard the swish of the piece fly over her. Had this hit her head, it could have killed her! It scared us all and especially me (about 1971).

I traded the motorboat at the marina that day with a man who owned a vacant lot nearby. I saw the lot and agreed to the trade. Neal bowed out of the new partnership, and so Jay and I continued ownership for the next 45 years, and each year we paid the real estate tax of $30 or so dollars every year. Until 2022 when we started getting offers on this worthless real estate lot. We went to see it that summer and decided that it wasn't worth much and certainly more than the motorboat that almost killed Susan! So, we sold the lot for $30,000, much to our surprise and never looked back. Jay Stanley and I got about $15 grand each.

POSSUM KINGDOM

I purchased a lot overlooking Possum Kingdom Lake from The Cliffs, a golf course development. The Lot was lot #156. I ended up assuming the loan balance on another lot (#287) under the high pressure of Cliff's salespeople, including a man named Jay Scott. About 3 to 6 months later, I learned that the Cliffs had hidden microphones in the respective sales offices/closures where Susan and I met with Jay Scott, and as he stepped out, they would listen to our discussions on the relative merit of purchasing a lot at PK. We ended up hiring a lawyer and accusing the Cliffs of fraud in the inducement. All was not lost because the Cliffs refunded all of our money.

DILLON COLORADO

Good investments I made during the 1990s included the purchase of 1/3 interest in the Colorado townhome called Lake Haus. Paul Rider, Mike Maraist, and Gary Tuna had purchased the condo in the late 70s, but Tuna ended up being a "flake" such that Paul and Mike offered me his share for $25,000 if I would assume the management and bookkeeping of the place. Maggie Mariast, Mike's sister and attorney, drew up the papers, and I assumed my role as manager.

Our family had been there many times before, enjoying Paul's generosity, and we all knew it would be a good investment. It was and continues to be so. We skied, hiked, toured, and entertained many people as our guests. We have auctioned off the condo for charities many times—American Cancer, CDRI, Hugely Hospital, to name a few.

Over the many years (at least 25) after 1994, I told my partners, Mike Mariast and Paul Rider, that we should sell the townhome, especially since their children did not know ours and when one of us died, we would have legal problems and other issues. They both agreed. So, Susan and I spent a week up there in Dillon, near Breckenridge, hired a realtor, dumped a lot of dated stuff and furniture, and sold the townhome in 10 days for about 10 times the amount we paid for it. We split the proceeds up three ways, and we took our share and purchased another townhome in Ruidoso, New Mexico, for our kids and grandkids.

HIGHWAY 114 32 ACRES BOYD, TEXAS

Another good investment was when Gary Kirkland and I purchased 32 acres of land on Highway 114 near Boyd, Texas. We hunted quail and dove on this property until Gary Kirkland, my partner, was considering bankruptcy. We partitioned 16 acres for each of us. We had kept the gas royalty, and the quarterly gas production amounted to about $30.00, but as gas drilling became more important in that area, the production increased to monthly checks and around ten times that amount and more periodically. The Texas Highway Department planned on expanding Highway 114, so they compensated us substantially for the 1.6 acres they needed. Then about ten years later, I sold the remaining 14 acres for twice what I paid, but I kept the royalties that still produced a handsome monthly income for us to enjoy.

Early in our marriage, Susan and I considered retirement a long way off, and she did not hesitate to cash in her Teacher Retirement Savings.

When she left the profession to have our firstborn, Jay. We also needed a new car, so we purchased a Volkswagen and named it BC (Baby Car). We actually had another Volks earlier, and it, too, was named BC. During the 90s, however, we contacted the Teacher Retirement System and arranged to purchase that retirement back on a monthly basis. Sure, glad we did because the monthly retirement is currently used and enjoyed by us both!

Chapter 41
Sierra Club Working and Camping

Susan and I were members of the Sierra Club, and although we did not agree with everything they offered, we did agree on many of their ideals. We enrolled in one of the SC's summer work camps. The camp was to be in Colorado on the mountain road between Leadville and Aspen. The Lost Mine Trail was located on the Continental Divide at about 9,000 in altitude. Our camp included about 25 volunteers, lasting nine days. We were assigned three paid staff members to lead, cook, and organize our work.

Our work included rebuilding the main trail after much damage had been created by melting snow and by hikers on the trail that hiked around the mud bogs creating a bigger mud bog. We called those people "Mushroom Pickers." Some of the more distinct water bogs had to be built up with rock and rock bridges sufficient to support pack animals and horses. We learned a lot about trail building and really appreciated those who came before us creating water bars and the like protecting the trails. I learned that if I needed large rocks to be the foundation of a bridge, that I needed to roll the large rocks down the hill rather than lifting or moving the rock up the hill! The trek lasted nine days, with every third day a "day off." Susan and I went exploring on our days off, and I tried my hand at fly fishing.

The work was at 9500 ft of altitude, and the peak of the trail (where we fished) was more like 10500 feet.

We made some friends, but the food was not that good—lots of tofu, short of meat, and anything worthy of our hard work.

The second Sierra Club two-week adventure and work assignment was not real far from Cody and Marteese, Wyoming. Cody's museum was where I saw Garrison Keeler the day we arrived.

We were to hike with our camping gear up to 11,000 feet to help restoration carpenters with the rebuilding of AA Anderson's home that was listing down a hill toward a water stream. Teddy Roosevelt had appointed his friend, AA Anderson, to be the Special Superintendent of the Yellowstone Forest Reserve. There were several water streams near the large house each had names of various women that entertained Mr. Anderson. The house had hot water heated downstairs and pumped into the large tub reservoir.

Our imagination went wild. Or was that only me? Mr. Anderson had a ranch several miles away and lived in these two-storied homes in the park.

Our food, provisions, and tents were carried by mule. Our saws, hammers, and other tools were also carried by mule. We were to cut trees in the forest and carve our lumber and carve our own wood-carved pieces to fit the house. Manual jacks were also provided to jack the house up to level again. All of the volunteers would work three days and then be off one day to fish, explore or go on hikes. One day we stared and stared at a rock that we thought to be a grizzly bear for the longest time.

There were about 18 to 20 volunteers like Susan and me and about nine hired restoration carpenters that lived in nice tents and feasted on steaks and great food every day while the Sierra Club volunteers ate rather skimpily on protein supplements and some packaged food. Fortunately, I brought lots of beef jerky.

Chapter 42
White Owl and LCAD 1998

At about that time, the real estate taxes that the Fiji's owed on their new house got my attention. The house is owned by the White Owl Housing Foundation and leased to the fraternity of Phi Gamma Delta, aka Fijis. I was the treasurer and got the appraisal notices of value changes and tax rates to be assessed on the value. These real estate taxes, also known as ad valorem taxes, were assessed on the house, based on formulas, comparable sales, etc., but did not include the land. The land lot was leased. Each year, these ad valorem taxes increased, so I filed a formal protest and asked for a hearing before the Lubbock Central Appraisal District. The protest year was 1996. The hearing was scheduled with three appointed laypeople who volunteered to conduct such hearings. The LCAD was represented by one of their employees, who was also an appraiser. At the hearing, I learned that the house was being valued on the rolls in the same manner that any other house in Lubbock was valued and that they (LCAD) had made an adjustment for the land lot. At the hearing, I asked for a discounted value for our house because we had no market for our house and that it should not be considered in the same market as residential housing in Lubbock, Texas. The chief appraiser with LCAD presented five simple houses in Lubbock for comparables, stating what he thought should be the fair value. I claimed that there was no market value for our house since only fraternities could purchase a house that was on land set aside by the Texas State Legislature, especially for Greek fraternities. I asked for a discount against our value because of the lack of a market and contrasted the multi-listing opportunities not available for the Greek circle houses.

The hearing concluded, and it was disclosed by the committee that they were planning on raising the value of our house to $85,000! I was flabbergasted and totally surprised. My response was that the ruling was not fair and that I would be forced to file a lawsuit against the LCAD for a more just and proper hearing. The Chief Appraiser told me that he thought it was fair and that no one ever sued the LCAD.

It did not take me longer after I returned to Grapevine to call and hire a Jewish law firm, Brusniak, Clements, and Cole, to represent White Owl in a lawsuit against the Lubbock Appraisal District. The law firm had no fraternity members. This lawsuit was not a fraternity issue; it was an issue of real estate value. The more we could emphasize the separation, the better we were. Both sides needed an expert witness to investigate and report their professional opinion as to value. We hired Mr. Larry Cantrell, a local Lubbock appraiser who is board-certified as an MAI appraiser. He also was not a fraternity man, and LCAD hired another Lubbock appraiser.

LCAD lawyers were Perdue, Brandon, etc., a prominent law firm with offices in numerous cities in Texas that specialized in Appraisal District values and related disputes.

The lawsuit preliminaries of expert witnesses, depositions, and generally throwing paper between law firms lasted four years! The lawsuit was finally docketed for trial in December of 1999 in Judge Blair Cherry's District Court in Lubbock.

Since our lawsuit dealt with value (our desire for a discount), I felt that all other fraternities and sororities should help with our legal expenses as they should benefit from a favorable decision by the court. We had some limited participation from two other fraternities, Sigma Alpha Epsilon and Phi Kappa Psi. But that was hardly a dent in our legal fees thus far, which exceeded $40,000 at the time of trial. White Owl did not have that kind of money, so Susan and I funded most of the legal fees.

The selection of a jury was rocky at best, especially since the jury pool consisted of hourly workers, truck and cab drivers, housewives, and a variety of other people, all from Lubbock. Only about a third of the jury pool had attended college, and none of them were in any type of social club. This did not matter because we felt that the issue involved real estate values. The stigma of "fraternity" was played down by our attorneys.

Perdue brought in a special litigation attorney to represent them in the court, and John Brusniak represented White Owl. George Nelson and I sat in as plaintiffs while David Kimbrough, the Chief Appraiser of the LCAD attended as the defense

APPRAISER OF LCAD AS A DEFENSE.

One of the jury candidates was a woman who stated that her husband was a journalist for the Lubbock Avalanche-Journal, Lubbock's sole newspaper and that he wrote several articles about Texas Tech and the fraternities. The Perdue "hot dog" litigator asked her what the subject matter was and what fraternities were involved in his writing. The juror responded and related to one article involving a fraternity and the Ku Klux Klan, with the fraternity being the plaintiff in this lawsuit. Our attorney moved to strike this juror. But I was upset since this article and story did not involve our fraternity (perhaps another, Kappa Alpha).

The damage was done—the same parallel as throwing a skunk in the jury box! I told my attorneys to ask Judge Cherry for a mistrial. Brusniak argued with me, stating we had too much money and too much time in this lawsuit to abort at this point in time. I had to remind John Brusniak that it was me who was paying his bill and that I insisted that we ask for a mistrial based on the false testimony by a potential juror. The entire jury panel had heard the testimony in the selection process, and it was my opinion that a fair trial would be impossible.

It took Judge Blair Cherry about two minutes to declare a mistrial and dismiss the entire jury panel. The lawsuit then took another road. Judge Cherry made known his views of this lawsuit and told Dave Kimbrough that he had 60 days to settle with Jerry Pittman and White Owl with a discount! He further admonished the special litigator. If a satisfactory settlement was not attained, then he would take matters into his own hands.

We settled on a 35% look-back discount, and a 30% look-forward discount for all fraternities and sororities. The look back helped us in that the refund we received for prior years almost reimbursed Susan and me for our advanced legal fees.

A couple of years later, I was inducted into the Texas Tech Greek Hall of Fame.

Chapter 43
Longaalan Wedding

Jay was living in Washington, DC, working for George Sexton & Associates, lighting experts in the architectural world. Janann Mohring, the girl of his life, worked for another architectural firm near the Pentagon. They lived in the same apartment complex, but their lives were soon to be inseparable. In the spring of 1998, he proposed marriage to Janann, and she accepted! They had been dating for some time now, back in Houston when he was finishing at Rice, and they ventured off to Europe for a summer tour before they jumped into the working world. That's when I first met (at least by phone) Janann's parents because Jay had not exactly kept us informed as to when he was coming home. Ken Mohring did not have a much better clue than I did, so we continued to "wing it," realizing that Jay would eventually call us and inform us as to his intentions.

The wedding was set for September 5, 1998, in Wading River, New York. That is in Long Island, and as some New Yorkers say, "Longaalan." It was the Catholic church where Janann grew up, and Ken was a member of their board (they might have been chairman for all I know).

Plans began to brew for parties and travel to New York. We had a wine and cheese party for our Grapevine folks to meet them. Several of them decided that they needed to journey to New York for the wedding, namely Eddy and Barbara Windom, Rick and Diane Stacy, Paul and Charlotte Moore, and Bill and Leonora Byrd, to name a few. The wine party was at Dr. Bobby Smith's winery.

We were giving Jay and Janann the White Jeep Cherokee or at least giving them a deal. They couldn't turn it down, so I needed to take it to Washington, DC.

I asked Rick Stacy to leave with me early for the wedding so he and I could play golf all the way or almost all of the way to New York. We left around August 10. We needed plenty of time to play golf. We played every day and drove at least 300 miles each day. Our first stop was at Hot Springs Village, where I had a membership there to dine and play golf. We played on the golf course with two other men who had their wives or girlfriends with them. After they heard of our new adventure, the two women wanted to go with us rather than stay with their boyfriends! We turned them down and then moved on to Alabama to the Robert Trent Jones golf courses.

I never had any reason to visit Alabama until I heard of the Robert Trent Jones Golf Trail in Alabama. The teacher retirement system of Alabama financed the courses, and the revenue continues to look after Alabama teachers' retirement. The RTJT asked about ten or so very small communities near an Interstate Highway to contribute about 600 acres of land, and the retirement system furnished the money. Soon, motels and restaurants were built nearby, and economic progress evolved as a result of the golf course. The courses are beautiful and very inexpensive to play. Rick and I play a round of golf, then take showers in the men's locker room at the Clubhouses, then drive to the next golf course.

The first stop was in the northern part of Alabama at The Shoals in Muscle Shoals, Alabama, where we met Eddy Windom and Jim Shin (Eddy's boss) for a round of golf. Each place has two 18-hole courses. Rick and I took along a bottle of scotch whiskey but never opened it because we were too busy driving to or playing golf. We were also very tired at the end of each day.

We then drove to Opelika, Alabama, where we played the two courses called The Grand National. Eddy and Jim joined us there as well. Rick and I then drove on to Raleigh, North Carolina, to play Pinehurst's famous golf courses. We stayed in the Pinehurst Hotel as well. We played two rounds of golf there. We stopped by Augusta, Georgia, to try to view the golf course there where the Masters is played every April. But the course is closed except during the Masters time and a few months before and after.

I put Rick on an airplane bound for Dallas in Raleigh and picked up Susan the same day as she was flying to join me on the rest of the trip to Washington.

We drove over to Myrtle Beach to spend the night and played golf at one of the 100 or so golf courses in Myrtle Beach. The golf there was right after a hurricane had been through there, leaving a trail of destroyed trees and messes everywhere. From there, we toured the East Coast, took walks on the beach, and meandered into Washington to give Jay the White Jeep Cherokee. There, we rented a Suburban to drive to Long Island. The wedding was at least a week away.

We drove through New York and connected with the LIE, which is short for the Long Island Expressways. One thing was for sure: there are many freeways in the New York area, and you really have to plan ahead. We did not have a GPS to guide us through to Wading River, where our hotel was and the wedding to be.

I had arranged to take three two thousand dollar cashier checks. I used one or most of one of them for the trip to New York—golf, lodging, and fun. So, I needed to cash another, but when I got to a bank in Long Island, I was informed that they did not cash Texas cashier's checks legally. What a dilemma. I thought that cashier's checks were good any place. I went to two different banks and got the same story in both places. So, I used my master card for the fishing and the rehearsal dinner.

We hired a fishing boat to take the wedding party or any part fishing in Long Island Sound the day before the rehearsal dinner. We caught a lot of fish, namely "Blues." Most of the Texas folk that came to the wedding went fishing. Ten to fifteen people went fishing, including Greer, Jay, Rick and Diane Stacy, Eddy Windom, and all of the groomsmen in the wedding-Scott Foster, Tim Hagan, Takao Kamibeppu, Rusty Morrison, and Kenny Mohring. We caught over 300 pounds of the Blues and had them filleted and delivered to Jane Mohring—Janann's mother.

Long before the wedding, Jay and Janann were instrumental in drawing architecturally the sanctuary of the Catholic church where they were to be married. Ken, Janann's father, was on the church building committee and experienced frustration with the hired architect, so he sent the plans for revamping to Jay and Janann (while they lived in Washington). They did! They sent the revised plans for the sanctuary to Ken, and the hired architect added his AIA stamp of approval. Neither Jay nor Janann was licensed to certify building plans. Nonetheless, the sanctuary was built following Jay and Janann's plans.

Bill and Leonora Byrd drove up for the wedding! I was so pleased. Leonora, a certified public accountant, had been my right arm as an employee for over twenty years, and she had made a beautiful quilt for a wedding present for the kids. Paul and Charlotte Moore, long-time friends and clients, came. Eddy and Barbara Windom were there, and we attended all of their sons' weddings. Jay and Jackie Stanley, whom we had nicknamed our son after when he was born, were there. Of course, Linda and Less Allison from Houston were there as well.

Long Island was beautiful—many trees and lots of water. Golf before the wedding and after was great even though Kenny Mohring was to get tee times for Bethpage golf course but was unable for residential reasons or whatever (we were not NY residents). Bethpage has been the site for the US Open golf tourneys.

The lobster was plentiful on Long Island. In fact, lobster tails were sold by street and highway vendors for ten bucks. Rick, Eddy, and I frequently stopped to buy some lobster tails and a six-pack of beer and have a momentary pause in whatever action we were pursuing at the rehearsal dinner went off without a hitch. We had Llano Estacado Winery prepare private labels for two cases of white wine celebrating September 5, 1998, and Julian and Janann Pittman. We gave wine bottles to each of the Texas couples that ventured to NY as well.

At the wedding, the groom's friends sat on the right side of the church, and the bride's friends sat on the left. I was pleased to see so many of our Texas friends at the wedding! The Priest's name was Father Joe Mundy, and we called him Father Joe. He was a really cool and fun-loving guy. After we were seated and before the service began, Father Joe leaned over and whispered in my ear, "How are you hitting them?" meaning, of course, my golfing swing and related hangup!!

The sanctuary was beautiful, with high ceilings and much attention given to the skylight. Before the formalities of the wedding began, Father Joe told the story about how the two people about to be married were the design architects of this new sanctuary. Susan and I were so proud. My tux buttons were about to pop off!

It was a Catholic wedding, and most of the time, I had no clue whether I was to sit, kneel, or stand up. But the reception was coming up.

The reception was at a private club with a disc jockey playing music from tapes and CDs. I had brought plenty of music with me, especially those tendered pieces like "Waltz Across Texas" and "Faded Love," sung by Ernest Tubbs and Willie Nelson, respectively. I also brought many other country and Western albums, all of which I gave to the DJ operating the music for the reception. After about two or three different times requesting that he play this music, I was getting a bit frustrated. Also, no one was dancing to his mood music either. Les Allison, Linda's husband, went to the DJ and slipped him some money, and said…PLAY "WALTZ ACROSS TEXAS" now!

He played Ernest Tubb's Waltz, and the ice was broken! All of the Texans sprang to their feet and commenced to dance, and the New Yorkers followed. The dance floor occupied the balance of the evening!

Ken and Jane Mohring had breakfast at their home the next morning. Jay and Janann had left the night before on their honeymoon. Susan and I drove out of Long Island through Rhode Island and onto Cape Cod that afternoon with the intention of touring a part of northern New York before we departed by airplane from Washington, DC. The irony would have it that we discovered after a trail hike in Cape Cod their white Jeep Cherokee with "Just Married" signs on it. It was parked in the same parking lot where we parked. We did not wait for them to return, and we left not to interfere with their honeymoon.

Chapter 44
Mexico and South America

When I was growing up in Sweetwater, I went to Mexico maybe three times, and the visits were only to the border towns of Cuna and Juarez. Mexico intrigued me, although I had only experienced the nightlife, beer, and whatever the border towns offered. There was no trouble down there, as this was during the 60s, long before drugs and violence erupted.

Susan and I honeymooned in Acapulco, Mexico, right after our wedding (1966) at the Las Brisas Hotel. We had a pink jeep at our disposal, and the beach was ours. We decided to go fishing for sailfish. We saw Glenn Jennings, a fraternity brother from Tech, there as he was recovering from a massive car wreck with two steel pins in his legs. He was living in Acapulco with two girls from New York. So, he went fishing with us. We chartered a small boat (we could not afford a bigger one), the Ma Christina. Susan caught an 8-foot sailfish. She had fallen asleep at the time when the fish hit, and with the help of the captain, she managed to land the huge fish. Glenn also caught a sailfish, but it was much smaller. I had gotten seasick and threw up over the gunnels for most of the trip. We had a grand time, especially on the return boat ride, because our boat was flying two red flags, signaling that two sailfish had been caught, while the larger boats sported mostly black flags, signaling that only sharks had been caught. We were so proud. To mount the fish was prohibitive, so we donated the fish to the natives after pictures were taken. Our honeymoon was great as we dined every evening on fresh fish and violin music there at Las Brisas. Each room had a private swimming pool, and the only drawback was the twin beds that we managed to scoot together as you expect honeymoon couples to do! Yes, the smell of a woman in my bed was the most wonderful event of our honeymoon. We jumped into bed morning, noon, and night! Wow!

After Christmas in 1973, we drove in a Volkswagen to Mexico. Susan was pregnant with Greer at the time but certainly felt like traveling with me to Mexico. We had celebrated Christmas in Sweetwater, where Mother and Eddie were to keep Jay, while we went to Mexico. Of course, Santa Claus was coming to Sweetwater that year for Jay, who was three, and GI Joe toys and related toys were high on his wish lists. His mother and I stayed up most of the night before we left for Mexico, assembling the GI Joe Helicopter (he called the Hellofacopter) and the platform for the helicopter.

We left Christmas day after Santa Claus, of course. We had purchased insurance for the car and had our papers current to cross the border. We had mapped out our course, including hotel reservations. We spent four nights in Mexico, touring San Miguel de Allende and Guanajuato principally. The hotels were colorful, the food was delightful, and the people were most gracious. The last night in Guanajuato, we attended a Rotary Club meeting. We were their guests, and it was their official Christmas party. A great many of the Rotarians were college graduates in mining (Colorado School of Mines), and almost all of them spoke fluent English. In fact, they converted the entire club program to English as a favor to us, the visitors. They also were fluent in drinking! We had before dinner, after, and during dinner drinks. And the food was good but really greasy. So, we stayed for the entire time drinking along with my fellow Rotarians.

That night, the hotel almost ran out of toilet paper for Uncle Jerry as he caught what is commonly called Montezuma's revenge. All of the night's drinking, along with the rather greasy food, did a number on me. We were to drive back to Texas the next day, and after a very rough night, we climbed into the Volkswagen with these huge pottery pots we acquired in San Miguel and headed home, stopping every now and then while I either threw up or squirted in a bar ditch.

Sometime around 1973, Adventure Tours advertised in the Dallas Morning News about all-inclusive trips to Puerto Vallarta, Acapulco, and Cabo St. Luis. We were intrigued about going back to Mexico on such a trip, except all-inclusive turned us both off. That meant three meals a day staying at a popular hotel wearing bracelets on with scheduled meals and nightly entertainment—a real regimen. At the bottom of their newspaper advertising, they indicated that they had "air only" fares to these various Pacific coast cities for a lesser price.

Susan and I purchased the air-only fare, and off we went to Cabo on the southernmost point of the Baja peninsula... We had no place to stay and no transportation. When we got off the plane, we found ten or so car rental companies and rented a Volks for $10 per day. Then, we drove 20 or so miles to town to find a place to stay. It was off-season for Cabo, the hot summertime, and the hotels had plenty of inventory. They were practically giving rooms away. We found a beautiful room right on the ocean side with lots of room and a really neat porch overlooking the Pacific. The price was right!

The next day, we arranged to go fishing. We found a small boat and an owner who was willing to take us out for a few hours the next day. Since I had melanoma cancer occurrences two different times in 1979 and again in 1994, more exposure to the sun was not acceptable. Two hours were negotiated with the boat owner, not a half day. We caught a large Dorado and a nice Tuna. After they were cleaned, we had a large amount of fish steaks. We gave the rest of the fish to the boat owner, and he was happy to take them to his family. We took ours to the hotel, and the chef in the restaurant there cooked them over garlic butter. We stuffed ourselves.

Another thing we tried in Cabo was golf. Oh, brother, it was hot, and all I remember about the game was that one time I threw my club almost as far as my ball traveled because my hands were so hot and sweaty that I could not hold on!

Greer, Susan, and I flew to Puerto Vallarta on some occasion during the 90s. It was one of those all-inclusive trips that included three meals per day and entertainment. Jay was in college or traveling Europe at the time, so it was just us three. Greer and I went fishing and caught a boatload of Tunas, which were cooked for dinner that night. Puerto Vallarta was the most charming Mexican Navy Seaport, and natives lived in a real Mexican city.

Greer and his Tuna

When Greer finished his degree at Texas Tech, he enrolled in a Texas Tech-sponsored total emersion Spanish study in Cuernavaca, a town about two hours south of Mexico City. He lived with Hector and his wife and children at their home in Cuernavaca. His study lasted for four or six months, and it was a very extensive study. He had classroom study during the day, plus living with Hector, and was confined to things Spanish in the evening at home. On the way down to Cuernavaca, his wallet was stolen, and he enrolled in another program as there were several Spanish courses offered in the city.

Susan and I wanted to visit him and Cuernavaca, so we flew to Mexico City and caught an Executive Bus from Mexico City to Cuernavaca. That was a real experience for us which made us realize that with my broken Spanish, we could get along fairly well with travel in the interior of Mexico. We stayed at a hotel there in the city and witnessed how Greer had developed relationships with the town's people. One very poor little girl had adopted Greer at the Zocalo, where she confided in him and trusted him with the money she had collected selling Chiclets (chewing gum).

We took Hector and his family out to dinner at a famous restaurant there, and we walked around the city exploring, realizing at one point in time we were in a bad area of town; we quickly exited for a better part. We rented a car and drove over to Taxco, a city known for silver production and many silver jewelry stores. That was when we learned that Greer had developed a sweetheart in a nearby town. He had some sort of relationship with her, but nothing ever developed as far as we knew.

COLUMBIA

Sometime around the year 2000, Janann's (see the Chapter on The Wedding) brother Kenny was to marry Adrianna in Bogota, Columbia. We met Kenny and Adrianna and much of their family at the wedding (Jay and Janann's). I had played golf with Kenny several times on Long Island, so we were invited to Bogota for the wedding.

Columbia was not the safest place to travel as the drug cartels were stronger than the government itself. Our US State Department had issued warnings not to travel to Columbia. But Susan and I were intrigued once again, and off we went to Bogota. Adrianna's father and mother, Miguel and Alicia, were especially concerned about our welfare, so bodyguards were hired for us, especially when we traveled by van to various parts of Bogota. One such trip involved a visit to Simon Bolivar's mansion. No sooner than we arrived at the mansion, we were hurried back into the Vans because of the presence of various unsavory characters carrying long guns.

The wedding reception was at the Bogota Country Club. I had played golf with the guys earlier at the Country Club, where we all had caddies. However, Jorge Ramirez had two caddies—one to carry his clubs and the other to carry and hold his liquor as he played golf. He and I became great friends. Jorge was married to Lilliana, a sister to Adrianna. Jorge and Lilliana lived in Venezuela with their three children, Erica, Elana, and Miguel. They later took political asylum from Venezuela and lived in the US with us for over two months. Every female at the reception wanted to dance with me for some reason, especially Marta, who also wanted to give and throw me kisses.

After the wedding and festivities, we flew out of Bogota in a small airplane to Belize, where we stayed for a few days. The exit from Bogota was eventful in that the family wanted to make sure we got safely onto the airplane. So, Alicia and her oldest daughter Monica accompanied us to the airport and made sure we got on the airplane safely. Our plane stopped in Guatemala for the night, so we walked into the city but did not see much. The next day we flew to Belize. We played golf on an island once owned by the singer Frank Sinatra. The water holes were full of alligators or crocodiles. It did not matter because if my golf ball went near the water, I would not go after it!

Another sister was Catalina, and she was 14 or so and rather bashful. She would later receive a tennis scholarship to Tyler Junior College in Texas and spend a lot of holiday time with us in Grapevine along with her niece Erica (Jorge's oldest daughter). They both loved Susan and Jerry because we fed and entertained them well, allowed them to call home (Venezuela and Columbia), and converted our computers to Spanish only (which took me forever to convert back to English!) Catalina Isasa and Erica Ramirez spent Thanksgiving with us. Catalina was the sister to Monica, Liliana, and Adriana, while Erica was the daughter of Jose and Liliana from Bogota, Columbia. Susan and I loved them both and were thrilled that they wanted to stay with us over the Holidays. Both were students and tennis scholarship recipients for Tyler Junior College, and they were too far away from home to travel there for Thanksgiving. Catalina was from Bogota, Columbia, while Erica was from Caracas, Venezuela. Both were fluent in English and spoke Spanish to each other. I converted my computer completely to Spanish, which took me several days, if not weeks, to convert it back to English! Catalina and Erica mused themselves by continuing to laugh for some 20 years!!!

Chapter 45
Grapevine's Outreach: Sister Cities

While on the City Council, we reached out to establish relationships to share ideas, cultures, and understandings. These locations included Parras de la Fuente, Mexico, Krems, Austria, Traverse City, Michigan, and Foley, Alabama. Each of these was selected having common ideals as Grapevine.

Parras, for example, has the oldest winery in all of North and South America. Krems housed another winery on the Danube, while Traverse City and Foley merely wanted to exchange ideas, services, wine, cherries, and beer or provide common ideas and relationships for their and our festivals.

PARRAS DE LA FUENTE, COAHUILA, MEXICO

Grapevine purchased a used ambulance for Parras and had it fully equipped at Baylor Hospital with all of the latest medical drugs and supplies, etc. (We later provided a school bus and two suburbans for their orphan home.) We had real problems trying to transport the fully equipped ambulance across the Texas border, as the US Customs arrested our fire marshal, Dick Ward, and detained the delivery of the ambulance for over a week. With the drug problems and the border scrutiny, no one trusted anyone. Mexico thought the US was transporting drugs their way into Mexico. Our US Senator, Kay Bailey Hutchison, had to get involved to get the vehicle across.

We drove to Parras de la Fuente in 2002, and we stayed with Lupita Arias and her daughter Adriana. The shocks on our Jeep Cherokee needed to be replaced, and Lupita arranged it with a friend. Lupita had dinner at her home and served delicious seafood, much to Susan's surprise and allergy to seafood. The next night was a BBQ when many of the town folk came to see us and wished us safe travels on Mazatlán, Mexico, on the Pacific Coast. Daniel certified that our car could travel safely over the two mountains between Parras and Mazatlán and further gave me his cell phone since he knew mine would not work in Mexico. The people were so gracious with us. The next day, we embarked, spent the night in Durango at El Governor, and took on the two mountains to the coast the next day. The road was narrow and with many curves (Cuevas Pelogrosas). The mountains were cool, and with our windows down, we could hear big trucks coming down the mountain such that we knew to get over and wait because these 18-wheelers would be taking up both sides of the road. Later, we came upon a truck that was out of diesel and blocking the entire highway. We were not going anywhere fast, so I taught the drivers to siphon diesel from another truck with a hose and slightly higher up the hill. Soon, we were underway and spent three nights at El Cid in the coastal city. We played golf at Mazatlán and ate a lot of fish!

We drove back through Chihuahua City and Ojinaga and finally spent the night at the Limpia in Fort Davis. We met with Scott Adams at the Fort Davis Water Company to determine if we could bring water to our land with our 7 acre future homesite which we had purchased on Cemetery Road there in Fort Davis in 1998.

We, citizens, took several trips down to Parras, small and large contingencies, to celebrate our City Accord with Parras, which was established. We met and made many friends there. On one visit there, I decided that I wanted to play golf at their only golf course, so I called a cab. With my limited Spanish, I was able to communicate with Daniel, the cab driver, that I wanted to go to the golf course. Daniel recognized me as a city official and took me immediately to the hospital to meet the ambulance drivers, show me the old beat-up ambulance, and explain how much they loved the new one, which they referred to as the "mobile hospital."

After getting hugs and many thanks, Daniel took me to the golf course, gave me his business card, and insisted that I call him when I finished. Golf was fun- a nine-hole golf course with elevated greens and my caddie

"Henry." Every golfer had to have a caddie on the golf course! Daniel picked me up this time in his wife's air-conditioned SUV with two of his friends, and Corona iced down in the back. We drove all over Parras, drinking beer and seeing all of the sights. I was especially interested in the aqueducts that conduct and direct water out of the mountains to the city. The water in Parras was always fresh and clean, and we never had to worry about unclean water there as you do in other parts of Mexico. About two hours later, Daniel and his two friends took me to my hotel, telling me that I owed nothing for the tour—"No Paga Nada."

Another trip to Mexico (2004 or 2005) involved driving to Parras to stay with Lupita and Adriana. We drove on to Mazatlán on this trip. We drove the black Jeep Cherokee down. We insured it with Mexican insurance and took out a permit to travel in Mexico with the Mexican authorities there in Piedras Negras, a border town on the other side of the Rio Grande from Eagle Pass, Texas.

Our departure from Mexico on this trip included a stop in Chihuahua City, Mexico, the capital of Chihuahua, a state in Mexico. Susan had read in her AAA travel books or someplace that there was a shop she could not live without visiting. So, we parked the car in an Estamineto Lot where we felt that it would be safe. And it was several blocks from this shop. Susan and I found the shop, and after an hour or so, I realized that she was purchasing more than we could carry back to the car. So, I left to get the car and bring it to the store. I stopped to purchase a new watch band on the way back and noticed there was quite a gathering of people in the town and park areas. Stands for multiple people to sit had been erected along a main corridor, and the men and women were dressed to the nine. Women with colorful dresses and men with suits and flower boutiques were everywhere. Driving the car from Estamineto to the shop was not easy because the traffic had picked up, and policemen were on every corner. A crowd was gathering.

Susan was a little concerned because it had taken me a long time to get the car. Susan does not speak Spanish, as she relied on my Spanish most of the time. She could not communicate with the shop owners or the taxis such that they thought she needed a ride to a hotel. She tried to tell them she was waiting for her husband, who went to get the car.

When I arrived, I had to tell a taxi driver that she did not need a ride. We loaded the pots and stuff and left Chihuahua City by some kind of freeway or highway that circled the city. Looking back, we saw the largest Mexican Flag flying half-mast in the downtown area. We learned later that some big Mexican official had been assassinated, and his funeral was scheduled that afternoon. The streets were about to be closed for the funeral procession. I think we left Chihuahua City just in time!

We drove on to Fort Davis, Texas, to spend the night. It was about 150 kilometers from Chihuahua City to Ojinaga, Mexico, the border town. It was raining when we crossed the border (the Mexicans call it La Frontera), and it was about 4:30 in the afternoon. The Mexican border office was closed, so we could not turn in our Mexican Tour Permit. We found out later that this was a mistake on our part!

We spent the night in Fort Davis at the Limpia Hotel. It was good to be back in Texas. It hailed cats and dogs that evening at the Limpia, and scotch whiskey tasted superb. It was a cool evening there in Fort Davis in July, and we were intrigued by the weather.

We attended the Chihuahua Desert Research Institute Member appreciation dinner there in Fort Davis. We were members of the Institute and wanted to get to know more people. We had already purchased our 7 acres of land on Cemetery Road (1998), and we spent some time looking over our land. At the CDRI dinner, we bid on a couple of items in the silent auction. One was offered by David Schmidley, the then President of Oklahoma State University. He formerly was at Texas Tech and is currently on the board of CDRI. He placed into silent auction two tickets to the Texas Tech and Ok State football game that fall together with a night's lodging at the Atherton Hotel on the campus of Oklahoma State in Stillwater, Oklahoma. Our bid of $100 was the highest bid.

Our next trip to Mexico was in 2005 or there, about when we drove my black pickup and crossed the border at Laredo, where we were detained by the Mexican border officials. It seems that when they fed my passport into the computer, I was rejected on the grounds that we allegedly had a vehicle that was never returned to the US—namely, the black Jeep Cherokee. Recall that we did not turn in our visa permit when we returned to the US a year or so ago, and as far as the Mexican government was concerned, that vehicle was still in Mexico!

Since Lupita was expecting us in Parras, we were in a pickle, to say the least. With my broken Spanish and our hearty attempt in trying to understand our plight, we figured out that we needed to prove somehow that we were married, transfer the title of the pickup to Susan, and promise that we would bring the Jeep to the border to prove its physical whereabouts.

With some very rough paperwork, we accomplished our objective, and we were off for Parras after at least a two-hour delay.

Jerry and Lupita in Monterrey Mexico

Susan and I played golf at the Monterreal Resort and Ski Club near Saltillo with Lupita's sons and son-in-law—Alfredo, Fernando, and Bobby. It was high in the mountains near Saltillo, and the weather was wonderfully pleasant and cool. The next day, I played with the guys again while Susan visited and shopped with Lupita, Adriana, and Gabriella

(Bobby's wife). We played at the Monterrey Country Club, where Bobby is a member. It was a beautiful golf course and simply a delight to play with those guys. We were unable to play only about 13 or so holes because we were to gather for a formal lunch with the entire family at the Hotel Continental where we were staying. Further, Susan and I were hosting the dinner as well. It was a typical afternoon dining experience in Mexico—lasting most of the afternoon in a very leisurely fashion. The hotel did a fine job.

The black Jeep Cherokee was given to Jay and Janann. I tried every possibility to clear my passport with the Mexican Consulate in Dallas, but I quickly learned that the only way to clear the blemish on my passport was to prove that the Jeep was in the US and not sold unlawfully in Mexico. So, I rented a trailer to take our 2004 Jeep down for Jay and Janann to drive while Susan and I towed their Jeep Cherokee to Laredo to clear the records. Janann did not want to drive our Jeep Wrangler, so she borrowed a friend's car in lieu. We parked the car and trailer at the Walmart there in Laredo and drove the Jeep to the customs office in Nuevo Laredo, Mexico. They issued a paper clearing my name after they inspected the vehicle. My passport was cleared.

On the way back to Houston to return the Cherokee to Jay and Janann, we stayed at the Hyatt Wild Oak Ranch with their compliments if we would attend a seminar about vacation home ownership, which we did. We ended up buying the Labor Day weekend at the Hyatt Wild Oak Ranch—it has been one of the best investments Susan and I have made in a long time!

A year or so later, Susan and I decided to drive to Parras and then to Mazatlán, Mexico. We crossed the Texas border at Eagle Pass, Texas (Piedras Negras). We stayed at Parras with Lupita and her daughter Adriana. Lupita was a superintendent of a private school there in Parras. We attended school the next day and witnessed the love the kids and parents had for Lupita. (Today, we have had Lupita and Adriana up to Grapevine to stay with us at least three times. Their thing is shopping at the mall!)

Lupita had a great seafood dinner at her home that evening, and the next night, Alberto and Aricelio had us all over for Barbecoa at their home. About 20 or so couples attended the Barbecoa.

Several of the men at the party wanted to inspect our car as we discussed our intent to drive from Parras to Durango and on to Mazatlán the following day. We planned to spend the next night in Durango and then the next day drive merely 120 kilometers to Mazatlán, except this involved climbing over two mountain ranges with many dangers on and only a two-lane road. That is why the men wanted to inspect our car to determine the adequacy of carrying us over a rather dangerous road. Daniel was at the party and gave me his cell phone to carry with us on the trip. My cell phone would not work in Mexico.

The curves on the road were narrow and indeed dangerous. We had a major advantage on the narrow curves with the big trucks—we could hear them coming! The mountains were cool, and we drove with our windows down. and none of the trucks had catalytic converters and made lots of noise! So, when we heard them coming, we merely pulled the Jeep Cherokee over to the side until the truck negotiated the narrow curve, taking his lane and ours, too. We yielded at least ten times during the trip as the signs said "Curvas Pelogrosas," and we could hear the rumbling of the big engines.

Mazatlán was fun. We stayed at El Cid, enjoyed the beach, played golf, and ate a lot of fish. We drove back across the mountains again but turned north at Durango to Chihuahua City and on across the border at Ojinaga, Mexico, and Presidio. It was raining in Ojinaga, and the Mexican Customs office was closed. So, we were unable to turn in our tour permit at that time. I did not think it was a big deal one way or another, only to find out later that it was a big deal. We had insured the Jeep with Mexican insurance and took out a permit to visit Mexico at Piedras Negras when we entered.

KREMS, AUSTRIA

We rented a car and drove into Germany, drinking beer at the Beer Garden in Munich, Germany. I got a speeding ticket on the Autobahn, where I did not recognize or honor the slow-down sign for an exit. Should have framed the speeding ticket! We turned the rental car in and tried the rail system. Found the trains to be quite efficient and fun to ride. More scenery was available on the train. We toured castle after castle until they began all looking alike. We went to Zugspitz, the highest point in Germany, where after riding a tram-train to the top, we boarded elevators and stepped out into the clouds really high up in the air on top of what looked like a big rock! We walked out on the viewing platform to imagine how safe Hitler would have been in this so-called Nest. I looked down and realized I was on some sort of grate that you could see through probably 600 or 700 yards below (it could have been 70 feet or even 70 miles). I am afraid of heights—ghastly so. I dropped to my knees and crawled back to the door where we entered. My fear was confirmed by the loose water in my pants.

The City of Grapevine established another sister city in Krems, Austria, on the Danube River, where the citizens produced a great white wine. A sister city accord was established with Krems, and we exchanged festival opportunities with them. Theirs was to witness the harvesting of their grapes on the banks of the Danube. Susan and I stayed at a vineyard owned by Eric. His vineyard had been in his family for many years, and his mother and father had been there before him. Doug, Laurie Evans, Tommy, and Patsy Hardy were also living at Eric's. On the primary festival night, we took a boat trip down the Danube, only to find out that Beethoven's waltz was never played on the boat!

We stayed the entire week in Krems along with Tommy and Patsy Hardy and Doug and Laurie Evans at Eric, a local winemaker overlooking the beautiful Danube River. His farmland or vineyard had been in his family for generations. Eric was not married, but we think he may have been smitten with the housekeeper who came daily to clean the rooms. Eric had his own wine cellar, and we partook of his hospitality and his wine. The rest of the Grapevine contingency stayed at a hotel down the hill. There were at least 20 or so of us from Grapevine to establish a Sister City Accord with the City of Krems. We were there during harvest time, a special and specifically festive date each year to celebrate the harvest.

We boarded a boat and cruised down the Danube while luminaries outlined the vineyards on both sides of the Danube about as far as you could see. It was beautiful, but the band never played the "Blue Danube" waltz!

We went to Vienna by train and admired the beautiful city. We lost Doug Evans for a while, but he showed up later without any explanation. Susan and I purchased some music from a great violinist.

We toured Europe a bit while over there. We flew into Zurich, Switzerland, took Euro Rail passes to travel to Munich, and then rented a car, a Mitsubishi. And yes, I tried the Autobahn for speed and got up to 140 kilometers per hour on the unlimited freeway.

FOLEY, ALABAMA, AND TRAVERSE CITY, MICHIGAN

Chapter 46
The Hammond Organ

During my junior and senior years in high school, I took organ music lessons at McMurry College in Abilene from Professor Macon Summerlin. My mother and father were in Houston most of my senior year at M.D Anderson Hospital, with my dad dying of melanoma cancer. Accordingly, I had more time for organ practice, basketball, and thespians. (Little Women, Meet Me in St Louis, and Harvey).

Going to Texas Tech, I got a job playing after-dinner music at the Plainsman Hotel. I got another job playing three or four hymns at a Lubbock funeral home for their almost daily two o'clock funeral and was paid $5.00 cash. That was good money in those days (1962) because gasoline was twenty-five cents per gallon, bread the same, and six packs seventy-five cents. So, two or four funerals each week was a bonanza!

I got some new music from my professor during Christmas when I was home and was trying it out at the funeral home before the family arrived. The deceased loved John Phillip Sousa's 'Stars and Stripes Forever'! But then, the family walked in, and the funeral director let me know rather sternly that the music was not appropriate! I thought I had been fired!

Later, I did not have time to play the organ, so I took up clothing sales, worked as a bread truck driver (Mrs. Baird's Bread), grading papers, etc.

I offered to purchase my mother's organ. She refused but much later willed it to me when she passed. In the meantime, I purchased my own organ, a Hammond C-1, for $2.0 for my own enjoyment. About 20 years later, we downsized our home to move to Fort Davis, so I had to dispose of this older Hammond.

I found a Church in West Dallas through Craigslist, which wanted an organ for their membership but did not have much money. So, I had them over to inspect and hear the organ. There were parishioners and the choir director with big lungs who showed up. I played 'True Hearted, Wholehearted, Faithful, and Loyal' for them rather loudly, then turned around on the bench and told them $300. They said 'SOLD' and handed me the money. They loaded the organ and separate speaker in their Suburban and drove off.

The Hammond organ at the Methodist Church in Fort Davis had not been played in twenty years; its wires were worn and dangerous. I replaced and rewired it. I cleaned all the tubes, oiled the motor, and vacuumed the rat pills up. It worked! The organ sat in the fellowship hall, where we worshipped most of the time. The old sanctuary next door was built in 1884 or so and was too small for larger crowds. It had an old pump organ dated 1884 that did not hold air. So, I removed the rotted leather straps screwed into the petals and replaced them with come along straps cut to fit; The bellows held air such that I was able to play the old pump organ when needed. It had a rather tinny sound, but the hymns were recognizable! But it's a real effort to PUMP and play very long songs.

One Thanksgiving service, we had the Presbyterian and Church of Christ as our guests for an Ecumenical service. Mat Miles, the Presbyterian Pastor, conducted the service, and the hymn selected was 'We gather to gather to ask the Lord's blessing." Matt insisted that we play all five long verses. I almost gagged before I finished!

Chapter 47
Our Misadventures

WRONG DAMN ROAD

One summer, we decided to go on a camping trip to the Great Smoky Mountains. We were going to tow a pop-up trailer behind a Volkswagen (BC). At each place we stopped, we merely detached the trailer and spent the night in the trailer. We had a Coleman stove that cooked most of our meals; we also had a small ice box where we kept milk and basic supplies. Jay got his first pocket knife for this trip. I had the Volkswagen (BC) worked on before we left to give me some assurance that we would not experience trouble on the trip. BC was air-conditioned and pulled the trailer quite well. We got to Gatlinburg and Pigeon Forge, Tennessee, and loved all the activities afforded us three, including the opportunity to fish on one of the rivers in the national park.

While fishing, Jay and I were casting our lines when we heard this big clap or crash of something upstream. Susan had walked off, presumably further upstream, while we fished. She heard the noise as well, and somehow, I surmised that a dam or some logs had released a gush of water upstream. I must have seen the water rising ever so slightly. I called Jay, who was in the water on a rock, to get out of the river immediately. He did, and I escorted him a few yards away from the river when all Hell broke loose with the river. A sudden gush of water, together with logs large and small, was being pushed by the onslaught of water. The rock that Jay had been standing on was at least three feet underwater during the rush. We were thankful.

We toured the area completely, looking for a particular place to stop and drop our hooks in the water, looking for that three-pound trout.

We drove up one road and down another, following the local map we had obtained. Susan's job was to study the map and give me instructions as to where to turn. After a few wrong turns, here and there, I got a little frustrated with Susan for getting us on the wrong road, such that I commented that "We are on the wrong damn road." Well, it caught on in the back seat because Jay thought that was so funny. He began repeating me steadily, saying, "Mother got us on the wrong damn road, Mother got us on the wrong damn road, etc... etc." This expression stuck because we all still laugh about map reading and being on the wrong damn road to this day.

CAMP WATONKA

7/8/09

Susan and I wanted Jay to go to Camp Longhorn near Burnet. Susan had been a counselor there for several years prior to our marriage. She knew every or almost everyone down there and made a few calls, and Jay was enrolled. He was intrigued with the western cowboy side of the camp: that is where he went during the summer of 1978, but it was not his cup of tea! He said he had no desire to return.

Jay was reading almost everything he could get his hand on, including a magazine from the Boy Scouts called Boys Life. In the magazine, he found a science camp in Pennsylvania that had a concentration on rocket ships. He was intrigued! He put up the howl and desired to go to this camp the next summer (1980). Susan and I could not imagine sending our nine-year-old so far away just because he wanted to go to a rocket ship camp. The camp (Camp Watonka) was to last two weeks, and we could hardly stand that either, but we relented. Jay had a relatively bad experience the year before at Camp Longhorn. He had been very good. He had met our and his expectations in school, advanced in rank in the Boy Scouts, and never caused any trouble at home—so why not?

We decided to let him fly to Camp Watonka, and we would drive to Pennsylvania to pick him up. American Airlines was most accommodating with a young boy's first air travel alone, as were the Camp officials who met him at the small airport nearby camp (I have forgotten the city). We talked with the camp and Jay after arrival and felt good about his circumstances. He wrote a few postcards about the camp and his rocket ship building, most of which were of little consequence, but they gave us comfort that the boy was having a good time. One postcard that he sent to Gayle Shumate included a line that nothing ever happens in camp these days except that an airplane crashed in the middle of the camp that day!

Since it was summertime and tax season long gone, driving to Pennsylvania sounded like a lot of fun for Susan, me, and Greer. We decided to leave a week before the camp was to end, giving us plenty of time to drive, stop in Nashville and Opryland, and camp through the Appalachian Mountains. We were going to tow the Holiday with our Buick station wagon. My friend, Bill Crabtree, insisted that we would be able to travel better if we towed the trailer behind his Suburban (vintage 1972). My Buick was 1978, but his Suburban did appeal to me for the comforts it afforded, not to mention the increased power a bigger engine provided.

So, off we went. We got to Sulphur Springs and had a little car trouble. The truck would not start when we stopped for gas, so we had to put a new starter on Billy's car. It was fortunate that we had trouble in Sulphur Springs because Jim Massey (Susan's cousin) came to the rescue to find and assess that we needed a new starter. We then drove to Hope, Arkansas, where the truck started to miss a few cylinder rounds of gasoline, leaving a funny sound under the hood. A mechanic in Hope, Arkansas, installed a new fuel filter, and we were on our way!

We got to Little Rock, Arkansas, and had to spend two days there. The car continued to hiss and miss, so the local mechanic convinced me that Billy's truck needed a new carburetor, spark plugs, and related spark plug wires. We were on our way again, stopped briefly in Nashville, and decided to drive further to the Blue Ridge Parkway to spend the night. We parked the trailer at a neat trailer park and then drove to a trailhead to do some hiking with Greer. The truck, however, would not turn off! After many attempts, I unhooked the battery connection, causing the engine to die after much hissing and moaning of the engine. Oh boy, more trouble from this borrowed car!

Realizing that more trouble may lay ahead, we drove/limped into Wytheville, Virginia, and parked the trailer. Hoping that without the trailer, the suburban with the new starter, carburetor, fuel filter, wires, etc., would get us to Camp Watonka in time to pick up Jay. Wrong! We drove toward Hagerstown, Maryland, when bam, bam, a loud noise came from the engine. We limped very slowly into a Chevrolet dealership in Hagerstown, only to find out that the cam had blown out of the engine and that it would need a new cam and drive chain. So much for Billy's Suburban!

I went to the new car sales department and promptly purchased a new suburban! It was a royal blue 1980 model. I called Billy to inform him of all the problems and that I had no intention of driving his car one mile farther. I asked if I could buy his truck; he replied that it was very valuable to him and it was not for sale. I planned on trading it in on my new suburban. My banker, Roger Cloud, was most accommodating and made my $9,800.00 check good for the purchase.

Jay was sitting at the Camp Watonka gate, looking for us to arrive! It was so exciting to see him. He certainly did not recognize the new blue Suburban but said, instead, that he recognized the burr haircut that Greer was sporting! We said our prayerful thanks for getting us there on time! We toured the camp, examined where the plane had crashed in camp, and examined Jay's rocket ships and other crafts.

On the way home, we toured Gettysburg and the battlefields of the Civil War. Then we spent the night in Hershey, Pennsylvania, at the wonderful Hershey chocolate park. We toured the plant and ate our We shared our share of Hershey bars, both with and without almonds! We returned to Hagerstown to pick up Billy's suburban and tow it to Wytheville, Virginia, to spend the night in our trailer. Leaving Billy's suburban at the trailer park, we drove to the Grand Old Opry theme park in Nashville and spent the night. The next day, Susan and the boys went to the park for fun and rides while I drove back to Wytheville to pick up the old suburban. I towed it back to the Little Rock, Arkansas, airport and called Billy to say that he could pick it up there.

I returned to Nashville to pick up Susan and the boys. We drove home. Wow, what a trip! What a vacation! I never borrowed another vehicle again as I had learned my lesson!

OUR LAST TRIP TO PARRAS

Our last trip to Mexico was a few summers ago (August 2015), and it was most fun and eventful! We had been spending our long summer here in Fort Davis since 2007, when our home construction was completed, while we spent our winters in Grapevine after we attended Grapevine's sister city committee meeting. We decided to join Grapevine's contingency in Parras de la Fuente, except we would drive down from Fort Davis, crossing the border at Presidio/Odinga, then onto Chihuahua City and Torreon, and Parras.

So, we purchased insurance for the Ford F150 pickup, and off we went. Parras had their usual festival in celebration of the harvesting of the grapes, and Lupita and Adriana insisted we stay with them in their home. After crossing the border into Mexico several times at Laredo and Piedras Negras, we thought we knew the ropes about customs, border registration, and rules. Wrong! We knew we had to register our car shortly after crossing and receive the famous sticker for our windshield. The customary stop was 5-15 miles inside the border (at least for Laredo and Piedras), but after driving 80 kilometers inside the border and not finding the issuance building, we doubled back to Ojinaga to find the office needed just inside the border. Whew! Our truck could have been confiscated if we did not have this famous sticker.

Lupita was a great host, as usual. We attended a dinner sponsored by the Rotary Club, another by the City of Parras, and then another by Casa Madera Winery. Every day included breakfast with Lupita and Adriana, and then we were off on tours and festivities with the 16 members from the Grapevine contingency.

Our trip home was the eventful part. We spent six days in Parras and then started back to Fort Davis.

Mexico has a lot of toll roads, and we confined our driving, for the most part, to paying the tolls because they were fairly nice and had clean restrooms along the way. The trip home would take 10 hours of driving, and we planned to spend the night in Chihuahua City. Instead of turning on the toll road to Durango, I missed it and went through Torreon and later Gomez Palacio, two cities comprised of about 2 million citizens. This was NOT a toll road. We were desperately trying to find the right highway to Chihuahua City.

Finally, we thought we found the right road, so we followed the appropriate signage. We were in the right lane, signaling to the right onto a one-way street when a postal worker on his Vespa scooter passed me on the right. He hit me on the right side! It was clearly his fault!

Two- and one-half hours later, soldiers, the police, Sanborn Insurance Company, and the postal authorities all had arrived and were scratching their collective heads. Some real nice people had stopped who witnessed the accident and rose to our help in that they spoke good English and offered interpretation as to the goings on....

The policeman had my driver's license and was telling me that I was going to appear before a Mexican judge tomorrow morning, and I was to pay a fine of $280. A fine? But it was not my fault! Apparently, I was outnumbered, and I was beginning to realize that the accident was 'my fault' by consensus! You see, I was the "gringo" in the crowd. Susan and the really nice lady interpreter started talking with the Police officer, asking him what it would take to get my license back and let us return to the United States. Another problem existed regarding our windshield permit in that if we did not return the sticker to the border by midnight tomorrow night, we would forfeit our $400.00 bond that we posted when we crossed.

The Police officer waited till everyone else had left when he said he would take $100 US dollars and return my license. I had to scrape $70, and Susan had $30, so we tendered the money and were on our way to Chihuahua to spend the night!

We spent the night at The San Francisco, a downtown hotel, and ate dinner in their dining room. It was a refreshing and good experience after a very trying day.

We only had about a three-hour drive the next morning to Ojinaga, so we had the truck serviced at the local Pemex station, and off we went. With only 22 kilometers left to cross the border, our truck started to heat up, and it eventually stopped. It was overheated! I raised the hood and noticed that the water cap was missing, and all of the engine's water had leaked out, causing the truck to overheat.

We had four beers, rodeo cool, in the cooler, and no water! I called 911, but there was no answer. I called AAA, no answer. I called Sanborn Insurance Company, who connected me to the towing department. The man who answered was in Mexico City, and he assured me that he could send a town truck out but wanted to know where Ojinaga was—close to Piedras Negras. He had no clue! So, I hung up. I talked with a hotel in Ojinaga, who told me to call back in 30 minutes that he had a friend with a tow truck. I did, and he never answered.

Finally, I tried calling the sheriff of Jeff Davis County, Rick McIvor. I Delivered a desperate call for help to his voicemail. By this time, we had consumed two bottles of beer. He called back and said he would do what he could. About 30 minutes later, I received a phone call from Mr. Pittman, and my name is Manuel Rohana. I am the mayor of Ojinaga, and I am sending a police car and possibly a town truck out right now."

A few minutes later, a white Ford pickup with lights flashing drove up, and two nicely dressed men with starched white shirts) with pistols on their belts, handed Susan and me a large bottle of water. It was only 104 degrees outside, and we were hot. He put two large bottles of water into our vehicle's engine and made a makeshift cap out of a plastic bag. He followed us into OJ, where we stopped at an auto parts store, but of course, it was closed because it was siesta time (2 pm). The mayor then arrived along with another police car, which just happened to have a Ford F150 water cap in a box. He screwed it on the truck, and everything worked! I offered to pay for their services, but they insisted that nothing was owed. "No paga nada."

Apparently, the Sheriff of Jeff Davis, Rick McIvor, called the Sheriff of Presidio, Danny Domingo, who in turn called the mayor of OJ. All of them were truly our angels from heaven!

I wrote thank you letters to The Mountain Dispatch, to The Marfa Centennial, and the Sheriffs of Jeff Davis and Presidio counties expressing our story and gratitude.

Chapter 48
Palace Theatre, Rawls

The year 2000 came in with no computers crashing, as everyone had predicted. All computers functioned, and the clocks turned over satisfactorily. Bill Clinton finished his second term, and the country then elected George W Bush. I voted for George Bush over Al Gore in a very close race.

A client of mine won the Texas Lottery prize of 24 million! His mother called me one that morning and told me her son (34 years old) won the lottery last night and needed to come to see me as soon as possible. We agreed to meet at 9 am, and in the meantime, I called the Lottery Commission to confirm the winning number. When Mike Parsons and Ann Parsons, his mother, arrived, we went to the copy machine, copied the winning ticket, and placed the original in an envelope. Mike said he was drinking beer with a few of his friends last night, and when the lottery numbers were called out, he quietly put the winning ticket back in his shirt pocket without telling his buddies of his fortune. I told Mike to put the ticket and envelope and place it in a safety deposit box at the bank while we had the necessary legal papers drawn up.

We agreed on a plan to hire an attorney to draw up a partnership/joint venture, allocating the bulk of the annual proceeds to Mike and sharing annual amounts with each of his two brothers, as well as his mom and dad. Coolio Enterprises was the named partnership, and Coolio's agent and attorney went to Austin, Texas, to pick up the first annuity payment later that month after the papers had been drawn and signed.

The Texas Lottery Commission never knew the name of the winner. That is the way Mike wanted it.

I decided not to run for a fourth term on the Grapevine City Council. Three (nine years) were enough. Darlene Freed had worked with me now for several years, and she coveted the job, so she decided to run and barely beat Harlan Jewett for Place 4.

Before I stepped down from the Council, there was a political disagreement brewing in Grapevine. A few years earlier, the City Council had purchased the Palace Theatre (my idea), a structure for movie shows built-in 1940 next door to the Buckner Cash Grocery Store. The Council formed the Grapevine Heritage Foundation, a nonprofit entity to own the Palace Theatre. The Theatre was in poor shape; it leaked rainwater and needed many repairs. The newly formed GHF wanted to restore the old Palace and acquire the old Buckner Cash Grocery that now housed a retail shop selling mostly blue jeans and other clothing. Under their leadership was Ron Emrich, who was soliciting money from the citizens of Grapevine to accomplish this massive restoration. Emrich had raised some money and began hiring consultants to devise a conceptual plan for restoration which involved sound and related needs of the new Theatre. Paul McCallum, the executive director of the Grapevine Convention and Tourist Bureau, took exception to the solicitation and spending habits employed by Emrich. They were truly at cross purposes. Emrich had enlisted support from Mark Manus and Marianne Charpentier, CPA, and Melva Stanfield, both members of the Grapevine Heritage Board. McCallum worked for the City Manager as Executive of the Convention Visitors Board. The battle lines were drawn.

Ted Ware, a City Council member, and Bill Tate, Mayor, asked me to chair the restoration of the Palace Theatre, including the creation of the Theatre in the round next door at the old grocery store. It would include raising money and restoring the political unrest that was created by Ron Emrich and his lieutenants. Ron Emrich was fired; Mark Manus and Marian Carpenter demanded a return of their money contributed to the cause. The tax-exempt entity under Section 501(c)3 for the Heritage Foundation was in jeopardy. Accordingly, all sums of money could be refunded.

I told Councilman Ware and Mayor Tate that I would accept the chair of the Palace Theatre with one provision. I estimated that it would take at least 3 million dollars, and to the extent that I could not raise all of the money needed, they would find or borrow the difference so that when we started construction, we all could see it to the complete finish. They agreed.

For the next three years, I chaired the restoration of the Palace Theatre and the creation of the Theatre in the round next door. Tommy Hardy, City director of Development, was to be my right arm in assisting me in any way, and Susan Batte at City Hall was to be my secretary and aide. We met every Wednesday at 1 pm, the minute Rotary was over. We continued to meet every week, sometimes more than that, for three years.

We hired an architect, we hired a construction company, and then we went for bids to complete the project. The final number exceeded 5 million dollars! The Council told me to proceed.

The Grapevine Heritage Foundation Board, under the chairmanship of Melva Stanfield, was initially mixed and divided on the political happenings. The first meeting that I had as the newly appointed member had an even split of 6 to 5 to approve the minutes of the last meeting. Melva later rallied to my side when she realized that the Palace was going to become a reality.

I needed to borrow at least 3 million to get started, so I went to six banks for a loan of $500,000 each, but each bank had to make a contribution of $50,000 to the cause. Drs Ed and Minnie Lee Lancaster gave enough money to have the new Theatre in the round named after them, namely the Lancaster Theatre. And CY and Shirley gave money for the Palace Theatre. Many businesses contributed money, including Classic Chevrolet.

We applied to the Texas Historical Commission for recognition and were granted. We had to go before the Grapevine Historic Preservation Commission for permission to extend the building size by 25 feet into the street. They approved, but one of their members asked why the "colored-only" entrance was eliminated. I replied that I was not interested in restoring that part of history! She made the motion to deny our application, but her motion died for lack of a second. The application for our restoration then passed 5 to 1.

The stage was extended 14 feet to accommodate live performances, the orchestra pit was removed, and seats in the Palace were named for $250 each. The green rooms were named, and hundreds of bricks were sold for $25 to $1000 each. We raised more than $3 million dollars when we finished. And the Council picked up the balance. Tom Durant at Classic Chevrolet, Drs. Minnie Lee and Ed Lancaster and Cyrus and Shirley Holley gave big bucks.

We had a grand opening with an official ribbon cutting and celebration of the new look on Main Street Grapevine. Our black-tie dinner included Bernice Hatcher playing Star Frank's piano during the dinner and Tenors from the University of North Texas singing for us afterward (my request). Jay, Janann, and Greer all came to the opening.

The National School Board convention was held in San Francisco in April of that year. Susan and I flew out later than most of the other school board members, and when we arrived at the Fairmont Hotel, they did not have a room for us except for a suite of rooms above the main entrance to the hotel. It was a great suite with all the beautiful flags outside our many windows. It was so large we had to throw a party for all the school board members and their wives/husbands. Penny Bigbie, Jack Dortch, Jeannie Hrnatsky, Walt Milner, Joe Deupree, and Steve Humphrey were some of the school board members who served with me during the six years I was on the School Board. Don Bigbie (Penny's husband) took all the spouses on a Napa Valley wine tour while we attended school board professional education seminars. Boring!

Susan and I had season tickets for Texas Tech football games in the Stadium Club. We have expanded our giving to Tech to include us as Scholarship Donors for the athletic department, which gave us certain annual perks. We started giving to Tech several years earlier when we purchased memorial bricks at the Market Center in memory of my aunt and uncle who attended Texas Tech—Aunt Iona Bennett, who lived in Roscoe, Texas, and Uncle Merlin H. Hastings, who lived and taught school in Kress, Texas.

We also purchased a bench seat at the Alumni Center at Texas Tech next to the Stadium and a grove of trees at the new English building. Two trees were planted in honor of Gayle Shumate and in memory of Bill Weiner, an old friend.

We got beaten very badly by Nebraska that fall, and somehow, I learned that Jerry Rawls, my old roommate, was at Tech that weekend making a large gift to Tech. I called him, and we met late that night at the 50-yard line restaurant and drank scotch till past 2 am. We spent the evening catching up and learning of his 40 million dollar gift to our university. We met Pam Peden, whom Jerry later married. It was good to catch up, lick our wounds after the Nebraska loss, and be proud of our university.

Jerry Rawls and Pam

Tech named the business college after Jerry Rawls. He also gave another 8 million to build a beautiful golf course, which they named after him. We had set up a foundation for our fraternity, and he endowed it with 5 million dollars to provide scholarships for all academically exceptional members of Phi Gamma Delta, our fraternity. For the house corporation, for which I continued to be treasurer, he perpetually endowed the insurance and real estate taxes with one-half million dollars.

Jerry's heart is as big as all outdoors! His generosity is unparalleled and clearly signifies his love and intent to reward his university for what it has meant to him. And I am very proud that he was my roommate in undergraduate school. His gifting has prompted Susan and me to endow undergraduate honors students with the opportunity to study abroad.

Chapter 49
Triathlon, Elberta

I sold the remaining land on Highway 114. Gary Kirkland and I had bought 32 acres in years past, and when Gary was to declare bankruptcy, we split the 32 acres into two 16-acre tracts. The Highway Department condemned 2 acres for Highway 114 expansion, and they paid me cash in condemnation. I kept the oil and gas royalties. I made a handsome profit while it continued thereafter as I collected the royalties, as will Jay and Greer after we die.

I paid the real estate taxes on the 7 acres in Fort Davis and Susan, and I had started dreaming about its future.

George W Bush was elected President, and Greer flew up to Washington to join Jay for Bush's inauguration as the 40th President of the United States. I was a Republican at that time, as I had voted for Regan and other Republicans before. When Bush declared war on Iraq, it was obvious that such a war would cost a billion dollars per month. The very next week, Bush helped get a massive tax cut for the rich people in our country. Capital gains, interest income, and dividend tax rates were lowered to 10%, which helped the rich immensely and did nothing toward paying for a recently declared war. I then became a Democrat!

ELBERTA, OUR LAKE CABIN

Lake Elberta was a private lake south of Sulphur Springs, Texas, where a long history of Waits and Sanders owned a cabin or two periodically from the 1930s or so. Susan's grandfather wrote the bylaws for Lake Elberta Fishing and Hunting Club in 1939. A cabin still existed when Jay and Greer were living at home attending school in Grapevine, and we would go to the Lake on occasion. Aunt Susan and Bill Riddell frequented the cabin more than Jane and Dub. It was a one-room cabin with a separate porch and kitchen. During the winter, the cabin was heated with a wood-burning stove, and in summer had a window cooling unit. The cabin leaked during rainy conditions. You could feel the wind blowing through the walls.

The ownership of Lake Elberta is in the form of a stock certificate. The land is owned by the Association of Members. Susan Riddell and Elizabeth Waits owned their one certificate together. Susan and I made an offer to Susan for her one half, and she accepted, while Gram gave us her half. Jay designed a cabin to our satisfaction, and we hired Joe Jennings to build it. We hired a bulldozer to raze the old cabin. I put a red dye in the concrete trucks when they arrived to pour the slab, which was red from top to bottom.

We designed a metal cabin with Galvalume corrugated metal, and when the truck came to deliver the metal. All Hell broke loose with some of the other owners at Elberta. Chibby Turner told the board that the Pittmans were building a barn at Lake Elberta. A board meeting was called immediately, and I was invited to come to the Lake to explain my construction with metal.

I had already read the club's bylaws, and there was no mention of the type of materials required for cabins. It did preclude modular and manufactured homes but was silent about constructed corrugated galvanized construction. Since this was happening during my busy tax season (February 2000), I could not attend, so I wrote the board a letter with magazine articles of homes with metal in varying parts of Texas (Jay had supplied me with Texas Architectural Digest and other magazines). I explained with a metal façade that did not have to be painted, termites could not eat it, and it would not burn. It was chosen to enhance leisure and minimize repairs. I also explained that their bylaws were silent regarding building materials.

About a week later, Bob Weaver (who must have been the President of the club) called to tell me that the board could "live with your cabin."

I sent airfares to Jay and Janann to come to inspect Joe Jennings's construction. I rented a van at Caps to accommodate our entire family, including Gram and Greer, and we drove over to Longview to eat some seafood at Johnny Cases. Jay was pleased with the construction. I later found out Jay was using our cabin's design in his architectural portfolio of drawings for his degree program at Texas A&M.

We were the first to install a dish television reception at Lake Elberta and the first to have a sprinkler system to water the flower beds. Now, almost everyone has satellite televisions and sprinkler systems.

Later, I was elected to the Board of Directors at Lake Elberta to serve as their treasurer and bookkeeper, and I was elected to the Board of Directors of Linkside Homeowner Association and appointed their treasurer as well. I paid their bills, collected the dues from the 29 or so cabin owners, published quarterly financial statements, and reported to the President and Board of Directors.

Highway 2305 was in poor repair and awfully neglected by Hopkins County. Potholes and water-worn asphalt were everywhere on the road. I compiled a listing of assessed values of the cabins on our land and surrounding neighbors to present as a lobbying effort to convince this country to repave our road. I demonstrated that there was more assessed value down our road to convince them to pave our old, worn-out road. It worked! They put a new asphalt layer down over the old.

I served as treasurer and business manager of Lake Elberta for ten years and stepped down in 2022.

The Pittman Trail at Lake Elberta

Chapter 50
Family Affairs

THE TWINS HAVE ARRIVED

Texas Grandpa feeds his grandson, Jack

I lobbied long and hard to convince Janann and Jay to allow the birth of their twins to occur in Texas. I even offered to hire a private jet and pilot to fly them all to Texas, including her doctor, but insurance or something else prevented the occurrence of 7th-generation Texans. The twin boys were born July 19, 2002, in MARYLAND, some foreign country or state. Noah Waits Pittman was born first, and then bringing up the rear was John Caulder Pittman. We drove up to Bethesda, Maryland, to see our new grandsons. I wore my ten-gallon cowboy hat to greet them at the Hospital. They were not really impressed. Ken and Jane Mooring were at the Hospital when we arrived in town but left before we got to the

Hospital.

About a month later, in August, the twins were to be Christened at the Catholic Church there in Maryland. Catholics baptize or christen their babies VERY soon after their birth. So, we flew up for the big event. There were many people coming to this event, mostly Moorings, so a house needed to be rented, and lunch needed to be catered. Many pictures were taken, and much celebration followed.

GRAM'S CAR

Linda and Susan shared various issues regarding the care and upbringing of their mother, Janie, Gram, and Dainty. One issue was her car, especially when the dent in the side of her Mercury Marquis occurred "when a building hit my car," her response when asked. They were dubious about her driving skills; her safety was paramount. I told Gram that when negotiating major streets like Preston, Hillcrest, or Mockingbird started to bother her, including changing lanes, speed, and red lights, she might let me know.

It wasn't much longer that she called me. I sold her Mercury on eBay. She was happy, and Linda and Susan were happier.

Later that year, I flew to Washington in November to help Jay and Janann load their worldly possessions on a truck to be driven to their new home in Houston. What fun I had helping my son return to his home state. When we crossed the state line, Jay kissed the Texas ground! The pink bedroom was repainted before I flew home to Grapevine. Pink just would not do even for the twins!

My Aunt Vesta Stephens, who lived with her gay son Kenneth Ray in Van Horn, Texas, died. She was my mother's oldest living sister. Aunt Vesta was married to Lee Stephens, who worked for the Texas Pacific East/West railroad. Her brother, Mildred Hanson Hastings (Uncle Buddy), survived her and all of the family of 11 children.

Dorothy Brown celebrated her 80th birthday, and I sent her a bouquet of roses. She lived in Fort Stockton. She was my surrogate mother in 1944 when I was born. Her husband was killed in Normandy. She moved in with Mother and Daddy during those tough times for her. She changed my diaper as much as my mother during 1944 and 1945!

THE TEXAS WEDDING

Greer and Angie announced their wedding plans to be at Comfort, Texas, at a B and B on the Guadalupe River. Susan and I were so pleased that we immediately went to the Kerrville/Comfort area to begin our planning and learn how we could participate. Clark Pfluger, my pledge brother, introduced me to the Comanche Tres Country Club, a new club with a beautiful golf course. We arranged with the club to have the rehearsal dinner there and a prenuptial golf tournament with all of Greer and Angie's friends, as well as mine and Susan's. My foursome included Clay Allison, Hal Hunter, and Floy Wallace Pittman. Clay Allison was 12 years old, Linda and Les's son. My roommates from college were all there: Jerry Rawls, Dennis Rawls, and Keith Winslow. Hal Hunter, the husband of Susan's best friend, Sarah, was a Parkinson's patient and a good sport all around about his plight; Floy Pittman was my first cousin and about 78 years young and a lot of laughs and fun. Jerry Rawls was my roommate in college, and he and his wife, Pam, flew in from California; Dennis Rawls from Medford, Oregon; and Keith Winslow, a dentist in nearby Kerrville. The golf game (best ball) was so much fun! Thank you, Angie and Greer! The rehearsal dinner at the Country Club included party favors of a bottle of Angie and Greer specially labeled white wine from Llano Estacado Winery in Lubbock.

Gram, Susan's mother, arrived at the Riverside wedding via golf cart, and Rick and Diane Stacy arrived late for their grand entry.

The reception and dance were spectacular. The dance included an eclectic group of people: Aggies, Red Raiders, and Fijis. And all of our friends. There were many war chants, school songs, and hand signals. An Aggie was getting married to a Red Raider! Joe Love and George Nelson stole the show by leading the chicken dance!

GREER'S MEDICAL TRAUMA

Several years later, after Crawford Dill Pittman had been born and just before Adelle Elizabeth Pittman was here to rule the roost, Greer began having vision problems out of his right eye. He consulted with an ophthalmologist and others. His eye was examined, and it was determined that there was a tumor the size of a grape behind the eye. Greer consulted with Dr. David Barnett, the head of Neurosurgery at Baylor Hospital, and it became clear that the tumor had to be removed. Barnett and a leading eye surgeon performed the surgery at Baylor with the risks of damaging and perhaps severing the optical nerve, which would blind that eye forever.

The surgery took several hours, and the tumor was carefully removed with brilliant success. After the very risky and delicate surgery, Dr. Barnett told me and Susan that God's hand was involved in the surgery.

I spent the night at the Hospital with Greer after the surgery. He was heavily sedated for a long while, and I think my son was pleased that I was there in the room with him when he came to early the next morning.

TEXAS TECH FINAL FOUR

In the winter of 2020, Texas Tech basketball was the shining star for me, Susan, and our son Greer! Under the astute coaching of Chris Beard, the team amassed an outstanding record of 31 wins and 7 losses for the year. They lost to West Virginia in the Big 12 tournament and later received an at-large bid to play in the NCAA tournament, which included victories against Northern Kentucky, Buffalo, Michigan, and Gonzaga. They qualified for the final four in the NCAA tournament and beat Michigan State. The NCAA National Championship game was for Texas Tech to play Virginia in late March of 2020 at St Paul, Minnesota.

Susan, me and Greer followed the team to watch every game, including losing to West Virginia in the Big 12 championship, the Sweet Sixteen, the Elite Eight, and the Final Four, with the Tech Red Raiders winning all of them to qualify for the National Championship game against Virginia.

The better or best was still to come, and that was how I could join my son, Greer, in St Paul for the game on such short notice. Greer was already in St. Paul since his boss, Steve Tabor, was so generous to purchase and give him tickets for the final four!! Needless to say, Tech fans booked every flight out of every town in Texas, but I found an early flight out of Midland, Texas, to Madison, Wisconsin, where I rented a car and headed only 320 miles to St Paul off for St Paul. By the way, there were 22 other avid Tech fans who also rented cars in Madison for the long drive.

I called Greer about my itinerary regarding my progress to the twin cities, and when I got there, I drove down the street where he instructed me with the windows open and was thrilled to hear "Dad" three times. I picked him up to get a beer and our game memorabilia (shirts, hats, Final Four, etc.). We could not sit together, but Texas Tech people were really loud and in force.

Tech lost the game with Virginia after one overtime period. The score was 85 to 77, and Culver, Odiase, Moretti, Owen, Mooney, and Chris Beard made us so proud of the grand moment!

Greer and I drove 230 miles South to Des Moines, Iowa, for me to catch my plane back to Texas while Greer then took the rented car west to Sioux City, Iowa, for him to fly home with about one hour's sleep.

Greer and I had a fine time.

A GREAT FATHER/SON MEMORY AND EXPERIENCE.

Chapter 51
Buy Low, Sell High – Passions And Pride

Overwhelmed by grandchildren

I have had more successful and profitable results in my life than losses. I have had a very successful and fulfilled marriage. I have enjoyed good health and out-of-door experiences.

Financial and early on in our marriage, we borrowed money to finance washers and dryers, purchase a second car (BC), and purchase a sail boat. Each time I viewed debt and particularly the payment or reduction of debt to be a way toward our nest egg. Every payment was building equity. I bought vacant lots, discounted Braniff Airway bonds, and real estate of sorts where there was always a clear upside view of possible profit. I kept all of my investments in minerals and never waivered. Oil and gas royalties were always maintained and never sold.

I practiced a philosophy of buying low and selling high, and it worked.

Dear Noah, Jack, Crawford, Adelle,

You guys were born between chapters, and you seemed to be having fun and establishing values of character on your own. I funded your college nest egg with a 529 plan for each of you that should help out with your college expenses. I have also created a Vanguard Account for each of you with some starter investments. This is intended to teach you to save and invest your dollars wisely.

I want the best for each of you, and I hope to leave this world with something greater than a hot check for each of you.

Thank you for loving your grandmother and me, or perhaps you fooled us both!

SEX, CIGARS, AND CIRCUMCISION

Sex is wonderful!

Our typing teacher in high school was so good-looking in the eleventh grade that we guys all got excited when she gave us close-up instruction. The typewriter above our erection rose an inch or two every time. Some things create this male drive more than others. A very active date that got sexually involved by the size of an erection, wet pants, and wet dreams were sometimes common, and manual means of relief occurred occasionally, namely masturbation. Sex with the female was a dream but certainly to be enjoyed with adequate intelligent thinking, namely, after marriage. The consequences for me to think otherwise were dire, namely pregnancy, career-ending, and fatherhood. Not unlike the Johnny Milsap song, "I am a one-woman man; our world lives by a little gold band..." Susan has my love and all of it.

Susan and I honeymooned after our marriage (1966) in Acapulco, Mexico, at the Las Brisas resort. The rooms had a private swimming pool for each and twin beds in each. We finally had big plans, and the twin beds were immediately combined morning, noon, and night!

Sex is wonderful.

Smoking started in college as I studied late for accounting and working the problems. I smoked little cigars and water pipes. I never smoked cigarettes. Cigars were celebration vehicles, but they started an addiction, and I inhaled the smoke. In college fraternities, we had 'smokers' in lieu of rush parties. Smoking, for me, lasted probably 35 years of my adult life. Cigars, both large and small, were habit-forming. I quit smoking about ten years ago when I realized that my lungs had been damaged and my stamina was not the same. I am gaining some of them back, but they will never be perfect again had I not smoked at all.

I am glad that I stopped and wished I had never started.

My father, my grandfather and all of my uncles were not circumcised. That is, the skin surrounding the penis had never been removed as in a tradition or some study that was published. It was sometimes a bit embarrassing in the basketball gym dressing room for me to expose my privates in the shower or dressing room because most of my fellow basketball players were circumcised with their skin removed. In those days, I did not know why, but It really does not make any sense to me. Sex has been easy and wonderful as well as masturbation when I was younger being uncut. If God did not want to protect the penis then why did he design the foreskin? Think about it before the issue or decision arises for you!"

Chapter 52
Citizen Of The Year and Golfing

George Bush was president, and 911 occurred in New York. I was a Republican in those days, voting for Reagan and the Bushes, both George H W Bush and George W (Molly Ivins called him Shrub in her book) When he declared war on Afghanistan in response to the New York bombing and the next week declared a tax reduction for the wealthy, which basically cut dividends, interest income, capital gains to a flat 10% percent, I had no idea how we could finance a war that cost billions of dollars each month at the same time the rich got a tax break. So, I turned Democrat or Independent to vote intelligently.

Susan retired from teaching in 2003, and we rented her a convertible. We went to Padre Island in celebration of her retirement. The pressure was soon to be mine to retire as well. We took the Rocky Mountaineer train trip through British Columbia, which included Banff, Canada, Jasper, and Lake Louise glaciers, and beautiful railway scenery. The food on the train was fabulous!

I purchased a twenty-five-long camper trailer and entered into a hunting lease at Eddie Hodges' place near Cameron, Texas. Greer and his new father-in-law John, Hob Gibson, and Larry Flynn all agreed to join me in the hunting lease. I installed a water tank to feed the trailer, but the hunting was not stellar. We did harvest a few deer, turkeys, and quail. Greer started to work on his Masters of Horticulture at Tarleton in those days, so his interest in hunting was a bit diluted, and understandably so! He was pursuing his dream of working out of doors doing what he loved and wanted. November 2004, we went to Nebraska and met Pam and Jerry Rawls there for the Nebraska Texas Tech game. We beat them like a drum there and loved it. That Christmas, we gave Greer and Angie a special shotgun for Christmas that I fell in love with at Bass Pro. Susan gave me handmade boots for Christmas that I later took to Fort Davis.

We went to Lafayette, Louisiana, to accompany the Tech golf team in a tourney there. We went through Houston to see the twins, but Ken and Jane were there, so all we could do was have dinner to see the twins there in Houston. We stayed in a local hotel after dinner with all. We were thrilled to see Jack and Noah!

My friend and partner, Mike Mariast, was pleased to see us in Lafayette. He and Paul Rider are my partners in the ownership of our townhome in Colorado, Lake Haus B-4. Mike owns a drilling company among his various other investments, which includes the La Triumph Country Club and golf course in Lafayette. He is a true Cajun and a very enjoyable fellow. He asked me continually when I was coming down to Louisiana to see him and Naomi. He says, "Jerri, (that's Cajun for Jerry) when u comin down to Lafayette---I cook you Cajun fuud, we play golf, and then we both go get drnk"!

We went to California to see Jerry and Pam in January 2004, played a lot of golf, and ate well, but we did not play Pebble Beach, much to my disappointment.

Jay Stanley was President of the downtown Rotary Club in San Antonio. I flew down for his last or one of his last meetings as President. He did not know I was going to attend. He was totally surprised, and it brought a tear to both of our eyes. He was pleased, and so was I! In the Spring of 2005, at the annual Grapevine Chamber of Commerce banquet, Ted Ware, my former fellow City Council member, announced and awarded me the Citizen of the Year Award! I was surprised but not unexpected. Six years school board member, nine years City Council member, and three years as Chair of the Palace Theatre restoration were announced as some of my accomplishments. It was a real honor and thrill to be named DE Box Citizen of the Year and to join many great pioneers from Grapevine dating back to the early 1960s.

The twins were growing like weeds, but more importantly, their twin beds were getting shorter for them and me, especially when we stayed there, so we bought them new twin beds! Much longer and more comfortable! That is when Ken and Jane were not there at the same time.

My desire to retire was creeping up on me and getting louder in my ears. I hired Joe Jennings to build us an outdoor porch to add to the existing one with red concrete. In later years, we encased the initial area with galvalume left over from the Fort Davis home construction to close in and air condition the porch. These improvements expanded the cabin and gave us some most enjoyable living areas with large windows.

Susan and I worked diligently for Main Street Festivals in May each year and Grapefest in September for twenty or so years. Susan was the official photographer and walked up and down the festival with her camera capturing magnificent photos of every volunteer possible. I was the captain of the Rotary Club's beer booths annually. These festivals started in the early 90s with the mere closing of Main Street down for fun, beer drinking, and, of course, a little dancing. Grapefest was always the larger festival since it dovetailed with wine-tasting events, which brought in crowds estimated to exceed 250,000 for one weekend.

In 2005, Susan and I were asked to be the honorary chairs of Grapefest. This was truly an honor acknowledging two people who have dedicated their time and talent for the love of our town—Grapevine. We were chairs of the volunteers and the liaison to the TV and radio media, which were solicited to lure the people to Grapevine.

GOLF

Jerry and Ricky

I loved golf as a recreation and played a round of golf in many places in the world. My best golfing friend was Rick Stacy. I scored one hole in one. I won a few tournaments and placed in some others, which really depended on how good all four players could play. On another, I won a raffle in the Make a Wish Foundation tournament and won the grand prize of airfare anywhere American Airlines flew for four people and $3,000 vouchers to spend at any destination, all of which I gave to our sons.

Grapevine built its own eighteen-hole golf course in 1969 behind the Grapevine Lake Dam. I started to play golf then periodically and took a few lessons from Jim Smith, the manager or pro of the course. I played in the many golf tournaments that followed in the years to come. Those having tournaments included the Grapevine Chamber of Commerce, AMBUCS, the Convention Visitor Bureau, and the Rotary Club. It was a great fundraiser, and I chaired one of their tournaments; we made good revenue for the scholarship programs that we sponsored annually. Grapevine built another nine-hole golf course adjacent to the original 18 while I was on the City Council.

Susan and I agreed to sponsor Texas Tech's golf team for a golf outing in Scotland. There were at least 15 other couples who also agreed to the elaborate trip. The team would play golf with other universities while the adult sponsors would play with each other. Scotland has many golf courses and it was my turn such that we all had a lot of fun playing golf for about five days at the birthplace of golf. I did not get to play the R&A course since it was lottery-driven, but I did play Turnbury, Prestwick, and a few others. Susan, Pam Rawls, Jerry Rawls, and I played one of the courses as well. In Scotland, everyone has a caddy. Some were good and helpful, and some were really bad. Especially those who kept saying, "Bunker, Mr. Pittman, your ball is in the Bunker."

One day, I had no one to play golf with, so I went to Bear Creek, the golf course at the DFW Airport. It was in the fall of 1997, and the pro assigned me to a three-some to play with. On the 6th hole, a par 3, my golf ball rolled into the hole. Yes, it was a HOLE IN ONE. It was my first and my last. I called Susan and Rick Stacy, and I bought the beer for everyone at the Bear Creek bar when we finished!

In July of 2000, Susan had an opportunity to attend an Advance Placement seminar/conference in San Diego, California. So, I felt that I should go with her as her bodyguard, taking my appropriate club or clubs as in golf clubs. We stayed at the Isle Palms Hotel, with two grand views of the bay, including the US Navy base. It was neat. I played Steel Canyon and Torrey Pines golf courses. Oh yes, I also attended a CPA seminar for one day while in San Diego. I needed to justify the trip for CPE and tax purposes!

When I purchased a residential lot in Arkansas at Hot Springs Village in 2001, Susan and the boys thought I was crazy, and perhaps so, but this year, it became more valuable than I thought because golf had reentered my passionate life. And there were six beautiful golf courses at Hot Springs Village (HSV). I was now 56 years old, and a passionate life could have included heavy drinking (beer, whiskey), wild women, or buying lottery tickets, but I chose golf. HSV offered their six courses for as little as $20 per round, including the golf cart. So, Rick Stacy, my best friend, and I started an annual spring HSV golfing trip. Other people who have gone with us include Bob Williams, Jay Stacy, Mark Leos, Randy Stacy, Ronny Stacy, Al Swarze, and Randy Stacy, all guys from the Grapevine and Southlake area. We always made the trip on Mother's Day weekend—it was also my birthday weekend. We had so much fun! Here, it is 2013, and our trip is scheduled for May 10!

Rick Stacy, Jerry, and Randy Stacy at Hot Springs, Arkansas

Before we made the decision to build a summer home in Fort Davis, I decided that golf playing would diminish, but the overall decision came down to the beautiful weather. Where else in Texas can one open up your windows and grab a sheet or blanket at night or enjoy very low humidity in the daytime? I realized that there were no golf courses nearby. The Alpine Country Club was a poor excuse for a golf course, and that membership lasted about three years. So was the golf course in Fort Stockton, eighty miles to the East, and we would leave our dog (Ebbie) in a cage in the back of the truck while we played that excuse of a golf course.

El Paso had Painted Dunes and Butterfield golf courses, and they were great comparatively. It was a three-hour car ride, and I asked Susan if she needed to go to Costco (also in El Paso) so we would spend the night at the Hyatt Place, purchase groceries at Costco, and play early morning at Butterfield. We also would have lunch or dinner at Landry's to satisfy our desire for fish, where we got acquainted with Juan, the waiter at Landry's. Another golf course that I loved was in Terlingua at the US/Mexico border, called Black Jack, named for the historic General Black Jack Pershing. A favorite hole was number 11A which was over the Rio Grande River and a par whatever because there was no ability to complete the hole, much less finish it. Generally, it was a gambling opportunity to bet with your foursome to see how close your ball landed to the hole. Your ball stayed there until a Mexican native ran and collected all of the balls. The same man sold the many balls collected later on the frontier highway! The golf course was a three-star course and expensive to play, but a lot of fun! It was always very hot there. I left home in FD at 6 am with a T time at eight and played 18 holes to leave and drive back to FD by 11 when the temperature was approaching 110 degrees by 2 pm! A BBQ sandwich at Study Butte for the two-hour trip home made my day!

Chapter 53
Retirement and Nest Egg

I played golf with Rick Stacy three days weekly at The Trophy Club and did not work overtime or at night. So, in the meantime, I was planning the sale of our office buildings. I hired a realtor, set a price, and a man from Southlake made an offer. We negotiated and sold it to him for $ 1.7 million) which was split with David Harris as an equal partner in Nerf. The sale occurred in early 2005.

I hated to sell the building for several reasons, one of which was the cottonwood tree outside of my second-story office since it housed a huge bee hive and I called them the most money-making bees in Tarrant County because I had many conversations about my bees with my clients about my tree and its inhabitants such that at my billing rate per hour or per minute as a CPA the bees were making me money.......

The sale of my CPA practice, the sale of the 1000 Main building, and the sale of the 114 real estate started my retirement fund, so I decided to pursue the sale of the 1701 and 1705 buildings.

In 1986-88, our country's financial distress created many changes in the tax laws, namely restricting the ability to prepay interest and limiting IRA contributions. Savings and Loan companies and banks were forced to repossess real estate loans that they had, causing them to have too much real estate on hand. Because the government had caused this problem by changing tax laws, they then set up the Resolution Trust Company to help these S&L companies out.

Darlene Freed and I were able to negotiate and purchase an office building (1998) at 1701 W Northwest Highway in Grapevine from the RTC for a very low price. It had 40,000 square feet and was new but not complete and certainly not occupied fully. I retained Jay, our son, to help with the design of the incomplete building. The duct work was totally incomplete, and Jay was super helpful in his heating. As time progressed and work pursued, we were able to identify the building leased and occupied within a year. And that was important because, after the purchase, I was strapped for cash. Wells Fargo, my bank, came through like a champ in those days and loaned money to me/Nerf to complete most of these tasks. Darlene Freed, a realtor with good business acumen, started to work for me, and because she was new to Grapevine, she was a real answer for me since my plate was full of City Council, CPA practice, Son in College (Texas A&M), and another son in Football at Grapevine High School.

There were about 2 acres behind 1701 that were also repossessed and now owned by another bank. I began negotiations with the bank to no avail, but I gained leverage with them when I realized that the only way to access their two acres was through my parking lot! Now, I knew Texas law guaranteed the right of ingress and egress, but that did not stop me from negotiating further because of the awkward access to their property, such that I had them agree that I was the only buyer for their repossessed real estate. They were asking $250,000. They ended up selling it to me for $50,000, which was my offer all along.

We built another 40,000-square-foot building there (Lakeview II), with the builder being Speed Fabcrete Inc. I became great friends with Ron Hamm, who was one of their officers, as well as his other officers, and later, they asked me to join their Board of Directors.

Lakeview II was a tilt wall construction built on a slab of concrete supported by deep piers. The driller of the piers hit the water in the majority of holes dug. I asked them to dig one more hole near the small lake that the buildings were named after. I installed water well with my new hole, sunk pipe, and pump, and I had enough water there to water all of the grass at Lakeview I and II!! I installed a complete irrigation system for the two buildings, and Jose Torres,

Oran Washburn and Greg Gray were employees of mine to helped me get many things done.

I hired Mike Lease with Structures and Interiors Inc. to finish out the interior with dry walls, doors, electricity, etc. Darlene Freed was right there with me in the planning of the office space in 1705. The buildings became known as 1701 and 1705 Northwest Highway. Now housing 80,000 square feet of rental space. Coupled with the building on Main Street, David Harris and I (Nerf Enterprises) was the largest rental real estate owner in Grapevine.

I had covered parking for those who paid extra. My philosophy in owning and leasing was that we must have green grass and good-looking landscaping, attractive lobbies, spectacularly clean restrooms, and excellent HVAC systems. Another motto for me was that rent payment would be due on the first of each month, and anyone who paid past the 10th would be noticed in writing and the 20th lock to their suites and changed with dollars for restitution, no exceptions. The lease agreement covered these aspects clearly. I wanted to be the best landlord in Grapevine! It all paid off! Air conditioning was the most critical aspect of rental real estate. My tenants were either hot or cold or too this or that. Some took control of the thermostats and overheated their neighbors. I installed a very sophisticated software-controlled computer that monitored and controlled each thermostat in all three buildings. I could tell in advance if I had trouble, like compressors malfunctioning or people taking advantage of thermostats. I laid down rules for tenants as to what temperature I guaranteed in ranges, i.e., summer 70 to 74 and winter 66 to 74. Space heaters were not allowed to influence the thermostats. My employees were able to understand this software, and accordingly, we were able to operate the buildings better, and the tenants were a lot happier. Our occupancy improved, and so did the cash flow!

Often, I consulted with David Harris, my partner, with Nerf on matters of importance. I was the Managing Partner of Nerf, and I received some compensation in exchange. We decided to purchase 5 acres of land on Wm D Tate in 1998 to build our fourth office building. The land planners, architects, and engineers were hired. We built a retaining wall on the North side, installed a cross street, and completed drainage, infrastructure, fire plugs, etc.

Our plans slowed when we experienced (about 2003) a few of our tenants closing their doors and a pattern of centralization and consolidation of branch services back to their home offices as a recessionary period was looming. We had a large vacancy upstairs at Lakeview! (About 12,000 square feet). We put everything on hold on the new proposed office building.

Susan was to retire soon, and I placed a price on our three office buildings. Hired a realtor, Jenifer Gray, and listed the buildings for sale. We went to Mexico, Fort Davis, and Colorado on vacations. The trip to Colorado was with Victor from Parras de la Fuente. He was in High School there, and we were good friends of his parents and his sister. We hiked the mountains with Victor and had a grand time showing him Colorado. He was our exchange student, and we previously had taken him on a trip to East Texas and his sister, Malena, to Houston.

On the trip back from Colorado, I got a telephone call from our realtor, Jenifer Gray, that we had three offers to buy our two buildings: one from Roger Staubach Company, another from Henry S Miller, and a New York company named Naveen Shaw. She said that all of the offers were similarly priced in line with my asking price, which was 8.6 million dollars.

Right before we left for Colorado, I had negotiated a new lease that occupied the entire second floor of Lakeview I with a five-year lease. This makes about 96% occupancy for our two buildings, making it a more attractive sale.

When I returned from Colorado, Jennifer Gray said that the New York company or Naveen Shaw wanted to meet me as soon as possible, like in two days, so I agreed to meet Mr. Sha this Friday at Lakeview I in the conference room. So, Jennifer made it happen, and ten members of Sha's family showed up, women, attorneys, and relatives of Naveen. They were convinced they were going to buy the buildings for CASH! That day. I told them that I could not make this decision until I had time to review the other two offers from Roger Staubach and Henry S Miller companies.

Naveen was insistent on his offer and gave me assurances that the CASH offer was sincere for $8.6 million. I told him NO, but he pursued the offer with "What is it going to take to agree?" by today (Friday) before he returned to New York. All members were in agreement—attorneys, his wife, and two brothers, as well as two Indian realtors that he brought to the meeting. He was being a pest, and I reacted by saying that if you had to buy them today, and before I reviewed the other offers, I would have to have $9.0 million! He privately huddled with his people and complained about my unwillingness to sell now for $8.6 and finally agreed to $9.0 million. I responded, "CASH"? He responded, "CASH"! We shook hands, and the offer was signed. An earnest deposit was made, and Jennifer notified the other brokers. David Harris was pleased, especially when I told him we would clear about $4.0 million each!

Jennifer placed the contract with Bill Tate's title office in Grapevine.

About two weeks later, when I was driving to Fort Davis as our home construction was well underway, I got a call from someone from Lehman Brothers, a mortgage company in New York. He said he wanted me to get attornment agreements from each of my tenants which basically assigned their rents to Lehman Brothers in the event of default. I told the gentleman that my sale was for CASH and that a mortgage was not involved. He said that Naveen must have a mortgage.

I told him that I planned on canceling this sale and that he should have Naveen call me to restructure this sale now that cash was not the deal. When Naveen called, I asked him what had happened to the Cash deal. He said that he changed his mind, and I said that I changed my mind, too. That our deal was OFF! Then, I was going to call other brokers. He asked what it would take for me to assist in a mortgage. I told him that an additional $100,000 would be required for me to put this deal back on the table.

He agreed!

Lehman Brothers wanted to fly out the next day to Fort Davis for me to sign the attornments. I told them that it would be impossible to fly to Fort

Davis since the unincorporated town of 800 people had no airport.

Crawford Dill Pittman was born in January 2008. He kept us up most of the night of his birth at Baylor Hospital there in Plano, and I ate the worst oatmeal that I have ever had that night, waiting for my grandson to arrive. I was thrilled when he did arrive and even more thrilled for Angie and Greer.

Our home was now completed (Spring 2007), and Susan and I were getting accustomed to six months in Fort Davis and six months in Grapevine. Yes, the winter in Grapevine and the Summer out west in the cool air. The low humidity and the high altitude appealed to us and everyone who visited. Our guests over the ensuing years included Jerry and Pam Rawls, Doug and Laurie Evans, Bill and Katherine Brink, Marget Telford, Ron Hamm, Harry Bowden, Fred Maldonado, Chris Chapman, Sonny Comfort, Sarah Hunter, Dale and Teddie Cherry, Richard Selinger, Eric Selinger, Carolyn Selinger, Tanner, and Darlene Selinger, Linda and Les Allison, The Dallas Book Club, The Boy Scout Troop ? from St Lukes Methodist Church in Houston. We cooked BBQ and Dutch oven cobblers for everyone's enjoyment. We played golf at Lajitas and Butterfield, drove the river road, and drove the famous loop. We went to Ojinaga, Mexico, to buy pots, eat at Los Comales, and drink a little cerveza. We attended star parties at McDonald Observatory and attended church at the Fort Davis Methodist Church so our guests could believe their eyes when I told them that I played the organ at the church.

My nest egg of money from the sale of the buildings, practice, etc., was not doing well. I hired two money managers to manage my money while I was busy building our home. Their monthly reports showed declining values for my investments. John Edrington with Deutsch and Bernstein were both losing money, my money! Now, I knew we were experiencing a Bear market, but it appeared that they were making money with their fixed percentage while I was losing money. Each charged me a management fee, and each was investing my money in their company-related mutual funds. Bernstein Alliance. This and Bernstein Alliance was their common investing pattern. And John Edrington was in charge of my IRA account as well as Susan's IRA account. The IRAs had declined $345,000. Bernstein got me to buy a Hedge fund, where I invested $750,000 initially, and now it was worth $485,000.

I had always thought that when investing, one should buy low and then sell high. Well, the two money managers and the Bear market had not learned that axiom. So, I fired them both and asked them to send all money and all investments to Vanguard in the care of an account manager who was prepared to receive them. In total, I lost about one and one-half million dollars. By mid-2010, all was intact at Vanguard, and I was in charge of my own money. I did extensive research, and Vanguard was a great help in providing me with the information and tools I needed to manage my own funds. The Bull market that followed the next twenty years helped a lot as well. By 2015, I had made more than what I had lost. I have been in charge of our money ever since, and after all, as a CPA, I was somewhat trained to do this. I am much happier!

Chapter 54
Fort Davis Construction

Jay and Jannan drew the plans after Susan, and I sent them a conceptional drawing that featured a three-bedroom home with a kitchen and two bathrooms with all plumbing in close proximity. When they had most of the drawings near completion, Susan and I had them fly out to Fort Davis via Midland to help us stake the new home out on the 7 acres. Susan and I had no clue, but they used the Pythagorean theory, but the direction and staking were perfect, which was proved correct for many years to come with the direction of the morning and evening sun! Construction could now begin.

We spent the night at the classic Limpia Hotel, and the excitement occurred when a mouse ran across the room and Jannan's arm as she was sitting on the antique couch. When I complained to the hotel, management brought down to our room "Tuxedo," the resident hotel cat! Not a mouse trap, but a cat! The Limpia was the only hotel in Fort Davis, a non-incorporated town in Jeff Davis County, of 800 people!

I hired Keith Jarratt in Fort Davis to complete the fencing around the acreage, install water to the site along with telephone wire, and build up the site with fill and rock for the building of the home.

Bake Turner, an older Fiji at Texas Tech who played professional football and lived in Alpine, a larger town 24 miles away, suggested that I call AG Hayes to install a septic system at our home. So, I called him to inquire and asked him if he knew Bake Turner. "That sorry son of a bitch" he responded. I knew then that A.G. knew him well. Bake told me he played golf with Bake every week. Knowing that he knew Bake well, I then asked him to install a septic system in Fort Davis. After we played golf that weekend, I asked him again, and I asked him when he could work it into his schedule, and he responded, "How about tomorrow?" And he did!

Clayton Shoot was a framer and highly recommended. At first, he was not interested in being my framer until he saw my plans and the 30-foot-high ceilings and the architect's plans. He then agreed, so I started seeking other contractors, including a foundation crew. I interviewed three and eliminated two as drug and bad references... I hired Luis Terrazas from Fort Stockton, who had a crew of about fifteen men, some direct from Mexico (wet backs).

The Framer Clayton Shoot

I moved my deer hunting trailer to Fort Davis for my living quarters. I hooked it up to my new septic tank and a water line and subscribed to Direct TV, and that is where's where I planned to live off and on the next year while I, along with my contractors, built our new home. The trailer was 29 feet long and quite adequate for all of my needs except showering. The shower was so small I thought I would get a hernia or never get out once I got in. So, I went to the Fort Davis State Park for my bathing needs. The showers were spacious and warm in the wintertime. Susan enjoyed going out there also when she was with me. We met a lot of people and got to know most of the rangers out there. We renewed our Conservation pass to use the park for this purpose. We have had and continue to purchase the unlimited pass for all State Parks.

I installed a canvas cover on the West side of the trailer and put up a table with three chairs which constituted my Office. I designed a CPM, Critical Path Movement schedule, weekly functions by sub-contractors, and a timetable for each. Some contractors overlapped, and the CPM accommodated. I maintained a CPM (Critical Path Movement) throughout the construction of the home. This CPM plotted out contractors' activity when someone stared, overlapped, stopped, etc. It was a great tool to plan.

All subcontractors were paid every Friday and were not expected to work Saturday or Sunday. Some wanted to balance my job with others that might have for which I did not tolerate. I expected them to work exclusively on my job until completed. I provided lodging at the Fort Davis Motor Lodge for those who had a long commute, like San Antonio, Odessa, and Lubbock.

Susan was with me to some extent, but her mother's health was failing, and she wanted to be with her. She so wanted to come out with me and did to some extent, but her calling was with and for her mom, too.

Lawson Allen was the President of Fort Davis State Bank. Lawson and I went to grade school and high school at Sweetwater, where we both graduated from Sweetwater in 1962. We were born one hour apart at Sweetwater Memorial Hospital on May 12 (11:23 PM) for me and (12:18 pm) on May 13 for Lawson. But he was very short, and we all called him "Squirt" in High School. Since I planned on borrowing money from him at Fort Davis State Bank, Susan insisted that I should not call him "Squirt" at the bank! So, I didn't!

Our Great Room was high in the ceiling, almost 30 feet, and required a large duct (like 25 inches in diameter hung from the upper ceiling, much like ductwork in large dining areas in restaurants. After some said, they could design flex ducts, and others said they might be able to construct some sheet metal to fit. Someone suggested Darville Plumbing and Air in

Odessa, three hours away. Mr. Darville asked me the right questions about whether I had architectural plans, so I sent him some of Jay and Jannan's plans, and we were in business. The ducts were large enough that one of Darville's men crawled inside of it to install the anchor of all thread bolts to the ceiling. He crawled about 30 feet.

Susan and I visited Bobby Mummy's stone company in San Antonio and purchased 18 tons of stone for our fireplace and other stone features of our home. Mesco Metal company delivered all of our galvalume metal.

My surrogate Mother, Dorothy Brown, lived in Fort Stockton, about 80 miles to the East. Susan and I had visited her several times. She moved in with my parents in 1944, about the time I was born. Her first husband was killed in Normandy, and during her grief, my mother asked her to move in with us. She probably changed my diaper as much as my mother did. Thus, I called her and loved her like my Surrogate Mother! She was so happy that we were building a home in Fort Davis, and she loved Susan and treated Susan as her own daughter! She recommended Gary Mills to do our stonework. Gary lived on a farm near Fort Stockton, raised Duroc Hogs, and I hired him. He was taller than me and took every stone and designed it to fit perfectly in our prow or fireplace. He was a very West Texas type of guy wearing a ten-gallon hat daily on the job, and when you would ask him how it was, he would slowly respond, "Okey, Dokey!"

Stone Mason Gary Mills from Fort Stockton

Barmore Plumbing was my choice for a plumber and probably the biggest mistake I made as the General Contractor of our home. They took forever to plan for the plumbing before the concrete was poured for the slab and then complained that the drawing and the slab were wrong. Then Leman Barmore overcharged me for labor and for a 3-inch sewer pipe. He charged me for 300 feet of 6 PVC pipe, with it only 30 feet to the sewer system. So, I wrote him a letter about these billing errors, for which he credited my next billing. HA!

Jay and Jackie Stanley's son, Andrew, was to wed his wife in San Miguel de Allende in Mexico. We had a grand time there and stayed at a very colorful home. At the reception dinner, we met an electrician named Richard, who owned an electrician company and was a friend of Jay's. Susan and I discussed our dream home in Fort Davis, and he replied, "I want to come to Fort Davis and wire your home"! When we got down to the need to hire an electrician, I sent Richard our architectural electrician plans section. He lives in San Antonio, and I gave him a general time frame of when we would need him. We flew to Leon, Mexico, for his wedding and stayed at a charming and very colorful, rather small hotel downtown. This trip was significant because the idea of building a home in Fort Davis was becoming a reality, and we ended up meeting and hiring Richard Francis to be our electrician, and we took a bus over to Delores Hidalgo, the ceramic capital of all of Mexico. We ended up purchasing three beautiful sinks and several Talavera tiles for accent purposes. We got lots of ideas about building the house, including the development of Susan's mind regarding colors for the new home in Fort Davis.

While we were in San Miguel, we took a bus down to Delores Hidalgo to visit a ceramic factory there. It is about 100 kilometers south of San Miguel, and we knew it would take most of the day. Friends at the wedding thought Susan and I were crazy on our wild hair bus trip. We purchased most all of our ceramics and three sinks there for the house. The sinks were shipped to Grapevine, Texas, and it cost more to ship them than it cost to purchase! The sinks were elegantly designed (Talavera Tile) and arrived in perfect shape, not broken.

Angie, working at The Container Store, measured, ordered, and furnished all of the fixtures for all of the closets, including drawers and rods. Greer and Angie flew out to install all of the orders. Susan and I provided the air flight, food, a place to stay, and most of the grunt work that Angie needed to complete the job. They did a great job, and we have received dozens of compliments on our closets.

I purchased a block of days lodging at the Fort Davis Motor Lodge for the contractors that needed to stay over night for a day or more. The electrician, stone mason, and the HVAC men took me up on the lodging offer. It was beneficial for them as well as me since their work overlapped days, and it was too far for the commute back and forth to their home. Travel time was saved.

Much of the furniture was purchased from Rick Stacy and delivered, while our beds came from Alpine.

I purchased 28 trees from Greer's Nursery, and we loaded them onto a bobtailed truck that I drove out to Fort Davis. Lalo and Sarita Hernandez installed all of the landscaping, including the trees. Lalo had to use a backhoe to dig the holes for the trees as we learned quickly rocks were plentiful and impossible to dig without one. I built the pergola, while Danny Urquizie built the BBQ pit out of leftover stone.

The house, and now our home, took ten months to build. Started August 2006 and occupied July 2007.

OUR COMPLETED HOME 910 Cemetery Fort Davis, Texas

Chapter 55
Margaret Goerke

Margaret Goerke

Another character that I met during the construction was Margaret Goerke, who rode a bicycle down from her home almost daily. She asked a lot of questions of me, and I answered each; ittle did I know she was making mental notes. The next day, she indicated that she had researched everywhere (on the web at the library) things I had said and then knew as much as I did, like the fact I was a Methodist and member of Whites Chapel Methodist Church in Southlake, Texas and how big that church is, etc. She rode that bicycle place in Fort Davis, but she owned a very old Ford van with a solar panel on the dash to keep the car battery charged so she could go to Mexico to see friends or to the airport to fly to see her son in Iowa. Susan often rode her bike with Margaret and tried to learn more about this very private person. She was extremely eccentric, as I will explain later in this chapter.

Margaret chaired the Mission committee at our Church in Fort Davis, the United Methodist Church. She rode her bike to church every Sunday and prepared the sacraments each month and, in all ways, was a true Christian in my view. She loved for me to play the organ at the church and oftentimes told me so and even requested certain hymns that she loved. She lived in a house trailer on a hill close to our home, and she watched our home from her trailer and noted when we had returned from wherever we had been, and called us on her landline to welcome us back to Fort Davis. We loved it!

Her trailer was not level and had no hot water as the hot water heater died some years back, she said matter-factly. It also had no heater, and she used the oven for heat. She was very guarded about her personal living conditions and never mentioned or discussed anything like that. It was mostly our observations. When we discussed anything personal about her, she would manage to change the subject to something else. One day, however, she and I discussed septic tanks and surrounding issues. Sure enough, she did not have any such tank or collection method. She had divorced her husband several years earlier, and he left her this trailer. It had deteriorated under her care, but Margaret did not want to call anyone to fix this or that. I explained very carefully what septic tanks and lateral lines did to dispose of our human waste, etc. She listened intently. A few days later, she called me for AG Hayes' phone number. And a few days or weeks after that, AG Hayes installed a state-of-the-art septic system for her little trailer. I was pleased Margaret had paid attention to me once and showed some trust in my advice and judgment. She had previously demonstrated her trust in me when, several times, I fixed a flat on her bike or repaired the chain. I was pleased that she asked me or said something like that to give me the idea she might use my help.

One day, she brought an empty quart bottle and asked me for a quart of water. Later in the week or next, I was up at her trailer adjusting her radio when somehow the dial was off the PBS station she enjoyed (this often happened when she thought the radio had broken). I tried her water faucet and noted the discolored water. I tested the water, and it was grainy like the well was drawing sand. I called Andy Prude, a noted well water mechanic in Fort Davis when he came out and fixed the well water problem. I told Andy to bill me for his service. He never did. Margaret and I never discussed the problem, and she did not ask for a quart of water again.

Margaret attended many of the book club meetings that Susan attended. She never hesitated when Susan invited her. She rarely read the book but instead enjoyed being among her other friends. Most people in town thought of her as being the "bike lady of Fort Davis."

A few years later, Margaret fell off her bike and broke her ankle. We were not in Fort Davis at the time since we continued to live six months in Grapevine. I do not know or remember how she fell and what the circumstances were. She was in rehabilitation at a rest home in Alpine. When I visited her there, she expressed that she hated this rest home and was ready to return home. After a few weeks or so, Dr. Lucke let her go home, and fairly soon thereafter, she was riding her bike again very gingerly!

Her son lived in Iowa City, Iowa, with his wife and their two children. Margaret went to see them about once each year. She drove her van to the Midland Airport parking lot and spent the night in it to catch a plane the next morning. She never talked about her family or even bragged about her two grandchildren. I knew she had a sister because she talked to her every morning at 7:30, and that time was off limits as to everything else going on! When we asked her about her living conditions (no heater, air conditioning, no hot water), she said it did not concern her. We learned over time that she had worked with her husband (the second husband), Rolf, in an Idaho Natural area in a log cabin for 30 or so years. The only way into the area where she worked was in a small plane, and her mail came that way as well.

In Fort Davis, Margaret lived as a pauper in a down trailer, and a bicycle was principally her means of transportation. Only on about two occasions did she ask for a ride from us. Once, it was raining, and we took her to Church, and the other, it was at night, and she was uncomfortable riding her bike at night. She really did not want to be an imposition on anybody anytime. Many times, she merely chose not to go. She was bright as a penny, and she could converse about current and political events. She always took notes on Church sermons and read the Bible often.

In the late Spring of 2020, as I recall, she fell again on her bike and broke (dislocated) her shoulder and had to be transported to a rest home in Fort Stockton, a much better place. We began seeing her at least weekly while she was there. I offered to bring her mail weekly, and I opened it for her to review and decide what she wanted to do. Much of her mail was trash bulk mail, and she wanted to throw it away. Some she wanted to pay, but much of her payments were on bank ACH auto pay like gas, electricity, water, the church, etc. I took all of her opened mail or bulk mail back with me to discard or shred, as she asked. She certainly did not want anything left at her rest home.

One day I took my organ music with me to play the organ there in the rest home. I told her I was going to, and she talked it up among her colleagues there, and they were all waiting in the public area for me to arrive to entertain them. I played for about an hour, and when I finished, many of them asked me to return to play again. Margaret was so proud!

In the mail routine of Susan and me going to Fort Stockton, I noted several items of bank notices: Bank of America, Vanguard, Puritan, Fort Davis State, and Wells Fargo. I discussed some of this with Margaret, who then wanted me to help her transfer some money from one bank to another so she would have enough money to pay her bills. I mainly helped by helping her use my telephone to call for the transfer.

She needed one of her bank statements and told me it was in her strong box and for me to bring it the next time I came. I asked her the location of the strong box as I assumed it was at the Bank. She replied that it was in her refrigerator. Sure enough, the strong box was an old metal candy or cake box about 4 inches wide and 12 inches long with a lid.

Margaret trusted me now without question, and I was honored and knew I would never let her down nor disappoint her. However, her strong box revealed information that we wondered about and now confirmed. She divorced John Rutherford early in their marriage, leaving him for another man, Rolf Goerke. She was the mother of a boy, John Jr., and left him with his father. Margaret did not love John and was intrigued and in love with Rolf. They left after marriage to work in the National Forest in Idaho. While in College, she earned her Master's degree from Iowa University in Sociology and lacked only a few hours to complete her Ph.D.

The statements from all of the banks are in the box. Margaret was a wealthy woman with substantial money scattered amounts in several banks and security companies. My guess is that it was upward of two million. I learned then more about John, her son, his wife Kim, and their two children, Aaron and Claire. She sent money to them periodically.

When Margaret was feeling better, I called John. She and John had talked numerous times about her going home after her injury was cured. However, as she told me, John told her that either we purchase a new trailer for her or she might have to stay in the nursing home in Fort Stockton. Her old trailer was simply not livable anymore, with no heat, hot water, or air conditioning. John and I talked about her finances and how she should be able to buy a new home. He agreed, and Susan and I started our search for a new mobile home. Margaret agreed, and I took out enough money from her accounts with her involvement to purchase the new trailer. We bought one in Odessa, and I hired Keith Jarratt to level and put fill dirt on her land. I also learned that Margaret had purchased the 35 acres behind and above her home. The new trailer was positioned neatly against a beautiful tree. I hired Danny Uqudize and Luis Aguilar to move the water, sewer, electric, and phone lines to the new trailer. Danny took Margaret's old trailer for his crippled son, and they moved it to a lot that Danny owned. John and his wife, Kris, purchased new furniture dishes to set Margaret up, and John flew down to help her move in. Margaret was all set and happy.

John stayed there a few days, and I informed him fully of Margaret's financial situation, and since he was the sole heir, he took care of Margaret thereafter. He purchased her a new tricycle which she never rode, and a television set that she rarely ever watched. She kept the HVAC off most of the time because it cost her money. Later, her caregivers during her last days needed those comforts. Margaret lived about four years in her new home before she passed. She was not the same but was pleased that her son was looking after her those last years. She donated her body to Texas Tech Medical School for research. In her will, she asked that I play four hymns at her memorial service. I did, and the whole town came to celebrate the life of the bike lady of Fort Davis, Margaret Goerke.

Chapter 56
The Flood

We were experiencing a calcium buildup in our hot water system, which caused plumbing stoppages in the pipes throughout the house. Consistently, I had to clear the sink delivery pipes from the calcium buildup. I called Barmore Plumbing to see if they had a solution, and they sent out Brian, their lead plumber, who installed a filter on our tankless water heater to clear the lines from the mineral buildup. Leman Barmore said they were closing their plumbing business, and accordingly, he sent his best plumber on this one of their last calls before the plumbing company closed down altogether.

The filter worked well in that calcium and mineral buildup had ceased.

Susan and I left for an extended vacation to the Northwest. We spent about three weeks in Victoria, Vancouver, tent camping and playing golf! We had high tea at the Fairmont Empress Hotel in Victoria and drove the entire time, playing golf, going and coming.

It was mid-2012. Our vacation was coming to an end, and we were on our way back home. I got a call from Scott Adams with the Fort Davis Water company telling me that my water meter at our home was running wild and asked if he wanted me to turn the water off at the street meter. I told him to please do so and assured him that we should be back in a day or so. Susan and I hoped the leak was outside the home and not on the inside. We had no idea.

When we got there and opened the house, there was a floor of water everywhere. The filter that Barmore installed was on the floor, cracked and broken. My laptop, still plugged in, was floating, and all furniture had been saturated. We opened all of the windows because the smell was bad. The water company said we had used 85,000 gallons of water; the propane tank was empty, and it was apparent that the water filter had busted open and that hot water had pumped into our home until the propane tank was empty. All baseboards and sheetrock had absorbed water, with black mold existing on the walls. Every room was wet; furniture, ceiling fans, computers, and stereo systems were saturated and ruined.

I called my insurance company, Farmers Insurance, and they got a restoration company hired to come to Fort Davis from El Paso to begin drying us out. I moved our washer to the garage and hooked it up to start some cleaning. Carol Nicks had us over for a drink and a place to live for two days. Members of our Church in FD got involved, including Nancy and Bill Davis, offering their rented house on the highway to the Observatory.

The restoration company heated up the house to 124 degrees to kill all the mold and began tearing out all of the pine baseboard and sheetrock. It was too hot to stay in the house very long.

I had cashed a bond for $50,000 to help us with the financial cost before the insurance rescued us financially.

I called Clayton Shoot, my framer and building foreman. He and all of his contractors came to our rescue: carpenters, drywall, finish cabinet people, and painters. We were back in our home after two months!

Initially, Trudy, with Farmers, arrived and measured our house, performed various calculations, and presented me two checks, based on her calculations, for $31,000 for the damages and another for the personal property items (furniture, computers), etc.

I was insulted as it was not even close to the damages to our custom-built home, and I told her to keep the checks. I called my attorney, Greg Standef, in Southlake, and he wrote Trudy and Farmers a brief letter that stated that either you deal with Jerry fairly and properly now, or you will have to deal with me in court later.

Farmers cleaned up their act, dismissed Trudy, at least from my claim, and a supervisor told me that whenever I needed money, to call him. Farmers subrogated the claim against Nationwide (Barmore's insurance). Nationwide tried to sue Culligan Filter Company, but gross negligence was proven since Brian, the plumber, installed the filter on the hot side of the tankless water heater while the instructions by Culligan to the plumber were clear to install it on the cold side.

Thus, gross negligence. The total cost amounted to $140,000, and Nationwide paid it all.

Chapter 57
CDRI

After a year in Fort Davis, I was invited to join the Board of Directors of the Chihuahua Desert Research Institute. My friend Kimball Miller was a member and asked me to attend in that vein. The non-profit owned about 500 acres and was involved in the study of plants, shrubs, and trees indigenous to the Chihuahua Desert and the expanse of land stretching from deep in Mexico, including much of the Trans Pecos area that Susan and I were getting accustomed to both living and enjoying the dry area of a desert. CDRI had a visitors center, a botanical garden of sorts, some walking/hiking trails, and a staff of two or three.

Many of my fellow board members were Sul Ross professors, while others included men and women from all walks of life, including nurseries, ranching, law, business, and economics. My expertise was, of course, CPA and nonprofit budgeting. We had meetings twice annually and an annual BBQ dinner for existing and prospective members. The Board got involved in hosting the annual BBQ by cooking all of the sirloin for the event. That was fun. At the annual dinner, I got to meet a lot of guests, including Clayton Williams and his wife, Modesta. Clayton (Claytie) ran for governor of Texas but was defeated overwhelmingly by Ann Richards when he was quoted saying that rape was inevitable and that women should grin and bear it.

The revenue for CDRI came principally from memberships, grants, and the annual. We did receive some bequeaths from an estate that was gaining in volume. Kathy Hoyt, Ph.D., was the current executive director. She paid the bills, reconciled the cash, and prepared the annual budget, for which I offered my help. She reported mostly to the executive committee and chairman of the Board, Tom Bruner, or vice chair, Rob Dunnigan. Over the years, I found that I had some issues, if not disagreements, with the manner in which Kathy prepared the annual budgets. I voiced my concerns at the board meeting, finding fellow board members both in agreement and in disagreement with my thoughts.

CDRI began to de-emphasize the research aspect and started more of an education aspect of the desert by getting school children to come to Fort Davis for mini-seminars on rocks, "Earth Rocks," and bugs "Bugs, Bugs, Bugs," and other programs. The educational aspect flourished.

I had gotten involved with Green Mountain Energy, an electric provider in Texas, with my interest in Renewable Energy when I installed a Sky Stream Wind Turbine and 30 solar panels at our home in Fort Davis. I joined their charitable division, Sun Club, and asked them if they had an interest in visiting CDRI to make a grant of money for building solar panels for a fellow nonprofit entity. They did! We applied, and they came through with money granted to CDRI sufficient to install 37 solar panels at a reduced budget for electricity by two-thirds! About six years later, I made another application with Sun Club for another grant for the Cactus Center at CDRI, and it, too, was granted.

Kathy Hoyt was playing imagination with her preparation of the budget, including taking money from our endowed funds, understating expenses, and recognizing certain revenue items twice, including bequeaths that were recognized and reported in the previous year or years. When, at a board meeting, I asked her about these missteps or mistakes in budgeting, she took exception to my comments, and Suzette Ashworth, a fellow board member and assistant chairwoman, told me before the entire Board that she did not like my Tone! Tom Bruner, the Chairman, agreed with Suzette. Larry Francelle and Robert Potts agreed with me.

Tom Bruner wrote an email to me and asked me to resign from the Board. I refused and cited her budget practices, to which I disagreed.

Tom then called a meeting of the Executive Committee to consider a motion expelling Jerry Pittman from CDRI's Board of Directors.

About this time, my longtime companion and best friend, Ebbie, a Labrador, died, and we buried her on our 7 acres in Fort Davis. We hired a backhoe to dig her grave since we grow rocks in Fort Davis. She had been the apple of my eye, our faithful companion for 15 years. Since we were distraught and without the love of our canine companion, Susan and I embarked on a three-weeklong tent camping vacation to Vancouver, Victoria, and British Columbia, including golf at Coeur de Lane.

CDRI had set the executive committee meeting to consider a motion to expel me to be held a few days after we returned from our healing vacation. I had plenty of time to prepare my response.

The Executive Committee of CDRI was comprised of Tom Bruner, Joe Duncan, Suzette Ashworth, Blaine Hall, Shirley Powell, and two others (I cannot remember). The committee met that Monday to consider expelling Jerry Pittman. Tom set forth his ideas and made a motion for expulsion. The second to his motion never came.

Apparently, your motion has failed for lack of a second to the motion, I said.

He was clearly not happy and was beginning to close the meeting. But I said I wanted to speak in my defense that I prepared and for the committee to hear. So, I cited the need to budget and how to prepare it, and that has been the thesis of my board involvement. I pointed out how expenses had been understated and revenues recorded twice by the executive director, Kathy Hoyt, etc. Besides Mr. Chairman, I am like a leopard with spots (CPA), and no matter how much I try, I cannot wash them off.

Hearing that, Tom Bruner stood up, folded his briefcase, and walked out. He had been chairman for 5-10 years. CDRI never saw him again.

Kathy Hoyt resigned, and a new executive director was hired. Some directors also resigned, and new appointments were made.

I served CDRI for a total of twelve years when my board membership was limited. CDRI is in the black now, a complete success, and a great organization serving the Chihuahua desert and visiting the public.

Chapter 58
Tres Hombres

BILL LEFTWICH

DICK SLAUGHTER

BILL WAGGONER

Bill Leftwich

During the home construction at Fort Davis (2006), I met our neighbors Bill and Mary Alice Leftwich, who treated me with much courtesy and coffee each day at their adobe-built home, which was fascinating. Bill built it with his own hands. He and Mary Alice had two daughters and two sons who were grown, and they, in turn, had married children. Bill was over at our construction site often almost daily! I gained a lot of respect and love for both, but many times at 5 pm, I wanted a beer in lieu of coffee, so I went to Marfa for beer and newspapers occasionally. Bill and I became great friends. He went with me to OJ, Mexico, to pick up much of our ceramics, which Susan and I had purchased in Dolores Hidalgo, Mexico. The ceramics were being shipped periodically on Mexico's timetable! Bill spoke better Spanish than I did, although my Spanish was getting better living around so many Hispanics, most of which became my friends. He was a fascinating man, about 80 at the time, and had written four books about his experiences. For the World's Fair in 1962, he designed the New Mexico Pavilion. First Lady Laura Bush selected Bill Leftwich to design the Christmas Tree ornament to hang on the White House's annual Christmas tree during George W Bush's term. It featured Fort Davis's Historical site. He was a great artist and designed and built art sculptures. He gave us some of his art and artifacts as well as free advice on building our home. We loved Bill and Mary Alice.

Bill Leftwich thought he would be a horse commander in WWII, but the next best thing was a tank commander, and that is what he got.

Susan and I had them over to watch The Battle of the Bulge by Ken Burns on TV. Bill was very quiet and solemn during the movie.

Several years later, Bill's heart gave out, and he died in 2012. He was buried at the National Cemetery Grand Prairie.

Another hombre was Richard Dick Slaughter, whom I did not know as well. Dick's reputation was well known. Historically, he was the auction hawk at the CDRI annual auction, and everyone knew it. He celebrated every Christmas at the historic La Fonda Hotel in Santa Fe, New Mexico, dressed as one of Santa's elves and gave out candy in the lobby. To this day, behind the concierge's desk is a photo of Elf Dick. His great bass voice was wonderful and totally in harmony with singing church hymns at the Methodist Church! And I told him so. As I started playing with Nancy Davis (the Church pianist), Dick came up to me while I played the organ to give me a peppermint lifesaver, symbolic of his approval of my efforts. Dick's wife, Joyce, was most supportive as well. Come to find out her brother was Pete Wehner of Arthur Anderson's days. Pete was the Chairman of Arthur Andersen & Co. in Houston, Texas. He was the one who sent me to Florida and looked closely after me when I was in the hospital (The Uh Oh portion). I also learned that her uncle was Ernest Tubb, a favorite country singer of mine.

Sometime later, my neighbor Bill Leftwich decided to connect his home to the Fort Davis water system by installing a water line from the street to his home. So, Dick Slaughter, Bill Waggoner (the third Hombre), and Bill Leftwich, all three in their mid-80s, were digging the fifty-yard ditch and laying the pexpipe to the house. I happened to drive by and witnessed this gallant ditch-digging effort and pulled into the driveway. I asked whether I could help. No! Was the response by Dick Slaughter. You are too God Damn young!

Dick died in 2013, and he was buried at Hillcrest Cemetery in Fort Davis.

Shortly after our home was finished and we had moved in (2007), I inquired about a wind turbine to generate electricity to supplement our grid costs. I purchased a 40 ft high turbine from Sky View company in Tucson. Their dealer was in Alpine, Mark Upchurch, and he installed it along with his brother and others. AEP and Blaine Burchard (also a Red Raider) from San Angelo arranged to have a Smart Meter installed that would merge wind energy with the grid energy, of course, after microinverters had converted DC current to AC current! Later, this Smart Meter handled the solar panels that I also installed and acted like a traffic cop, yielding first to the renewable energy I produced and then to the Grid. For example, when the wind was not blowing and the sun was not shining, then I had to buy electricity from the Grid. This never happens in Fort Davis!

My research discovered several other facts and political issues that were factored into my decision-making. Green Mountain Energy is the only Provider in Texas that is willing to purchase my generated renewable energy, and when contacted, they agreed to do so ONLY on a monthly basis. This means that they could pull the rug and switch the purchasing off. This risk was one I did not want to run, but my intrigue was overriding. I really thought that renewable energy was gaining popularity in Texas, e.g., 24% of Texas energy today is renewable energy. Another fact is that the States of Texas and the State of Idaho are the only states in the U.S. that DO NOT have laws that require all providers to purchase all renewable energy products in their respective states.

Bill Waggoner

I met Bill Waggoner at Cueva de Leon restaurant in Fort Davis. He was an 83-year-old outspoken, cussing sailor who became a fast friend of mine. Bill was Lubbock's answer to swimming pools back in his day when he installed swimming pools in Lubbock everywhere. Several of my friends in Lubbock remembered Bill. Bill, Susan, and I gather every Thursday evening between 5 and 8 at this restaurant to listen to Jim Hall and his Last Call Band play country and Western music. Bill loved the music, the Mexican food, and the beer, too! Not a bad combination.

Combination for any friend. Susan and I were there every Thursday and also loved the music and the beer in the Texas Tech cooler.

In one of those meetings, I mentioned to Bill that I wanted to build a stand to hold solar panels. He said why don't you weld the stands. I found out that he was a welder in the Navy! So, he drew off on a Big Chief tablet a drawing of how the stand could be built, taking into consideration the need to reposition the panels for the changes of the equinox between the summer and winter position of the sun.

My job was grunt work, so I dug the nine holes for the support to be planted in concrete, measured, and aligned with each other pursuant to his drawing. He welded the steel together along with the support to hold the 3x5 solar panels along with their microinverter to convert AC to DC electricity. The electrician that I hired connected the panels with my new Smart Meter at the house about 100 feet away.

In later years, 2014 and 2019, I installed 24 more panels on large steel stands on a single large pole buried in concrete holding 12 panels each. Now I had 30 solar panels and a wind turbine generating about 2000 kWh each month, creating a cash flow more than I needed. Green Mountain Energy attached to my monthly billing the meters at Grapevine and Sulphur Springs (Elberta), leaving an additional net cash flow of about $200 per month, and it was cumulative.

Waggoner and I continued our friendship at Cueva drinking beer, enjoying good music, and eating Mexican food every Thursday. I wanted to build a garage of metal and steel to replace the canvas awning I had erected at the beginning of the house construction. Bill volunteered. I measured and decided the size with his help. I ordered from Mueller and all of the steel; roofing was delivered along with one 8 x 11 drawing. Waggoner did not approve of the lack of instructions but cussed a bit and started to work. I hired Danny Urquidze and Luis Aguilar to help us. And if any work performed accurately and correctly Waggoner took all credit and pleasure for HIS great work, but if anything went wrong or was screwed up Bill Waggoner would complain that it was all my 'goddamn' fault! For example, the trusses for the garage fit each side but they were a bit crooked together from one end to another. and when I protested and asked "How did this happen? The trusses are connected from side to side yet they are crooked. "It is your fucking fault. I welded them together on your land outside the garage where your land is not level and that is where I welded them all together!. Therefore, it is your fucking fault!"

About three months later, Bill had cataract surgery on the right eye. He was at my house almost daily telling me some story after another. I enjoyed Bill's company always. He was becoming to be a real friend. I noticed that he continued to wipe his right eye with what looked like a dirty rag. After we returned to Grapevine, a few days later, I got a call from Loueda telling me that Bill was in the hospital in Fort Worth. His entire body was poisoned as a result of not keeping his eyes clean. I went to the hospital to see Bill and met his son-in-law in the hallway. He told me that Bill was dying. We visited, and he said goodbye. My friend died a month later. He died of the poison in his body. It was November 2014. His ashes were thrown in the Ocean at Maui, near where Bill took his family for a month at Christmas time each of the previous thirty years.

Chapter 59
Sailing the Ocean Blue

Lake Grapevine

Susan is the original sailor in our family. She sailed and taught sailing at Camp Longhorn during her staff days in summers before college. Then, after we married, I promised her that if we moved to Grapevine to start my practice, I would buy her a sailboat.

Eddie Morrison found a perfect sailboat for us to look at, and naturally, I joined him in the search and inspection. We bought it. A 22-foot Catalina that was already moored on Lake Grapevine. We shook hands on a gentleman's agreement, and I began making monthly payments to him as he was the lender. I would have exclusive use of the sailboat on even days, and he would have exclusive use on odd days. It worked out well since there was at least one day each weekend to use the boat. It was a promise to Susan that we would own a sailboat on Lake Grapevine. She longed for her Camp Longhorn experiences and also wanted to teach me how to sail. We spent many evenings on the lake when the water skiers were absent, and we had the serenity of the lake to ourselves. We took picnics on the boat, and Jay and baby Greer were always with us.

We sailed at night mostly because we wanted to avoid the speed boats, skiers, and traffic. We occasionally fished by trolling a baited hook behind the boat, and this intrigued Greer especially.

Over the years at Grapevine, as we sailed, Susan taught me the basics, and I studied the facets of sailing a larger boat.

We have sailed on Lake Grapevine, mostly at night, now for several years. We collectively had become quite good at sailing in most conditions the lake and weather provided. So, we decided to sail the ocean blue! I called The Moorings in the British Virgin Islands. They rented larger sailboats for a week at a time; It was called bareboating. The sailboat would be provisioned with food, maps and charts, two-way radios, sonar, and good sails, not to mention good and separate sleeping quarters. We all flew to Tortola, British Virgin Islands, to meet with The Mooring's initiation crew. The first day was used to provide the boat with groceries and receive sailing instructions. The boat was a 39-foot Beneteau and was the perfect size to accommodate our family. We learned how to hoist the Jib and the Main, how to manage the anchor, when to use the diesel engine to move around tight turns, or when the wind did not blow.

We mutually agreed that we should have an instructor with us for the first day and night to ensure our abilities to command the waters and the vessel. We had a female instructor who admitted that she was fairly new at instructing and further admitted that she was working for The Moorings because she was in hot pursuit of her boyfriend, who also was an instructor with the company. We sailed across the bay to another island. We practiced our tacking ability with many come-about turns. We even practiced a couple of jib turns, the trickiest of all turns.

The instructor was a great help in learning where everything was and how it worked. We sailed into a cove with full sails, then promptly dropped them and cranked up the iron jib (the diesel engine) to maneuver around several other boats to find the right place to anchor and begin our evening of cooking, snorkeling, or whatever. Jay and Greer were really a great help in raising and lowering the sails as well as paying out the anchor. The anchor had mostly rope with a very heavy chain at the end attached to the anchor. The anchor held firmly to the sandy bottom of the cove, allowing us to sleep securely without drifting during the night.

The Anchor was managed with an electric motor because of its weight primarily. To properly anchor a boat of this size, the anchor rope or rode had to be paid out seven times the depth of the water.

We had a leisurely breakfast and prepared to get underway for our next destination—Pool Island. We were to drop off our instructor at Pool Island as her mission was coming to a close. She had served well, and we felt confident in our ability to command the boat. We raised the Main immediately after we raised and secured the anchor. I had the diesel engine on and running in case we were unable to maneuver out of the cove merely with the main. We did not need the engine after all, and once we got out into the open waters of the Caribbean, the boys raised the Jib, and we were underway. It was late in the morning, and we were enjoying a good headwind. So, the boys had the job and the main rather tight for a solid close reach.

Another boat came up beside us and wanted to race us. They were about 100 yards to our left (port side). They also had a charter with The Moorings, and their boat was obviously longer—I later learned that it was a 50-foot Beneteau. Susan, Jay, and Greer were pumped that we were racing, and so was I. The instructor had no problem with the process but was mostly noncommittal.

Up ahead of us, I could see a storm brewing. There were dark clouds, heavy with obvious moisture, such that I instructed the boys that the race was over for us. I asked them to lower the jib, which they did. I started up the diesel engine and asked Susan to go below to bring me my rain gear.

The wind was picking up as we headed toward the storm clouds.

I looked over the other boat, which was still about 100 yards to our port side. They were still racing and certainly gaining speed on us. They had not lowered their jib in anticipation of the storm! Suddenly, the wind got worse, and I looked again at their boat. Their jib had backwinded, and they had lost total control of their boat! In fact, they were heading right at us! It looked as though their boat was going to cut us in half! They had no control over the high winds. I pushed the throttle on the diesel engine to full speed, trying to get out of their path.

The throttle of the engine to full in hopes to outrun them. A collision with their boat, as they got closer, was a real possibility. Our so-called instructor had only one thing to say, and that was, "Oh Shit"! Susan was coming up from below with my rain gear when she saw the boat coming our way. With the diesel engine at full throttle, I made a 90-degree turn into them in hopes that I could cause my stern to swing away from a collision with their boat, veering off to the left of our boat.

Our boats did not collide. Instead, our sides did touch each other, causing some minor damage to our boat. The two boats merely kissed each other in a minor and glancing blow. We motored onto Pool Island and met a rescue boat there. Our instructor had called the home office to report the near accident, and a rescue boat had been dispatched. After the inspection of our boat, we were authorized to continue with our Charter. The other boat, however, lost its charter and was told to return to the home base. They had failed to use good judgment in the face of a storm.

We continued on our charter. The instructor left us, and we were on our own. There were no more mishaps. We sailed, anchored, snorkeled, ate well, and had a marvelous time. We went from one island to another and stopped one time at Virgin Gorda and tied the boat to a floating mooring. We put the dingy in and motored to shore for dinner. The waiter wanted to know how we liked our "sticks," and Jay responded that they should be removed from the tree! He meant 'steaks, but his British/Island speech called steaks 'sticks.' Jay responded that he wanted his stick with the leaves off of it. This provided much family discussion and laughter thereafter!

Greer and I tried our hand at fishing by attaching a large hook on a 40-pound test line with chicken pieces as bait. We trolled the line behind the boat as we sailed. As I recall, we never caught anything on this trip.

CATAMARAN SAILING - BRITISH VIRGIN ISLANDS

During Main Street Days of 1995. We were the high bidder at the Vintner's Auction for a bareboating sailing experience in the Caribbean. It was a catamaran, and Larry and Jean Flynn joined us in the bidding. Larry and Jean had never been sailing before, and I had never sailed a catamaran, so we were in for a real learning experience. Jean had a severely broken arm with pins in it and could not assist much in the sailing adventure but lent a great hand in the galley and mixing drinks department.

This boat was 42 feet long, with cabins in each of the two hulls and twin inboard screws (propellers). The boat also had a desalinization machine that converted salt water to fresh, Nice but noisy, and it would only produce 2 gallons per hour. Water was priced at thirty-five cents at the various docks, so we mostly purchased water when needed. The Cat could fairly scoot across the water at a faster pace than any monohull that I had ever sailed. It was fun.

We sailed out of Tortola, BVI, then on to Pool Island, Lost Van Dyke, and several other islands, where we ate and drank like kings and queens.

We spent eight days and nights on this trip. We bathed in the Ocean and rinsed with fresh water because we had a limited amount of fresh water, and it was also fairly expensive ($.25 to $.45) per liter. The provisions were ordered by us according to our tastes, which generally included breakfast each day, plenty of snacks, and one large meal each day. We ate out at various restaurants periodically, which included great choices of fish, beef, and chicken. One stop was an exotic restaurant where the waiter asked Jay how he liked his 'stick.' (British dialect for steak) and Jay very astutely replied, "Without the leaves." Sometimes, we would order ahead at designated places, and other times, and natives came to our boat when we were anchored to offer a menu, braid our hair, and sell us groceries, beer, wine, or fresh fish. One native asked me if I would like some red snapper fish. I laughed and responded yes, thinking it would be frozen or a pipe dream. About an hour later, he came back with six fresh and beautiful red snappers that we ate for dinner for six dollars.

We sailed at least three more times with the Moorings company thereafter, and I was a full-fledged Captain, and they did not want me to have supervision thereafter. They only wanted our money.

LAKE HURON, MICHIGAN

The year was 1994—my 50th birthday was in May, while Susan had already celebrated her 50th—I married an older woman, and she had already rounded the corner. Neither one of us ever thought we were old or older throughout our lives. We loved sports, hiking, walking, hunting, fishing, and anything out of doors. I gave (and she wanted) her a glider flight for her 30th birthday, and when she turned 68, I gave her a hot air ride. We went sailing sometime along this time with Larry and Sandra Foster. We flew to Detroit and sailed out of Mantock Bay on Lake Huron. Sun and Sail leased and provisioned the boat, and we commenced to start island hopping. Larry was a Texoma sailor who had a lot of sailing expertise except none with the drain cock. He left the drain cock open while we were sailing on the last couple of days which let water in and melted all of our ice. The beer was no longer cold—a real downer and a disappointment to Susan and me. Touring the islands did not result in any kind of store to buy more ice.

SEA OF CORTEZ, BAJA

When the guys graduated from Texas A&M and Grapevine High School, respectively, we chartered a Moorings 50-foot boat and sailed Baja in Mexico. The wind was very mild, and the sailing was not that good, but we amused ourselves in many ways by fishing and watching two natives catch a huge sailfish and try to get it aboard their boat. The fish was about as long as their boat, and the fish pulled the entire boat many yards before it tired. Then, the real challenge started to get the huge fish on board the small boat.

We fished many times and caught Bonitas, sharks, and barracudas. Sailing on a calm sea, generally, under a broad reach, we were able to trail a chicken bone behind the boat to catch the larger fish. The barracuda was a feisty fish that we brought on board and tried to kill with a hoisting wrench, but we had more success with a bottle of rum down the hatch! It killed the fish instantly and also marinated it as well. It was a really pretty and delicious white fish.

These boats were fully equipped with ship-to-shore radio, cell service, and sonar equipment to identify the depth, which was really handy since we had to be anchored in a protective cove each day by 4 pm. This was required because we had to anchor in fairly shallow water, like 10 to 20 feet, and reefs could be identified with good sonar equipment. A BBQ pit was on board, and we charcoaled meals often from the stern of the boat.

We had another charter with Sid and Karen Cavanaugh and their friends Peter and ? in a 50ft Moorings yacht at Grenada and Coral Key. As we pulled into Beque Keys, we were anchored in 7-foot water near another boat from France with a nude captained by a man and wife who were nude, which gave us all ideas, but we were too old.

BARBADOS AND GRENADA

Doug and Laurie Evans

The most recent charter was Grenadine, Coral Key, sailing toward St Lucia in 2012. Our guests were Doug and Laurie Evans (director of Parks and Recreation in Grapevine), Shane and Paula Wilbanks (City Council member of Grapevine), Carol Nix (our neighbor and traveling partner from Fort Davis), and Susan and me. Doug, Susan, and Laurie were in charge of the anchors, and Shane was supervising the Main Sail. While he helped Susan with the furling jib, Paula was to help me with the charting. Susan, being my first mate, has always been my first and only first mate!) to be a floater and help with any facet of the boat. We had wall-to-wall music with Linda Ronstadt, Susan Boyle, and Jimmy Buffett.

Carol Nicks

The boat is a 55ft Beneteau, this time with an automatic pilot with five bedrooms and baths. Anchoring the boat is a critical operation if the Capitan wants to sleep at night. The boat has a swing radius and must have adequate room to avoid other boats and land itself! The anchor had to be carefully paid out of the rode and chain seven times our depth, and Doug, Susan, and Laurie did a great job. Carol was up every morning with me, making coffee and breakfast. She was having a good time as well. Doug got a picture of my morning, everyone, since I was lost on a hike on shore one time (at least they thought I was lost, but I really was not). Once, I had to moon Doug on one of our hikes. The last day was a really windy day, and we had to tack Back and forth with only our jib pulling about 8 knots with close reach. Paula Wilbanks challenged me a bit and questioned the directions periodically, especially when tacking positions with a sailboat was required.

OTHER WATERS, RIVERS

Susan and I always loved the water. Throughout these memoirs, one can draw those conclusions. As we got older and our abilities changed in new ways, we came up with a new idea to tour the Missouri and Mississippi Rivers by auto. We normally camped with tents, bedrolls, grown coves, and camp stoves. These rivers intrigued us since they are so large. I can throw a rock across almost all rivers in Texas because they are so small. That's impossible for the Missouri and Mississippi Rivers!

So, we decided on some guidelines or parameters: drive on the country, farm to market roads only, eat at cafes, not chain restaurants, spend the nights at selected boutiques and smaller motels, and never book anything more than one day in advance. Our first adventure was to follow Lewis and Clark's venture up the Missouri River. We rented a pickup truck in Spokane, Washington, and went to the area where three small rivers merge, starting with Missouri. We put our feet in each of the three rivers and then commenced to road drive down the river and crossed it 31 times in two weeks before we took an airplane home to Fort Davis.

We flew to Spokane to start the Missouri near, where three rivers merged and started the Missouri River. After we waded all three rivers that formed the beginning, we started our journey. We flew home about three weeks later from Kansas City, Missouri, after seeing and meeting great people, enjoying good home-cooked food, and crossing the magnificent river thirty-one times. We ate homemade hamburgers, attended local community plays, and tried to see a Major League Baseball game. We stopped when we wanted, especially Teddy Roosevelt National Park, which we almost missed. This trip took about two weeks.

Susan costumed as William Clark

Jerry as Merriweather Lewis

About two years later, we went to Minneapolis, rented a car, and drove North to Lake Itasca, the headwater of the Mississippi River, so we could wade across it, and we did. It was less than knee-deep. We did deviate a bit on this trip and drove a little out of the path since Duluth was about 75 miles away. We checked into the Fitseker Hotel, a quaint old brewery converted into a hotel on LAKE SUPERIOR. Walking along the shore that day, I was able to put my feet in the largest of the Great Lakes!

Tom and Patty Prody are friends of ours that we met at Port Aransas, and they treat us like family, and we do the same with them! They have a pontoon boat, and we cruised the Mississippi and had dinner on the river with them as well. We saw Bald Eagles nesting on eggs in trees on the river. We stayed with the Prodys for two days, met Patty's brothers, and had a delightful time.

From there, we toured the Mayo Clinic in Rochester, Minnesota, where I spent a week deciding against Cancer. I merely wanted Susan to see this marvelous place. We moved back to the river and found the Great River Road Signs that we followed most of the time.

We had dinner at the Throwed Rolls place, where they actually threw delicious yeast rolls for you to catch, or they might dip a huge spoon full of fried okra on your butcher paper plate before your ham steak arrived that was one inch thick and the size of a basketball flattened.

We went to St Louis, and I sang, "Meet me in St Louis, Louis, meet me at the fair." Another play I performed in High School was Thespians. We toured the NAACP museum, which used the backdrop of the motel where Martin Luther King was shot and murdered. The entire museum was most inspirational.

We stayed at the Hyatt Regency and flew home the next day after crossing the mighty Mississippi twenty-nine times!

Chapter 60
Now There Are Three Homes

Our home ownership grew to four, something not planned. This closes the chapter on one of them and redefines our plans for the final event in our lives. Susan is the non-numbers English teacher in our family whose attention to reconciling her bank account is less than three minutes (or is it seconds?). I, on the other hand, would attend museums at her request in Dallas, New York, or whatever, where she could spend 6 hours reading and studying everything that it would take me less than 6 minutes to get to the whole museum.

She has already purchased the book, "I am Dead, Now What," which I dutifully have filled out with appropriate instructions as to what to do, who to call (social security, Vanguard), and final plans. She has started parallel thoughts in the event that she might die before me. If in the unlikely circumstance that she would die before me, I plan to sell her BMW in about three minutes for almost any price. I hate that car! It is locked up in the garage in Grapevine. She loves it!

Every year now for 17 years, we have spent six months in Grapevine during the winter months and six months during the summer months in Fort Davis among the Davis Mountains. The altitude there is five thousand feet, with the temperature and the humidity very satisfactory for Texas summers. We have two pear trees, one apricot tree, and one Fuji apple tree. We also have three raised garden beds where I grow garlic, watermelon, tomatoes, cucumbers, cilantro, basil, green beans, bell peppers, squash, greens, and many other garden items other than marijuana. I did consider it, but I am not ready for jail time.

About three years ago, we met Alex and Diane Spencer. They live in Austin with a home on Lake Buchanan. Alex is a computer consultant with Samsung. They visited Fort Davis periodically, and we became acquainted with them each time they visited. They own a tiny home about five hundred yards from us, where they stay a week here or there.

One time last summer, we had Alex and Diane over for libations of sorts, and Diane announced that our great room would be a good home for her grand piano. That confused Susan and me until Diane expressed a desire to purchase our home.

Over the next six months, we negotiated and entered into an agreement for a binding agreement to be dated June 1, closing on September 30. The sale is most of the furniture and as is otherwise with our keeping most of the original art. Alex, employed by Samsung, likes my involvement with solar and wind, and Diane is occupied with their real estate holdings. So, it appears to be a good match.

Susan and I have been involved in planning our departure, planting our last garden, and planning the final harvest of our Fuji apples and pears. Taking clothing and other items to Ruidoso at our townhome there. We are going to Grapevine in July to carry more things there.

Susan and I are in a bit of shock. We never imagined that the sale would be this way. We always thought this event would be postponed until our mid-80s or so. We also knew that we should be the sellers, which is far better than shifting this burden onto our sons upon our deaths. We know by virtue of living in Fort Davis and witnessing several high-end sales of similar properties the timing of the listing and ultimate sale could be quite lengthy and maybe two or four years. So, because of our age and my health, we decided to accept the offer. We discussed this issue with both of our sons, and they at least understand and, for the most part, agree on the timing.

We will be leaving a lot of friends here in Fort Davis. Many others have already moved or died, and we will continue to miss all of them.

Lastly, we will miss the weather, the cool nights and days.

Chapter 61
Dogs and Cat

VIRGINIA

Our dogs probably should warrant a chapter by themselves. Virginia was our first. She was a dachshund who slept with us. We called her Gin lovingly. She was our companion while we were in Lubbock and later in Houston. She died tragically when in the street at Mother's home in Sweetwater. We buried her on Eddie's farm. Susan and I cried all night and missed her for some time thereafter.

CHRISTY

Our next dog was Christy (called Chrispy by Greer caretaker), another dachshund whose claim to fame was barking at a copperhead snake near our swimming pool in Colleyville such that Susan summoned our neighbor, John Ramey, to come and shoot the snake. She was another dachshund like Virginia. Christy was a very brave dog in that she barked a lot. Size did not matter to her as she was willing to take on any sized dog or other animal! She did not sleep with us like Virginia did and stayed outside full-time. She cornered another copperhead snake one time until Susan came outside to find the cornered snake. Susan called John Ramey again, and he shot it with a pistol. We were grateful for her alertness and John's pistol.

Christy and Katy, a Weimaraner, had cornered a skunk at our home in Grapevine while we were going to a football game. When we got home, we could smell the skunk. We found Katy over in the corner of the backyard throwing up as she had encountered the skunk directly. But Christy would not be denied. She was in full pursuit of the skunk, smell or otherwise. I called animal control with the City of Grapevine, only to find out that they could not come out right away. They informed me that it was unlawful to fire a shotgun in the city limits. I had no choice and shot the skunk with a 410 as soon as Christy backed away, enough to allow it. Animal control showed up later as we were bathing Christy and Katy in tomato juice. Unfortunately, we had the entire house windows open with the attic fan drawing outside air in, such that the lovely skunk smell was rampant throughout the house! It was a long night!

KATY

Katy had beautiful blue eyes. She was not really smart; in fact, she was rather dumb but became a famous guard dog when we sold our home in Colleyville. We were moving to Grapevine to live in a townhome on Choctaw Circle while Roy Stewart finished building our home on Pebblebrook. The title had passed on the sale of our home, but possession was not to occur for a few more days. The mover had come to move our furniture while we were moving the usual lamps, plants, and many other things. We left the dogs, Christy and Katy, in the backyard while we went to the townhome in Grapevine. The new owner showed up at our house to leave some telephone books. She went in the front door, which upset Katy immensely. Katy began to bark as the woman proceeded into the kitchen, where the bay window was that overlooked the backyard. Katy did not delay as she barreled through the bay window after the intruder! When we arrived back home, we found glass all over the kitchen and the bay window in shambles. Further, we found Katy all cut up and bleeding profusely. She required 30 stitches at various places on her body. We had no idea what had happened until the woman called and had the audacity to ask what and how I was going to repair the broken bay window. Dream on!

She repaired the broken window, and we paid our vet bill.

TOOTSIE ROLL

Tootsie Roll was our first Labrador. She was obviously chocolate in color. When she was a pup at the breeders and beside her mother and siblings, she ran to us and jumped into our arms. Susan and I knew she had to be ours. We knew she was going to be a hunter and generally an outdoor dog. So, we took her to a rattlesnake school where she learned with shot collars to be wary of rattlesnakes and all snakes in general. I took her hunting several times as she loved to retrieve birds. Once, we hunted ducks with Bob Mundlin in a boat on his bird lease near Stephenville. We shot nine birds. Toots jumped out of the boat and retrieved eight of them. She was unable to retrieve the ninth because Bob had shot this duck that fell directly into the boat. Toots were pissed!

I had a dove hunt in Sweetwater out at Eddie's farm north of town when Gary Fickes, Ken White, David Mahan, Barry Emerson, Terry Hall, and I went out to Eddie's farm. Toots had a blast. The hunt was successful as almost everyone got his legal limit of the dove. Toots especially liked to retrieve the dove because I pulled the head off of the dove and gave it to her as an award for a soft mouth retrieve. She performed beautifully with no dove harmed. She especially liked to retrieve a downed dove on the opposite side of the stock tank. Refusing to go around the tank on land. Instead, she swam across the pond, grabbed the bird, and brought it back to me. She hunted a little while with Gary Fickes but got real frustrated because Gary shot often, and no doves would fall anyplace. Gary could not hit anything. He was just a bad shot! Toots got really frustrated with Gary, what with ten or more false starts. She finally decided to sit with me for the remainder of the hunt.

EBONY PERRA

Bart and Ebony Perra were our labs. We hired a male dog in Lewisville to breed Ebony. It was a cold day in February when she delivered eight beautiful black baby Labradors. Susan came home from school and was so surprised to find her in delivery. Susan found one of the babies outside near a tree, and thankfully, it was still alive. Ebony was bored being a mother and wanted to play ball with me more than nurse her youth. After the babies opened their eyes, we took them all to Elberta since it was spring and warming up. We had Ebony and her tribe outside, and two little girls walked up to see the baby Labs when their large St Bernard walked up behind the girls, and that dog took one step toward Ebony and her pups, and she leaped up and rolled the large dog, while Bart, our black lab, did not know what to do about his new "nieces and nephews." He was not smart and tried to stay away from baby labs, chewing on his tail or legs. He was really good and would not hurt or harm Ebby's babies for the world.

Ebony Perra, a black Labrador and the apple of my eye. Ebbie retrieved everything I threw. She barked at cars that drove up to our home in Fort Davis. She caught frisbees in the air and swam the lakes and rivers in pursuit of whatever I threw. Many times, she retrieved things I did not throw. She merely thought I needed what she brought.

For Christmas, Susan commissioned Debra Allison, an artist in the Alpine, to paint an oil painting of Ebony and me as a present. We went to a Big Bend Museum function in the Alpine, and I saw a Theodore Roosevelt painting that Debra had painted, and I decided that I wanted to bid for it in the auction. Susan encouraged me to look again for anything else that I might want to purchase, and I looked up and saw the beautiful painting of me and my dog! I Cried big tears. What a wonderful gift!

Ebbie wore out and had to be put to sleep. We buried her under a large rock in the pasture of our home in Fort Davis. She was the best dog we ever had until we got Sadie!

SIMON AND SIMONE

Our first cat was Alice Blue Gown, as airy as her name, she was with us one moment and gone the next.

While we owned the 160 acres (the ranch) in Stephens County, we had seen more than one rattlesnake around the house. So, our neighbors began giving us the cats and kittens.

I return every two weeks to the ranch house to feed the cats and refresh their water. Each time I arrived, there were fewer cats, and several skulls were found in the yard that indicated the coyotes were very active at night, preying on our cat population. A white cat that I named Whitey, and another Siamese-looking cat that I named Simon survived throughout the entire time. I learned that Whitey and Simon spent each night on top of the roof of the house, safely away from the hungry coyotes. Greer and I went out there hunting during the cat ordeal and shot a turkey. We cleaned the bird in the backyard on a table we had, and during the process, Whitey and Simon were right in the middle of the cleaning routine. Neither would be denied and jumped right in on the carcass of the bird ripping off meat with feathers in their mouths. Many times, we took our dog, Tootsie Roll (Toots), with us, and the cats loved her. She was so patient, allowing them to ride on her back as well.

Finally, we were rattlesnake free, and we had only Whitey and Simon left from the original seventeen cats. On a subsequent weekend that I went to the PK ranch, I found Whitey's skull in the front yard that a coyote had left and could not find Simon. After searching for Simon, I heard the faint cry of a kitten in the back of the outside storeroom. I went back there, removed a box and other junk in the storeroom, and found Simon nursing a baby kitten, a calico-colored kitten, probably the ugliest kitten I had seen lately. Well, Simon had been bred by an old and wild Tom that I had seen numerous times out in the barn area, and now Simon was clearly not Simon anymore, so Susan and I renamed her Simone.

I took Simone and her ugly kitten back to Grapevine in a box because I knew she and her kitten were surely doomed if she stayed at the ranch.

The veterinarian in Colleyville gave Simone her shots and agreed to find a home for her kitten if we would allow Simone to nurse two other baby kittens that their mother had abandoned. Simone was a good mother and nursed the three kittens—how, we will never know because Simone was tiny herself!

Simone lived on top of our house for the first month or so before she felt comfortable with Toots and Bart, our two Labradors. I think she thought the dogs could be the coyote type, so she sought safety on the roof of the house. One of her nine lives expired when Susan ran over Simone with the car, which only dislocated her shoulder. As time went on, she would come inside on occasions where we kept her food, and eventually, she owned the place—the people as well (me, Susan, and Greer). Toots gave her a wide birth as she was clearly the alpha animal. Bart was not smart enough to get even close to Simone. But Simone did not ever get close or venture into their backyard either. Each animal clearly knew his territory.

SADIE

We spent three years getting over the death of Ebony. Susan and I had several thoughts about our next dog, including our age, the size of the dog, and our training. By the way, our first granddaughter had entered into our thoughts. Adelle Elizabeth Pittman was born in Dallas to Greer and Angie in 2009. Adelle was allergic to some dogs, so we needed to find a nonallergenic dog. Three grandsons and now the princess of all had been born. The grandsons better beware!

We found the right dog in San Antonio from our research in the newspapers. She was a miniature golden doodle. A mix between a poodle and a golden retriever except miniature from both breeds. She was a puppy and bonded with Susan in the back seat of my truck for the ride back to Grapevine, her new home. We named her Sadie.

Greer friend at his office recommended Brad Doolittle as a trainer for Sadie, so I hired him and had about 6-8 sessions with him for about $800.00. He was training me more than Sadie, especially since she was so young and still very much a puppy. He used a lot of hand signals to train larger hunting dogs. That did not fit the Sadie I was beginning to know. Mainly, Brad trained me. He recommended that I purchase a training collar that used a trainable dial for a shock with a switch for mellow music that reminds a dog to behave.

I only used the shock element for Sadie one time, and that was at the Fort Davis Cemetery when she started to bolt from me in hot pursuit of quail, rabbits, and road runners (chaparral). When she bolted and gave her #4 shock, I told her NO and came here at the same time. The next day I did the same thing, and I have not used the shock element since. From that moment on, we all knew I was the disciplinarian. I have never had to spank her or get a paper after her. When she misbehaves, I merely say NO, and she always falls in line. I do use music from time to time, especially on the beach, to fine-tune her training and discipline.

She now walks with me daily without a lease. She always stays with me, approaches dogs and people, and bikes without any interference. I love every person or other dog that likes her. When she encounters mean dogs, she will hide behind Susan or me. She is a happy dog who acts like a puppy all the time. Susan takes her out in the mornings, and I take her out at bedtime. She jumps into the bed with us both until we both are in bed, and then, when we are both in bed, she goes to her bed for the night.

The End.